Market Sentiments

Market Sentiments

Middle-Class Market Culture in Nineteenth-Century America

Elizabeth White Nelson

Smithsonian Books
Washington, DC

Grateful acknowledgment is made for permission to reprint the following:
"Charitable Contributions: Fancywork, Charity, and the Culture of the Sentimental
Market, 1830–1880," in *The Middling Sorts: Explorations in the History of the American
Middle Class*, edited by Burton J. Bledstein and Robert D. Johnson, copyright © 2000
by Routledge/Taylor & Francis Books, Inc.

Copy editor: Karin Kaufman
Production editor: Joanne Reams
Designer: Brian Barth

Library of Congress Cataloging-in-Publication Data
Nelson, Elizabeth White.
    Market sentiments : middle-class market culture in nineteenth-century America /
Elizabeth White Nelson.
      p.   cm.
    Includes bibliographical references and index.
    ISBN 1-58834-139-9 (alk. paper)
    1. Consumption (Economics)—Social aspects—United States—History—19th
century. 2. Middle-class—United States—Economic conditions—19th century.
3. Sentimentalism—Economic aspects—United States—History—19th century. I. Title.
    HC79.C6N45   2004
    306.3'0973'09034–dc22   2004045310

A paperback reissue (ISBN 978-1-58834-290-4) of the original cloth edition.
British Library Cataloguing-in-Publication Data available.
Manufactured in the United States of America

15   14   13   12   11   10   1 2 3 4 5

For Ethan

Phoebe, Cyrus, and Jasper

Among the many smooth mischiefs of sentiment, it is one of its sure and successful frauds to affect the most frigid indifference to those external and pecuniary advantages, which is its great and real object to obtain.

—Hugh Blair, *Sentimental Beauties and Moral Delineations,* 1792

Contents

Introduction 1

Introduction

In 1849, Esther Howland, the daughter of a prosperous stationer and insurance salesman in Worcester, Massachusetts, started manufacturing and selling fancy valentines. Intrigued by the imported valentines, covered in embossed lace, gilt paper, and hand-colored images of Cupid, she had seen in her father's store the year before, Esther saw a business opportunity. Her brothers, who were traveling salesmen in the family business, took her sample valentines with them and returned with orders for more than $1,000 worth of valentines for the next year's trade. Her father ordered fancy paper and engravings from New York merchants, and Esther launched what later grew into the New England Valentine Company. With the help of her family, she built one of the most successful early valentine manufacturing concerns. As the business prospered, she hired young women, whom she described as friends of the family, to help her. She moved her production out of the family parlor, first to a room specifically designated for valentine production, and then to a separate business address. In later years, as her business faltered, she moved production back into her home. There does not seem to have been any great moral outcry about Howland's business activities. The R. G. Dun reporter who assessed her credit in the 1870s, when the business was heavily mortgaged, did not castigate her for social or financial impropriety but pointed to the intersecting demands of family and business, suggesting the mortgages were not testimony to bad business practices but to the demands of her father's last illness.[1]

In an interview in the *Boston Globe* toward the end of her life, Howland described her business as an extension of a woman's ordinary leisure production, characterizing herself as more of a maternal figure than a managerial one and noting that several of the girls who worked for her were family friends and even lived with the Howland family.[2] Howland used sentimental language to describe the production and consumption of her valentines. Her business transcended the neat boundaries between the home and the marketplace described by the authors of etiquette books and domestic manuals, but this did not make the Howland family unusual. Esther's father, Southworth A. Howland, chose not to become a carpenter like his father, who was an entrepreneur in the artificial limb business. He left the small town where he grew up and moved to Worcester, Massachusetts, where his brothers followed him. They all prospered, becoming proprietors and entrepreneurs in their own right. Southworth Howland began his career in the printing business and owned a stationery store, but in the 1850s he entered the insurance business, as did his sons, one of whom became president of the company, Quincy Mutual Insurance, in 1885.[3] Esther's mother took advantage of her husband's printing business and published *The American Economical Housekeeper and Family Receipt Book* (1845). Howland had published his own book, *Steamboat Disasters and Railway Accidents* (1840), and in later years he published *The Ladies and Gentlemen's Sentimental Valentine Writer,* a book of valentine poetry for his daughter's business.[4] Despite the unusual products the Howlands manufactured—artificial limbs and valentines—these three generations of the Howland family traced the shift from artisanal trade to small manufacturing concern that described the transformation of middle-class commerce in the nineteenth century.[5]

In the story of Esther Howland's valentine business, we see much more than just a successful female entrepreneur and a growing market for luxury goods. Her interest in manufacturing sentimental goods and her success at marketing them reveals the complexity of middle-class market culture in nineteenth-century America.[6] The central oxymorons of this market culture were apparent in Howland's valentine business: domestic economy, fancy-work, marriage market, and sentimental value. The juxtaposition of pleasure and profit, heart and head, private and public, consumption and production, suggest how important the balance of these competing and complementary ideas were in defining the terms of market culture. Throughout this book, I am less concerned with whether sentimental strategies succeeded or failed to reform capitalism than I am with their influence on the development of a particular kind of market culture in nineteenth-century America and its legacy to our modern market culture. I contend that we owe much of the logic of contemporary consumer culture to the successes and failures of these sentimental strategies and to gentle ways they taught tough economic lessons.

Howland launched her enterprise in an existing market for sentimental commodities. By the late 1840s, a generation of consumers had grown up educated by sentimental texts and enticed by sentimental goods. This sentimental education about the market began in the 1820s as the number of prosperous Americans began to increase and the market for manufactured goods began to expand. As the urban population grew, the possibilities for commerce meant that market activity was no longer confined to a particular time of the week or the arrival of a peddler or ship. The opportunities and temptations of the market could be found every day in a growing number of commercial establishments. Choices about consumption became part of the rhythm of daily life. The increased presence of economic transactions with strangers created a market defined less by a particular location than by the nature of the exchanges. By the mid-nineteenth century, the market had become more than the sum of market places, and a culture of the market had developed that influenced a broad spectrum of social interactions.[7]

The growth of the population, particularly in cities, resulted in changes to the American middle class. In 1790, only 200,000 people lived in cities and

towns, but by 1830, more than 1 million people had moved into rapidly growing urban areas. In 1860, this number was more than 6 million.[8] With the
influx of so many people, cities changed dramatically. Only some of the people who lived in them fell within the economic parameters of the "middling
condition," but the visual impact of their homes and businesses was important and influential in defining market culture. In the early part of the century, new buildings grew up as part of the existing urban fabric, but as the
population increased, cities expanded. New urban inhabitants infused what
had once been small colonial cities with energy and life. Merchants created
business districts in which streets bustled with commercial activity.[9] People
worked in newly built commercial buildings that housed a wide range of new
professions. Women and men shopped in elaborate new showrooms and, by
the middle of the 1840s, amazing department stores such as A. T. Stewart in
New York. Some of the newly prosperous city dwellers moved into existing
houses, but many chose to build new houses, farther from the center of the
city, that suited their growing domestic needs. These new neighborhoods were
not as homogeneous as the streetcar suburbs of the late nineteenth century,
but like the new commercial streets, they were visual evidence of individual
prosperity.[10] The appearance of the parlor from outside the house was often
as important as its furnishings. Middle-class domestic architecture was
designed to represent a balance of modesty, refinement, and comfort, ideas
codified by figures such as Andrew Jackson Downing and Frederick Law
Olmsted, who wrote about the important synergy between middle-class ideals
and the built environment.[11]

Although commercial and residential districts became separate areas of
the city in the antebellum period, cities were still small by modern standards
and remained walking cities.[12] Middle-class men no longer worked in the
home, but they frequently dined at home in the middle of the day and
attended to shopping requests from their wives on their way home. Women
became more frequent consumers of manufactured goods, but male heads of
household continued to choose house plans and make most of the major decisions about household purchases until the twentieth century.[13] Husbands and
wives shared an interest in and responsibility for the furnishing of domestic

spaces, but it remained a husband's responsibility to provide and furnish the home. Consequently, we must reexamine the assertion that the rise in nineteenth-century luxury consumption was a process of feminization.[14]

The growth of cities and the spread of urban culture into the countryside after 1830 presented new challenges for class definitions. The cultural strategies of a small and relatively homogeneous middle class before 1830 were tested, challenged, and revised as the number of people concerned with questions of cultural and moral authority increased. As urban areas grew, older traditions of elite example and mutual social scrutiny that had been possible in small cities and towns were less effective in regulating social behavior. This sponsored a new kind of anxiety among the elite, a concern that they could not exert the kind of influence, particularly over behavior in the activities of the market, to which they had been accustomed. The expansion of the economy and the numbers of prosperous families after 1830, combined with the panics of 1837 and 1839 and the depths of the depression between 1839 and 1843, severely tested the elite definitions of appropriate market behavior and challenged the moral authority of this original small group, especially regarding questions of restraint and other "proper" forms of economic behavior. The anxiety about moral authority prompted an increase in economic advice, particularly in the form of fiction, to try to reassert a restrained version of sentimentalism in the face of the excesses of the newly prosperous.[15]

The fluctuations of the economy and a discomfort with European definitions of class hierarchy based on birth encouraged prosperous Americans to dissemble their claims to status and displace their definition of class hierarchy onto cultural and economic criteria. This did not belie a real investment in social distinction and social advancement, however. The fluctuations of prosperity played an important role in the dependence of these men and women on cultural definitions of class that could transcend temporary economic difficulties. Much of the energy spent on class definition was intended to maintain social hierarchy within the rhetoric of classlessness and define cultural limits that transcended the turbulence of individual economic fortunes. The antebellum middle class worried more about the lower boundary of class than the upper. Middle-class men and women embraced cultural definitions of status to prevent the newly monied from storming the citadel of the parlor without conforming to the dictates of propriety. In turn, they believed that propriety could preserve class status in periods of retrenchment. They insisted that prudence and self-control were the source of personal virtue and economic virtue, which underpinned class distinctions in a way pure economic distinctions could not. Class status was dependent on a particular kind of market philosophy as much as on financial success.

This market philosophy, which I call sentimental pragmatism, was a strategy of market relations. Middle-class Americans tried to reconcile the imperatives of market capitalism and Christian morality through the secular catalyst of sentimentalism.[16] Although nineteenth-century middle-class women and men did not use the term "sentimental pragmatism" to describe their market activities, the strategies they developed to define the relationship between sentiment and profit helped generate a vocabulary and a code of behavior that defined the market relations of both production and consumption in moral terms. They employed the language of emotion to achieve rational, economic ends. Sentimentalism was more that just an observation of emotion, it was the investment of that emotion in commodities and interactions that defined and delimited them in concrete ways. Sentimental pragmatism was a method of action rather than a model for acquisition. The term "pragmatism," in addition to its simple meaning of practical approach, suggests how middle-class women and men used sentimental ideals to resolve the contradictions of market culture and puzzle out new ways of understanding and reconciling the conflicts between public good and private interest, spiritual worth and worldly success, personal character and national identity.[17]

Prosperous men and women frequently chose to define themselves first in terms of national identity rather than class identity. By insisting that their domestic and market lives provided the perfect image of national sentiments, the middle class declared they were the central class rather than just the middle between the upper and the lower.[18] They often used terms such as "middling" and "middle" to describe themselves, claiming the virtue of moderation as much as defining their station in a larger hierarchy. The virtue of "middleness" had its roots in eighteenth-century notions of political economy, which linked economic and social development in a series of three successive stages. In the first stage, commerce merely sustained the mutual needs of the community. In the middle stage, commerce supported culture and provided for the refinement of society. In the final stage, commerce promoted greed, dissipation, and corruption brought on by immense wealth.[19] The desire to sustain the benefits of the middle stage without succumbing to the dangers of the final stage fueled the debates about the role of commerce in the early Republic and in the lives of a small but increasingly prosperous middle class. These debates supported the correlation between the virtues of the middle stage and a middle class, who embraced moral prosperity while rejecting gross luxury. Because the associations of virtue and the "middle phase" were so strong, some prosperous families insisted on their "middling" status, even in the face of substantial wealth.[20] These rhetorical strategies, however, did not preclude the aspirations of great wealth; they merely defined the terms of public self-fashioning.[21]

Sentimental enterprises were not just business ventures, they were a way of positioning oneself in relation to all aspects of business. Sentimentalism allowed an elevation of the material world to a moral plane that was a marked shift away from Calvinist suspicions about the seductions of the material world. A sentimental world view opened up new possibilities and justifications for consumption. Material goods became suffused with moral meaning. But the suggestion that sentimental associations could give all goods moral meaning worried conservative critics. They became concerned that this behavior encouraged moral relativism. If all goods and all transactions could be defined by sentiment, where could the line be drawn between sloth and industry, luxury and restraint, virtue and indolence? If the value of goods could be defined by sentimental associations, conservative writers on economic issues insisted that all forms of exchange must be rooted in a moral economy in which the possibilities of sentimental association were tempered by insisting that all forms of production and consumption should be dictated by good motives.[22] The status of goods was too precarious and sentimental value too fleeting. In a moral economy, the process of exchange must be determined by sentiment; only then could goods that passed the test of moral exchange, which was defined by good motives, be invested with sentiment and be part of the moral economy. This approach soothed conservative fears about material relativism and anchored market behavior in the practice of restraint rather than indulgence. For these conservative writers, the debate about moral economy did not hinge on a nostalgia for a pre-capitalist agrarian market.[23] They embraced the growth of market culture, insisting that Christian and republican ideals could temper the individualism of capitalist market behavior.

The dynamic relationship between the development of a middle class and the development of a capitalist economy was neither a teleology of triumph nor of decline, but a process of active and ambivalent engagement. The impulse to make peace with the contradictions of market culture by reforming the market from within rather than attacking it from without was a key element of middle-class identity. A history of consumption in the antebellum period does not show the replacement of an ethic of production with an ethic of consumption but the important interdependence of these ideas in the development of a middle-class market culture.[24] In antebellum America, production and consumption remained fundamentally linked; it was essential to be a producer in order to be a virtuous consumer.

I use the term "market culture" rather than "consumer culture" or "market society."[25] Although the interest in the history of consumer culture in the nineteenth century has pushed the search for origins back in time, the commercial activity of antebellum America should not be characterized as a consumer culture.[26] Using the term "market" helps reestablish the connection that antebellum Americans saw between the acts of production and consumption, a connection that was central to the way people understood their activity in the market. Using the word "culture" rather than "society" also suggests a form of active engagement in the activities of the market. Antebellum Americans used the language of political economy and business relations to describe and discuss many aspects of life that ostensibly lay outside the parameters of commercial relationships. This language and these relationships had a particular resonance for them and offered useful metaphoric and symbolic ways of thinking about the complexity of life. Ordinarily, middle-class Americans did not rail against the injustices of capitalism, but they persistently strove to reform the more troubling aspects of individualism, to shape the market with ideas that tempered self-interest with sympathy and acquisitive behavior with restraint. The popularity of these discussions suggests that ideas about the transformation from commerce to capitalism were debated in anticipation of change as well as in retrospect.[27] The readers and writers of texts that examined the problems of a moral market economy did more than just participate in a market society; they actively attempted to shape a market culture.

Antebellum Americans found sentimentalism a useful language for describing and defining the terms of a moral market culture. The rhetorical strategies of sentimentalism were well suited to puzzling out practical problems of all kinds. Sentimentalism offered rhetorical solution to the problems of moral diversity. A person who displayed incorrect sentiments could be excluded from the community, thus providing a way to eliminate diversity based on moral rectitude rather than material circumstance.[28] By defining the boundaries of community in these rhetorical terms, members of a middle class could restrict access to its ranks by either rejecting the cultural behavior of the lower ranks or domesticating it to suit genteel needs—rejecting the self-indulgent behavior of the wealthy as beyond the sphere of rectitude. This allowed them to both keep out the "rabble" below and quench the fires of envy for the possessions and society of the rich. "Feeling," therefore, became a tangible way to define the moral world and give not only the behavior of men and women in the market but also the very products of the market itself a kind of aesthetic regulation in the face of disruptive religious, social, and economic changes.[29]

In contemporary culture, sentimentality is a word that conjures up a host of negative associations, usually centering around a sense of false consciousness based on an indulgence of insincere or delusional emotional attachment. At its best, "sentimental" is used as a synonym for "nostalgia," but it is most commonly used as a foil for the tough, hip realism of a modernist sensibility. To be sentimental is most often a sign of weakness, often self-proclaimed, and it has largely been defined as a form of feminine consciousness. In addition to having connotations of weakness, this weakness is conflated with judgments about lower-class taste. This contemporary assessment of sentimentality is in part a product of the disgust of historical exhaustion, but these condemnations were present at the very height of the vogue for sentimental literature. The popularity of sentimentalism has always been defined by a concurrent ambivalence about the possibilities and perils of a world view based on the idea of legible emotion. "Sentimental" is such a complex word, and so often dismissed in favor of its seemingly more refined cousin, "sensibility," that it is important to recover a least a little of the history of its cultural use to understand what antebellum men and women meant when they used the word and how they understood those ideas to be useful.[30] It is also important to note that twentieth-century scholars use the word "sentimental" to describe nineteenth-century cultural production far more often than nineteenth-century men and women used the word to describe their own actions or production. The word has become a moniker for antebellum culture, collapsing difference rather than describing it.

Sustained scholarly interest in nineteenth-century American sentimental literature was sparked in 1977 by Ann Douglas's *Feminization of American Culture*. Douglas approached sentimental literature from a new and compelling vantage point—its connection to modern mass culture—only to throw up her hands in disgust and despair at what she saw as the inability of nineteenth-century women to replace masculine, Puritan culture with a compelling and rigorous feminine alternative.[31] The firestorm of scholarly retort to this book is testimony to the brilliance of its initial insight: sentimental literature and its world view were fundamentally at the center of the process of defining American culture.[32] Many subsequent scholars have disagreed with Douglas's conclusions about the value of sentimental literature, but few have really explored her insights into the relationship of sentimentalism and the rise of capitalism. *Market Sentiments* questions her assessment that sentimentalism and feminization are synonymous and that sentimentalism was an alternative or external or marginal commentary on the development of market culture.[33] I argue that sentimentalism is not dismissed as a process of feminization until it is no longer a compelling market strategy. The demotion of sentimentalism to a process of feminization is concurrent with a loss of middle-class interest in sentimental aesthetics after the Civil War. Sentimentalism was not merely a commentary on the development of capitalism but one of the central strategies of market development. Men and women used the language of sentimentalism to insist on and describe an acceptable form of integration of those two spheres. Sentimentalism was a conscious strategy rather than a paradox, a social delusion, false consciousness, or assertion of cultural difference as a critique of mainstream culture. Whereas literary studies of sentimentalism have found the market in the home, I extend this analysis by finding the home in the market. I reexamine the definitions of domesticity by asserting the importance of men in the cultural work of class formation and the importance of women in the economic work of class formation. Sentimentalism did not function as the marker of difference between a private feminized domestic sphere and a public masculinized commercial sphere; it was social and cultural phenomena that provided complex connections between those two rhetorical worlds.

The heart of my argument begins with the ambivalence of sentimentalism itself. Recently, scholars have brought the important links between eighteenth-century moral philosophy and nineteenth-century sentimentalism to our attention.[34] In the eighteenth century, philosophers, particularly members of the Scottish Enlightenment such as David Hume and Adam Smith, often discussed moral sentiments. At the heart of this discussion was the relationship between sentiment and reason. Sentiment was much more than mere feeling; it organized the insights of sensibility through the structure of moral reason. Far from being a manifestation of excess emotion, it was the core of moral thought.[35] Moral sentiments dictated a form of sociability that was defined by gentility and politeness that made possible a public sphere that replicated the refinement of the private sphere.[36] Moral sentiments were discussed not only by philosophers but also in novels such as those written by Samuel Richardson, Laurence Sterne, and Henry Mackenzie. As interest in these discussions increased in America, less prominent philosophers such as Dugald Stewart and William Paley made these ideas accessible to collegiate and popular audiences.[37] These ideas were further popularized through new sentimental magazines that became common in the United States in the 1790s. Fearing that this tendency toward popularity was evidence of a decline rather than an increase in moral behavior, conservative social critics cautioned against the profligate use of the word even as they encouraged a broad adoption of the best behavior it described.

The roots of the relationship between sentiment and reason predate these eighteenth-century discussions. In *The Passions and the Interests: Political Arguments for Capitalism Before Its Triumph*, Albert O. Hirschman astutely observes the importance of the relationship between the passions and the interests that were molded to conform to the needs of the changing economic culture, frequently with consequences entirely unanticipated by those who participated in the transformation.[38] In his pathbreaking book on market culture, Jean-Christophe Agnew demonstrates how important Adam Smith's *Theory of Moral Sentiments* was to the understanding of market relations. Like Hirschman, Agnew reassess the traditional dichotomies of property and propriety to show how those relationships changed and developed to respond to the developing market rather than to resist it.[39] In reexamining Smith's interest in the relationships between strangers and friends in market transactions, Agnew drew on the work of anthropologists such as Clifford Geertz, Arjun Apppadurai, Mary Douglas and Baron Isherwood, and Chandra Mukerji, who have shown how important the understanding of the meaning of goods is in determining the means of their circulation in every kind of economy from simple to complex.[40] Their studies of other cultures and other models of economy have borne out Smith's own observations of the relationship between an economy of strangers and one of friends.[41] The insights of these scholars have shown us how complex the relationship of exchange is, and how important the cultural relationships of the marketplace are in the history of economic development.[42] In his reassessment of Max Weber's theory of the Protestant work ethic, Colin Campbell demonstrates the simultaneous development of a romantic ethic along with the Protestant ethic. The history of consumer culture, he asserts, is defined by an ongoing relationship between consumption and production rather than a linear progression from a culture of production to a culture of consumption.[43] Literary historians have used these insights to demonstrate how sentimental literature incorporated commentary on the developing market culture into its vision of middle-class culture.[44] However, literary histories rely heavily on the idea of feminization to explain the relationship between sentimentalism and capitalism. By focusing more on abstract ideas about capitalism than the concrete negotiations of nineteenth-century commerce, they often do not address the fluctuations of the antebellum economy. Novels, by definition, are a form of constructed reality in which the plot demands a series of resolutions to the conflicts raised by the actions of the novel. The function of a happy ending is fundamentally ideological, modeling anticipated cultural coherency as much as reflecting existing cultural conflict and complexity.[45] Novels remain formulaic, and the vision they provide can be expanded by juxtaposing them with other contemporary cultural texts and artifacts that derive their structure from different cultural imperatives.

Until the eve of the Civil War, sentimentalism resonated with the citizens of the new Republic as a description of personal comportment and social relations in a world in which challenges to older forms of hierarchy and new possibilities for prosperity brought the importance of the relationship of individual character and social status into high relief.[46] Like "sentimental," the word "genteel" also grew in popularity, but because "genteel" implied a form of social aspiration, its use often became a subject of mockery.[47] To use the word as a form of self-description suggested aspiration rather than achievement. The increased fluidity of society that the growth of economic prosperity seemed to promise meant that any term could easily be turned on its head. The anxiety about the sincerity of social behavior increased. Despite the slipperiness of a term such as "sentimental," it proved to have longevity as a term that defined social and economic success. As the ranks of the newly prosperous grew, a cultivated detachment from the sincerity of sentiment was replaced by an appreciation for its theatricality.[48] The devastation of the Civil War called into question the persuasiveness of sentimental rhetoric. After the war, sentimental explanations declined in popularity, especially as sentimental strategies of class identity were associated with those women whose economic independence had been irreparably damaged by the war. In the 1870s and 1880s, sentimental rhetoric was replaced by new languages of naturalism and realism, in literature and culture. Those who clung to the rhetoric and strategies of sentimentalism were increasingly seen as relics of another era, and their productions and methods of self-presentation were often described as mawkish. It was these images of sentimentalism that the proponents of modernism and antimodernism alike, used as their foil. The legacy of these definitions still informs our understanding of nineteenth-century sentimentalism whether we condemn it as mawkish or champion it as alternative.

In order to understand the earlier definitions of sentimentalism we must detach them not only from these late-nineteenth-century definitions but also from late-nineteenth-century definitions of capitalism. As sentimental ideas lost their cultural currency, they became merely a form of failed commentary on the problems of industrial capitalism and the rise of a mass market. But antebellum ideas about commerce grappled with different issues. "Commerce" and "capitalism" cannot simply be used as synonyms, just as the appearance of a growing middle class cannot be confused with the stability of individual families. Commerce was defined in fundamentally positive ways, connoting industry, moderation, economy, and independence, whereas capitalism, a term that came into more common parlance after the Civil War, connoted a hierarchical shift in the way business was conducted and the ways men related to one another in the world of work, in particular the problem of dependence raised by the specter of a permanent working class.[49] The negotiations of commerce within the confines of the middle class, however tenuously that group was defined, tell a different story about the rise of market culture than the struggles between capital and labor after the Civil War. These two stories are clearly related, but there are different issues at stake, particularly the economic and cultural relationship of production and consumption.[50] We cannot fully understand the economic struggles of the late nineteenth century without more careful attention to the market negotiations of the middle class in the antebellum period.[51] The virtue of work and the pragmatic nature of beauty underpinned their claim to social, cultural, and political power. To detach consumption from production was to threaten not just their claim to power but also their identity as the central class in American society.

Sentimentalism played an important role in helping to mediate the anxiety attendant to the cultural upheaval and shifting class structure of in the antebellum period.[52] In the early Republic, the spectacle of political parades employed sentimental strategies to represent social order and elite leadership through the medium of popular culture as a way of making reassertion of the social hierarchy, especially by the Federalists, palatable to a growing and diverse electorate. Both Federalists and Republicans appealed to the moral sentiments of participants and spectators, not only to shape the spectacle of the parades but also to craft the terms of national identity, merging political, social, and moral notions of sentiment. Sentimental rhetoric was useful as a tool of reform because it insisted on a universal recognition of moral sentiments and reframed traditional forms of social and economic hierarchy in cultural terms. It suggested the possibilities of mutuality, even as it insisted on the reestablishment of traditional hierarchies. Sentimental rhetoric served the conservative purposes of the Federalists even as it appealed to notions of self-determination championed by the Republicans and the democratic leanings of the crowds these politicians sought to educate.

Sentimental rhetoric provided a way to discuss values—moral value, personal credit, patriotic sentiments—that seemed to shed older notions of inherited rank with earned social position. This appealed to Federalist and Republicans alike, who sought to equate elite virtue with public order, and helped establish boundaries to respectability without relying on older methods of defining it. The vision of class identity was more frequently focused on the lower boundaries of class than the upper. The optimism and sense of exceptionalism that circulated through popular consciousness provided the promise of upward mobility for those who earned it. If people felt anxiety about their class position, it was either a fear of falling or concern about the inability of those on the rise to conform to the dictates of respectability. Defining the terms of respectability, in terms of both personal and national virtue, helped give weight to these definitions and alleviate some of the fears of personal and national failure that could be brought on by a slackening of personal and public virtue. In this vision, respectability and patriotism came from correct sentiments rather than calculated interests. If the public good could be defined in these terms, commerce was also susceptible to domestication and could be restrained by correct sentiments rather than controlled by rapacious self-interest. Americans perceived commerce through the lens of political economy, which insisted on the moral dimensions of economic life.[53] This promise of market refinement made the language of exchange seem particularly useful as a description of all kinds of actions, not just those of commerce, and made it possible to define not just respectability in non-economic terms but also economic success in sentimental terms.[54]

Market Sentiments is a history of this ideological transformation. It is not a social history of nineteenth-century consumers, although I owe a great debt to the excellent social histories about nineteenth-century America.[55] In these pages, I join the ongoing debate about the history of the middle class from the perspective of cultural history. By looking at both material culture and written sources, this study brings together evidence that is often studied in isolation and demonstrates how an integrated look at sentimental culture lets us see a more diverse audience for sentimental texts and performances.

Chapter 1 and Chapter 2 explore the models of moral economic advice available to readers in the 1820s before the explosion of sentimental advice literature and novels. In Chapter 1, I begin with the discussion of moral market culture in Sarah Josepha Hale's *American Ladies' Magazine* because her definition of a market economy organized by "good motives" demonstrates how much of the rhetoric about moral economy that defined a middle-class market culture derived from debates popular from the earliest years of the Republic.[56] Hale was particularly interested in the problem of integrating the demands of political economy and domestic economy. The persuasiveness of her sentimental rhetoric demonstrates the power of conservative ideas to create the possibility for real and sometimes radical change that was not always the intent of those who articulated the ideas.[57] This change was subtle and powerful and sneaky. Understanding the contribution of conservative ideas to social change helps reconcile the seeming anomaly of a woman like Sarah Hale, who advocated women's traditional roles while conducting a lifelong career in the literary marketplace.

Hale was not the only woman who struggled with the disjunction between life and ideology. Magazines, gift books, advice books, and etiquette books provided an abundance of information about market negotiations and opportunities, especially for women. The audience for these publications was primarily an urban, northeastern population of aspiring middle-class women and men, but as they circulated more widely, the ideas they contained had an increasing influence.[58] The sustained discussion of economic issues in popular writing for women from the 1820s on suggests that it is important to trace the development of this sentimental economic discourse before the rise of the best-selling American sentimental novel, the majority of which were published after 1835. Although Americans read many British and French novels of sentiment, the relationship between sentimentalism and market culture that appears in American novels speaks to a particular interest in the problems of class and culture. With the exception of Sarah Hale, Catharine Sedgwick, Lydia Sigourney, Eliza Leslie, and Lydia Maria Child, most prominent female writers were born after 1810. Best-selling authors such as Harriet Beecher Stowe, Susan Warner, and Maria Cummins were part of a second generation of literary sentimentalists.

Chapter 2 explores the marked increase in the 1820s of the circulation of popular religious texts by the American Tract Society and other charitable religious organizations. The intent of these tracts was to circulate Christian teaching, encourage conversion, and prepare for the Millennium, but they also participated in the project of defining moral market culture. This was augmented by the contributions of tracts and Sunday schools to the development of children's literature. The generation of readers who came of age in the 1830s were profoundly influenced by this kind of reading and learned to depend on didactic fiction for economic advice.

After 1830, *Godey's Lady's Book* became one of the most influential sources of advice about behavior in the marketplace. Chapter 3 demonstrates how Louis A. Godey capitalized on the reading audience trained by religious tracts and earlier magazines to create the first commercially successful magazine. Evidence from *Godey's* figures largely in my study. Its wide circulation demonstrates how sentimental ideas that originated in eastern cities circulated throughout other areas of the country. Also, the editors and contributors to *Godey's* produced a wide variety of additional novels, essays, advice books, cookbooks, and other kinds of popular manuals that added to and elaborated on the ideas expressed in the magazine. *Market Sentiments* is not exclusively a study of *Godey's*, but *Godey's* was a powerful source of information for its readers. Louis Godey and Sarah Hale actively tried to create and control the debate about a moral market culture that circulated with their magazine.

In July 1852, Godey addressed his subscribers from his "Arm Chair," as he called his monthly column:

> READER! You may not be aware of the fact, but this first day of July is, indeed, the birthday of "Godey's Lady's Book!" Twenty-two years ago this day, we commenced the publication of a magazine which had but few friends or admirers when first ushered into life, but which has lived and prospered, while many others, apparently of a more sturdy stock, have breathed awhile in sorrow, then early sickened, and finally died in utter neglect. We mention this fact, not because it ministers to our vanity, but because it inspires us with the most lively sentiments of gratitude.[59]

Godey calls his readers' attention to the longevity of his enterprise and the particular way of thinking about market relations that he and Sarah Hale helped popularize during those twenty-two years. Business was like life. Magazines were anthropomorphic, thriving or sickening based on the exchange of sentiments. This kind of discussion of business had become commonplace, not just in the pages of *Godey's Lady's Book* but also in all kinds of sentimental publications that instructed middle-class women and men how to navigate the new possibilities of market culture. Just as Esther Howland firmly situated her manufacture of valentines as part of the family enterprise, popular sentimental writers insisted that their products were defined by family enterprise, writ large.

Women shared with men the burdens of economic responsibility that the new market culture brought. Frequent bankruptcies and illness made the financial lives of the nineteenth-century middle class turbulent. Adverse circumstances often drove women to renegotiate their understanding of the rhetoric of separate spheres.[60] Although women were held up as a moral antidote to the corrupting forces of the market and the home was cast as a pure arena of rejuvenation after the quotidian entanglements with Mammon, the insistence on the separation of spheres was, at most, an indication of the desire for separation and a congratulation of the moments of its success. Chapters 4 and 5 examine the education popular authors, both male and female, offered about the mutual dependence of political economy and domestic economy. Economic advice writers constantly reminded their readers that a successful middle-class existence depended on the balance and integration of home and market life rather than their alienation. The market economy was, from the beginning, intimately bound up with domestic economy, and the home rather than being immune to the imperatives of market culture was one of the first places where people explored a new understanding of goods as commodities. The home was not separate from the new market relations, it was at the center of those negotiations.[61]

In the new market economy, both women and men took on new managerial roles, carefully drawing the distinction between mental and manual work.[62] Women experienced change in the nature of their domestic production as factories took over the production of cloth, soap, candles, and other traditional domestic products. Despite the freedom from these tasks, the amount of work required to care for larger and more elaborate houses increased.[63] Middle-class domestic production encompassed not only the more abstract kinds of cultural production that shaped middle-class family relations but also the adaptation, in an urban context, of women's production of goods made to sell for "pin money." Middle-class women developed a language of the market and conventions of production in order to represent labor as duty, thereby distinguishing it from that of working-class women. "Duty" was an important code word that camouflaged the nature of their work.[64] Middle-class women chose not to discuss the domestic work they did alone, or in cooperation with servants, because they aspired to an ideal of genteel womanhood that seemed inconsistent with manual labor. Duty, however, also made it possible to regain economic activities by describing work in moral rather than economic terms. This protected women from the scrutiny of the market but allowed them to participate in the growing market economy and, most important, allowed them to lay claim to the ideas of virtue associated with production.[65]

These ideas about women's work and moral market culture were tested in the production of fancywork for the sentimental marketplace of the charity fair. Chapter 6 uses the role of the fancywork "expert" and the production of fancywork for profit to examine the impulse to create a new kind of market based on a gift economy. Charity fairs are examined in Chapter 7. Women tried to define the terms of exchange at these fairs and the relationship of the production of fancywork to social production. The marketing of fancywork as a genteel labor of leisure gave legitimacy to its production for charity fairs and personal profit; it allowed middle-class women to represent their labor as *fancy* work and their leisure as fancy *work*. Charity fairs demonstrated concrete ways that sentimentalism could be harnessed in the service of profit, but this raised important questions about the relationship of moral profit and pecuniary profit.

Anxieties about this relationship were particularly evident in the discussions of love and marriage that fueled the popularity of romantic love and celebration of Valentine's Day at midcentury examined in Chapter 8. Parents, anxious about maintaining family status, saw the marriage of their children as a time of both great opportunity and significant peril. At the moment new households were formed, the relationship between the economic and cultural definitions of class was most fragile. The explosion in the celebration of Valentine's Day at midcentury was in part due to how the circulation of valentines offered a symbolic economy in which to explore the relationship of property and propriety and seductive, but potentially perilous, possibilities of investing goods with sentiment. Like Valentine's Day, spinoff products exposed the tenuous nature of sentimental value, a concept essential to the idea of moral market culture yet fraught with the possibilities of fraud and inversion. Chapter 9 explores the fluidity of sentimental meaning after 1850 and the reassessment of sentimental value through an examination of the spinoff products from sentimental performances by Fanny Elssler and Jenny Lind and the best-selling novels of the 1850s and 1860s. The question of sentimental value was of particular concern when it came to slavery, a subject that dominated popular debate in the 1850s. These debates brought home the serious nature of the quest for a moral market culture. Sentiments, both moral and economic, defined not only the domestic economy of the parlor but also the political economy of the Union.

One

GOOD MOTIVES

The Sentiments of Middle-Class Market Culture

*I*n 1815, Lydia Howard Huntley, an aspiring poetess and schoolmistress, published a slim volume, *Moral Pieces in Prose and Verse*, supported by an impressive list of subscribers from across New England who were sympathetic to Huntley's need to raise money to support her aging parents.[1] In this volume, Huntley collected her poems and a few essays on moral topics, ranging from natural beauty to filial duty to politics, gleaned from lectures to her pupils. The political poems were topical and reflected her Federalist politics: the Fourth of July, 1814; the burning of Washington, DC; the election of 1814; the Hartford convention of 1814–15. The essays, which digested Huntley's own education in moral philosophy for her pupils, touched on the subjects of memory, novel reading, the estimation of character, self-knowledge, happiness, and the government of the passions. The volume was introduced by an advertisement, written anonymously by her employer, Daniel Wadsworth, a prominent citizen of Hartford, Connecticut. Wadsworth emphasized the spontaneous nature of Huntley's writing and her youth, defining her authorship as the product of nat-

Figure 1. Sarah Josepha Hale, portrait painted by W. B. Chambers and engraved for *Godey's Lady's Book* by W. G. Armstrong, 1850.

ural emanation rather than calculated ego. The volume was well received, and Huntley became a popular poet. Four years later, she married Charles Sigourney, a successful businessman, and ended her teaching career. She continued to write, using the proceeds to contribute to charitable causes and, after a while, to augment the declining family finances. By the middle of the 1830s, Lydia Howard Huntley Sigourney was one of the most famous and beloved poets of the new tradition of American literature and an important contributor to her family's financial stability. Her early foray into the literary marketplace helped define the terms of authorship for American women writers.

Lydia Sigourney (1791–1865) was the first of a generation of women writers, born and raised in New England, who not only called attention to the possibilities of an American poetry and prose but also used literature as a venue to define a national culture based on the principles of conservative Christian thought and Federalist politics. Catharine Sedgwick (1789–1867), Lydia Maria Child (1802–1880), and Sarah Josepha Hale (1788–1879) admired Sigourney and followed her into print. They wrote on a similar range of subjects, historical, political, philosophical, and economic, as well as domestic.[2] Their early novels, *A New England Tale* (1822), *Hobomok* (1824), and *Northwood* (1827), offered moral lessons on more than just domestic life. Like their male contemporaries who edited and contributed to the *North American Review,* they participated in debates about the development of national culture and identity through the media of prose and fiction. All of these authors, male and female, used literature to illustrate the ways virtue linked politics and religion and provided a framework for social reform. Washington Street, Boston's publishers' row, was the hub of this cultural activity. Bowles and Dearborn, a prominent conservative firm, published the *North American Review,* the *Christian Examiner,* and the *Literary Gazette,* as well as novels by Sarah J. Hale, Lydia Maria Child, and other aspiring writers. Just down the street was Putnam and Hunt, later Marsh, Capen and Putnam, the publisher of Hale's *American Ladies' Magazine.*[3] This firm also published books by Sedgwick, Hale, and Child. The authors and publishers who shaped Boston literary culture attempted to educate a generation of readers who came of age in the 1830s by articulating a debate about moral culture that laid the ground work not just for a definition of national culture but also for the development of their own literary careers.

These authors, whose vision was strongly influenced by Federalist politics, hoped to shape the reading practices of both women and men by engaging in the central cultural debates of the day. It was, Federalists argued, the responsibility of the best educated and most virtuous to create social harmony through judicious leadership. Deference remained a crucial element of the social fabric. Without it, the potential for chaos was great. In order to maintain social harmony, it was essential that the general public acknowledge the continuing importance of social deference by emulating the behavior of the social and economic elite. This second generation of Federalists used literature to articulate a conservative philosophy that justified elitism through social responsibility. Their philosophy instilled a respect for the individual tempered by the understanding that the individual could only be fully realized in the context of community. At the center of the Federalist world view was a critique of the rapacious nature of liberal capitalism that they associated with a growing middle class.[4] When Federalist writers addressed the growing class of prosperous men and women, they counseled restraint rather than celebration of the rewards of progress.

In addition to their Federalist sympathies, Sigourney, Sedgwick, Hale, and Child were committed to integrating Christian teachings into the practical actions of everyday life. All abandoned the Congregational faith of their families. Sedgwick converted to Unitarianism.[5] Sigourney and Hale became members of the Episcopal Church.[6] Child, much to the disappointment of her brother, Convers Francis, who became a prominent Unitarian minister in Watertown, Massachusetts, became a member of Boston's Swedenborgian New Church when she abandoned the Congregational Church.[7] Child was an anomalous member of this group of literary women. She was the youngest and the least conservative of them. With the publication of *An Appeal in Favor of That Class of Americans Called Africans* in 1833, Child fell out of favor with her colleagues. Even Sedgwick, who was the most sympathetic to Child's abolitionism, was alarmed by the extremity of Child's position, and their friendship suffered.[8] Many of Boston's social and literary elite, who had received Child so enthusiastically ten years earlier, dropped her from their social circle. In addition to the loss of her social life and literary patronage, Child's free library privileges at the Boston Athenaeum were terminated, which was a significant blow to her ability to do scholarly research. She became an example of the dangers of evangelical fervor. Like her brother Convers, she counseled a tempered tolerance of southern slavery and advocated a gradualist approach to abolition organized around colonization that did not jeopardize social order.[9] In their eyes, it was the social upheavals in the North that demanded immediate attention, and despite their denominational differences, they all based their vision of a Christian society on their religious faith and experience, as well as on the moral essays of British writers such as Hannah More and Maria Edgeworth, whose works provided models for the translation of Christian sentiments into practical action.

Sigourney, Sedgwick, Hale, and Child were educated beyond the ordinary provision for girls in the early Republic. Sigourney, who came from a poor family, received her education from a wealthy benefactress who allowed Sigourney to use her library.[10] Sedgwick also gained more from reading in her father's library than from her education in a series of girls' schools.[11] Child and Hale both benefitted greatly from the intellectual generosity of their brothers, Convers Francis, who attended Harvard College, and Horatio Buell, who attended Dartmouth College.[12] Hale, who was educated at home by her mother, appreciated her brother's willingness to share his education with her. "To my brother Horatio, I owe what knowledge I have of Latin, of the higher branches of mathematics, and of mental philosophy," she wrote. "He often regretted that I could not, like himself, have the privilege of a college education."[13] Their educational opportunities made it possible for these women authors to engage in the same debates as their male contemporaries.

Dartmouth and Harvard were centers of Federalist thought. Each provided a conservative education that emphasized self-imposed restraint of those in power to balance the tendency toward democratic excess inherent in republicanism. Moral philosophy was at the core of the curriculum. Students read Dugald Stewart's *Elements of the Philosophy of the Human Mind* (1792) and William Paley's *Principles of Moral and Political Philosophy* (1788). These texts resonated with the Federalist concern with social order rather than resistance to tyranny and continued to be standard references for moral philosophy throughout the nineteenth century.[14] Hale expected her readers to be familiar with Stewart, Paley, and other moral philosophers, but she encouraged the translation of their ideas into new forms of prose she hoped her readers would find appealing. Her references to these works indicated her sense of their value and her hope that they provided a common vocabulary on moral subjects for her readers.[15] In an 1855 review of a revised and abridged edition of Stewart's *Elements of Philosophy*, Hale praised the editor, Francis Bowen, professor of moral and intellectual philosophy at Harvard College, for providing an edition well suited to the studies of female students, who might have been deterred by the length of the unabridged work. Hale reiterated her opinion of the excellence of Stewart's work but acknowledged that in its original form it was "too diffuse for general use."[16] Throughout her tenure as editor of *Godey's*, she continued to recommend works that had been a formative part of her own education and offer examples of their practical application in her own writings on moral subjects. Like Paley, Hale advocated the illustration of morality through "situations which arise in the life of the inhabitants of this country and in these times"; she used this pragmatic approach to moral philosophy to craft a vision of a national culture defined by a "common Christianity."[17]

Moral philosophy helped these women authors articulate, in concert with their intellectual brothers at the *North American Review*, a conservative opposition to the frivolity of light reading and superfluities that were a subject of Federalist concern. The economic prosperity of the 1790s had prompted a wide range of discussion about the temptations of luxury.[18] It was the connection of commodities to fashion that caused the most concern. As more families were able to afford domestic furnishings, carriages, clothing, and books that imitated the taste of American and European elites, magazines, moral essays, pamphlets, and novels argued for the importance of virtue to restrain the emulative desires of the newly prosperous. With the rewards of prosperity came new responsibilities for maintaining personal and national virtue. Although successful businessmen and their families were able to afford more domestic luxury goods, an insistence on restraint rather than a tacit approval of emulation characterized the middle-class view of the market for luxuries. Unchecked emulative behavior was at odds with the notions of moral economy. Prosperous individuals who resisted their emulative desires, maintained a balance between virtue and commerce, staving off the excesses of luxury that would lead to social decay. Underpinning this rhetoric of restraint, however, was the acknowledgment that the line between necessity and luxury was often blurred. Newly prosperous men and women needed help understanding not only which luxuries to avoid but also when a luxury could be considered a necessity.

Sigourney, Sedgwick, Hale, and Child shared these intellectual concerns, but their fiction, which often addressed economic issues, was also influenced by the economic difficulties in their own lives. With the exception of Sedgwick, who remained single and came from a family of economic means, Sigourney, Child, and Hale were independent economic actors throughout their lives. Each woman taught school before her marriage. Sigourney and Child began their literary careers as single women but continued to publish within the context of their marriages. Hale embarked on her career as a widow, but she had published a few poems before her husband's death.[19] She often championed the importance of an intellectual as well as emotional bond between husband and wife, and, indeed, her husband had provided a continuation of the intellectual relationship she had shared with her brother. She discussed their practice of evening study in the preface to *The Ladies Wreath* (1837), a gift book of poetry she edited.[20] In 1822, after a brief illness, David Hale died, leaving his wife to support five young children, the last born after his death. Although he had been a prosperous lawyer and a Mason, he was at the beginning of his career and did not have significant savings or property at his death. After an unsuccessful attempt at millinery, Sarah Hale published a volume of poetry, *The Genius of Oblivion* (1823), with the financial backing of the Masons. By combining the intellectual capital of her education with the economic assistance of the Masons, she created a viable economic persona for herself.

Hale fashioned a place for herself in literary culture that did not jeopardize her social standing or her womanly modesty. She used the skills and knowledge she had learned in domestic life to enter the market and support her family without challenging traditional definitions of womanhood. In the preface to *Northwood*, her first novel, she defined the terms of her authorship and her relationship to the reading public. A novel must have a good introduction, she noted, if an author hoped to engage the majority of readers, who only read the beginning and end of a novel, merely skimming the remainder. It has "cost me much study and not a little vexation," she admitted, to discover "how to please those restless readers who can find gratification only in constant excitement." Hale worried about the corrosive effects of a hunger for novelty on literary culture, but she was honest about her desire for success in the world of literary enterprise: "That I am anxious to obtain the approbation of the public, it would be folly to deny—worse than folly, it would be falsehood."[21] By admitting her desire for profit, Hale was more forthright than many authors. She was even more pointed in her instructions to her readers in the final paragraph of the novel. "I am confident," she wrote, "that were the circumstances under which this book was written, known, and the motives which have induced its publication revealed, it would receive from the most, toleration, and from the benevolent, patronage."[22] The exemplary nature of her motives was justification for the production of a novel, and for its consumption. Good motives, a theme she pursued throughout her career, underpinned the market philosophy she used to justify all her literary enterprises.

In the preface to *Flora's Interpreter* (1832), one of her most successful publications, Hale evoked Hannah More's poem "The Importance of Trifles," which was frequently republished in anthologies for young girls, to warrant both the production and consumption of her book.[23] She offered a market philosophy that resonated with the middle-class desire to distinguish between acceptable and excessive consumption. "Good motives may mingle a little of the useful even with trifles," she instructed her readers. "If this were not often the case," she insisted, "life would be a sad blank; for its greatest portion is occupied about trifles." Because so much energy was expended in "the invention and production of trifles," their pervasive nature made them impossible to ignore: "And when trifles occupy so much of the grave business of society, it is excusable that they should be considered of consequence in its amusements."[24] Even a book as seemingly frivolous as a flower dictionary, Hale argued, if it were written correctly, could play an important role in defining the terms of a moral market culture.

The conservative tone of Hale's writing attracted the attention of Rev. John Lauris Blake, the principal of the Cornhill School for Young Ladies in Boston. In 1827, Blake invited Hale to be the editor of a new magazine for women.[25] As editor of a monthly magazine, Sarah Hale had an unusual opportunity to contribute to the definition of the terms of moral culture central to the Federalist literary project that united male and female writers. As Hale often reminded her readers, hers was the first periodical intended expressly for women. Addressing a female audience allowed her to write with an authority that a mixed audience would have precluded. She imagined a female readership, but not in a world devoid of male readers. Her literary models were periodicals designed to be read by both men and women, and she knew that men would read her publication as well. Hale was well aware of her financial dependence on fathers and husbands who controlled women's spending. She not only assumed they read her publication but also, in her first issue, addressed them directly to assure them of her good motives. She recommended her magazine to fathers, husbands, brothers, and lovers as a worthy companion for women in the absence of male conversation. In order to create a happy home, Hale argued, women must be conversant on a wide variety of topics.[26]

From the beginning of her public career, Hale was an advocate for the education of girls and women, a position influenced by her own experience with the precariousness of family fortunes. Her economic advice for women was rooted in the "correct understanding" of moral sentiments that encouraged restraint rather than indulgence. The public and private spheres of market and home, Hale instructed her readers, were interdependent. The home could not be a haven from the market unless it was bound by the same understanding of economy. Political economy and domestic economy must be in balance, just as production and consumption must be. Women, therefore, were central to definitions of both domestic virtue and national economic virtue. Her own experiences had made her a pragmatist, and her practical approach made her advice influential.

Hale's version of this conservative economic philosophy was not unusual. Traveling in America in the early 1830s, Alexis de Tocqueville observed a common acceptance of what he called the "Doctrine of Self-Interest Properly Understood," which was based on a pragmatic rather than idealistic vision of virtue. "It cannot make a man virtuous," Tocqueville noted, "but its discipline shapes a lot of orderly, temperate, moderate, careful and self-controlled citizens." This doctrine supported Tocqueville's general assertion that democracy did not lend itself to the achievement of excellence, but he conceded that "the doctrine of self-interest properly understood appears to me the best suited of all philosophical theories to the wants of men in our time." He saw it as Americans' "strongest remaining guarantee against themselves." Private interest was bound to become, he asserted, "the driving force behind all behavior," but Europeans could learn from an American's ability to "sacrifice some of his private interests to save the rest." Properly understood, the doctrine of self-interest made this possible. Unlike the age of aristocracy, Tocqueville argued, the modern era was not one of "blind sacrifice and instinctive virtues."[27] Men must choose strategic sacrifices and this required careful education. This was just the education that Hale wished to offer to her female readers.

Hale regarded the instruction of proper behavior in the market sphere as part of a woman's necessary education. Presenting an image of disinterested profit based on duty, she offered her own experience as a good model for other women. At the end of her second year as editor of the *American Ladies' Magazine,* she reassured her readers that her continuing efforts as editor were still based in duty to her family rather than on her own desire for fame. It was the sense of duty that sustained her, she informed her readers, for although "the *author* might grow weary, the *mother* must continue her efforts."[28] A woman's preference for private life, in conjunction with her aversion to the scrutiny of the market, Hale opined, was insurance against the egotism of commercial enterprise. "It is only in emergencies, in cases where duty demands the sacrifice of female sensitiveness, that a lady of sense and delicacy will come before the public, in a manner to make herself conspicuous," she demurely admitted. "There is little danger," she assured her readers, "that such a one will be arrogant in her pretensions." In case her readers misunderstood her purpose in defining her own market persona, she made the reference explicit: "These remarks may be considered as allusions to our own case."[29] By framing women's public economic activities in terms of duty, women could engage in public activities without transgressing the boundaries of traditional female roles. The passive construction of this caveat helped give legitimacy to her description of a woman's public role because the grammar made it sound like a truism rather than an opinion.

The importance of good motives in all economic activity was a theme Hale returned to again and again. In a fictional exchange about courtship, modeled on Hannah More's *Coelebs in Search of a Wife*, she scornfully rejected the assertion by "Coelebs" that he was unable to marry because he could not find a wife who was industrious and intelligent as well as accomplished.[30] "Lucilla" responded that women were too wise to let men know that they are accomplished in the science of domestic economics. "You may, to be sure, write very sage essays about female influence, and praise industry and prudence, and condemn extravagance, and sentimentalize about the loveliness of domestic virtues," she noted, "but after all, you never choose, for a wife, the original of such a humdrum portrait."[31] Worse than the hypocrisy of claiming to value one set of virtues while only considering superficial beauty, "Lucilla" chastised, were the mercenary interests of men who really wanted a wife who would "help them to gain a fortune!" Nothing exposed the "calculating selfishness of the era" more than the fact that "the refined and civilized gentlemen of the nineteenth century want wives who will be profitable!"[32] This desire stood at odds with the very nature of chivalry, and putting the wives of the fashionable classes to work created larger economic problems in a national economy already beset with difficulties finding work for the laboring classes. Manufacturing was at a standstill because merchants could not find a market for their goods. The only way to balance production with consumption, "Lucilla" argued, was to make it unfashionable for women to work, except to raise their children. To allow men "to seek wives for pecuniary profit" was a dangerous trend: "How supremely selfish and commonplace the social world has become!—Every man taking care of himself, and caring for nobody else; and women expected to contribute their share to the support of their families, and engaging in business with all the calculation of financiers."[33] A husband's expectation that a woman would work destroyed the fragile balance of economic action that defined political economy and allowed the home to offer a refuge from the travail of the market. Unless men as well as women relied on good motives to guide their economic behavior, social harmony would not be possible.

Although Hale characterized her participation in the market as a temporary solution, her continued presence in the magazine business after her children had grown offered silent testimony to the rewards of her public role,
despite her advocacy of women's domestic roles. As long as a woman did not
neglect her duties in the private sphere, Hale saw no reason why she should
not pursue activities in the public sphere.[34] A literary career seemed to offer
the perfect balance of the two spheres. Hale painted an alluring picture of literary enterprise, imagining a woman author "seated by her own fireside, with
the simple apparatus of pen, ink and paper." From the tranquility of this
domestic vantage point, "she converses with the world at large—admonishes
others by the admonitions of her own conscience—imparts her own experience to warn the inexperienced, and 'if in the vein,' sends forth cheerfulness
to enliven the heavy heart and wit to amuse the dull."[35] Her public role was
an extension of her private one, and in this formulation, despite her public
economic persona, Hale could insist that she never left the private sphere.

Despite this rhetorical modesty, Hale was well aware of how frequently
women found themselves in need of a public economic persona. Because of
the expectations of middle-class family life, in times of retrenchment, women
struggled to maintain economic opportunities for their children, especially
their education, rather than dismantling the family circle. No one knew this
better than Hale, and she often offered advice about women's economic
responsibilities: "'What can she do?'—is a question frequently propounded
when a woman is left, either by loss or misfortunes of her friends, to struggle
for herself. What can she do? There are but very few venues of business in
which women are privileged to walk. The wages paid for female labor is [*sic*]
very trifling; and when she has others besides herself to provide for, it seems
almost impossible that a woman can succeed."[36] The difficulty of women's
economic roles further emphasized the importance of strict adherence to the
dictates of womanly behavior in economic activities.

Obliquely, Hale reminded her readers of her own success on this front, but
she also marshaled new examples to inspire hope in the breasts of those in
need: "We seldom see the good effects of female enterprise better set forth
than in the following sketches of Western manners and character, which we

extract from the letter of a Boston lady, a friend of ours, now residing in Tennessee.—Should any New England woman, feeling her lot is hard, complainingly inquire, what can a woman do?—let her be referred to the examples her sisters in the West have given, and *do all she can.*"[37] These western women turned their domestic labor into services for others traveling west. One knitted purses to sell, another made cups from gourds to provide traveling cups for milk. Each woman made substantial profits from these enterprises and played an important role in her family economy. Women could not afford to be ignorant about the principles of economy, and they should not, Hale instructed, be constrained by a false understanding of the duties of womanhood. In Hale's opinion, these western women demonstrated that good motives rather than social conventions should be the basis of both political and domestic economy.

In 1828, the first year of the *American Ladies' Magazine*, Hale reviewed *Political Economy*, published by Bowles and Dearborn. She called this book to the attention of her readers not only because she thought it was a worthy subject but also because the author, Mrs. Bryan, was a woman: "We assure our readers, that a book with the above formidable title (formidable to ladies, we mean—the men in this age of politics and economy, ought to comprehend the matter as clearly as Adam Smith himself,) has been written by a *woman*. We hope that females will feel a curiosity, not only to read this notice, but actually read the work."[38] The principles of political economy were introduced in a series of "conversations between two ladies" and explained in familiar terms. Quoting from the definition of political economy given in the book, Hale summed up the accessible nature of the argument: "I once heard a lady ask a philosopher to tell her in a few words, what is meant by political economy. Madam, he replied, you understand perfectly what is meant by *household economy*; you need only extend your idea of the economy of a family to that of a whole people—of a nation, and you will have some comprehension of the nature of political economy."[39]

This pragmatic vision of the links between domestic economy and political economy was central to Hale's formulation of a community organized by good motives. The study of political economy in the early nineteenth century emphasized the relationship between ethical behavior and economic behavior, rather than a split between the two. Hale defined the national Christian society she championed by insisting on the necessary relationship between virtuous politics and moral economics. The economic advice she gave throughout her career was based on maintaining a balance between the two. Even if women did not read political economists such as Adam Smith, she argued, they were obliged to understand these ideas. In her vision of domesticity, the home was linked to the nation, not as a refuge from the public sphere but as a barometer of its condition.

Political economy and domestic economy, Hale argued, must be kept in balance to create the possibility for "doing good." It was as selfish to save for the sake of frugality as it was to thoughtlessly consume luxuries, she cautioned her readers. Her review of Lydia Maria Child's *Frugal Housewife* is particularly pointed on this subject: "Nothing in creation is more unlovely than a selfish avaricious child, except a miserly woman."[40] Hale complained about the title of Child's book. Frugality, she insisted, must be prompted by the good motives of Christians and republicans rather than by selfishness. "The *motives*, make the excellence, or the evil in the character of actions, as respects the performer," she wrote.[41] Only through the development of good motives could the dangers of selfishness be tempered. Hale distinguished between seeking to be rich and seeking to enrich and took Child to task for failing to explicitly make this distinction.[42]

Hale frequently admonished her readers to teach their children proper lessons about economy. "Will not the free people of our Republic be among the first to endeavor to shake off the dominion of selfishness, and make the object of their ambition, moral and mental excellence, rather than wealth?" she asked. This transformation could only be possible through education, and the "women of America," she declared, "are deeply responsible." Women were the first to "awaken the moral feelings, and it is by them that the moral sentiments are directed, and the habits which finally stamp the character, fixed."[43] In order for mothers to fulfill this important responsibility, they must learn to teach by example. Benjamin Franklin's adage "Time is money" must be revised, she insisted; instead, mothers should teach their children that *time is their oppor-*

tunity for doing good.[44] The virtue of this approach, she argued, allowed women to participate in public fund-raising efforts, such as the campaign for a monument to the Battle of Bunker Hill, a cause near to her heart, without transgressing the boundaries of propriety. A mother's efforts were an object lesson to her children about the relationship of "enobling sentiments" and the true value of money.[45] Hale participated in the campaign to create the Bunker Hill Monument with William Tudor and joined Edward Everett in his crusade to preserve Mount Vernon.[46] She linked these campaigns to her crusade for domestic economy by suggesting to her readers that they could raise as much as fifty thousand dollars by giving up the unnecessary luxuries of fashionable dress and frivolous literature rather than asking men for money.[47]

In 1832, Hale reviewed Harriet Martineau's *Illustrations of Political Economy,* also published by Bowles and Dearborn. "Whoever dreamed the subject of Political Economy could be made susceptible to romantic interest?—and illustrated by stories, which should make its principles appear simple and practical as household management?" Hale marveled. "But trust the ladies for invention," she rejoined, "they can and do prepare the truths of philosophy for practical use in a manner more captivating than men."[48] Although Hale was confident about her own commitment to intellectual rigor, she worried about the stamina of her readers. Rather than insisting on the purity of education, she understood the virtues of recasting complex ideas in an accessible form. From the earliest years of her editorial career, Hale claimed an important educational role for this kind of interpretive text. She did not invent the practice of using the entertaining nature of romantic stories to weave moral sentiments and political economy together for practical purposes, but she promoted it. In this way, her approach differed from that of the contributors to the *North American Review,* whose commitment to purity limited their influence. The interest of Bowles and Dearborn in Bryan's *Political Economy* and Harriet Martineau's *Illustrations of Political Economy* demonstrates that this kind of education for women was part of mainstream conservative thought.

Despite her pragmatic approach, Hale still struggled to make her magazine a financial success. Her primary difficulty, which she shared with every other magazine editor, was the failure of her subscribers to pay faithfully for the magazine. As her financial situation worsened, her gentle reminders became more insistent. The financial "panic" in the winter of 1833–34 diminished Hale's subscriber list significantly. In January 1835, she wrote to her readers, bravely predicting that with improved fortunes, her subscriber rolls would grow. She was now, she informed them, "part proprietor of the work" and thus bore a greater share of the responsibility for the magazine's financial success. Hale was discouraged by the sagging profits of her enterprise. "We intend the Magazine shall be a profitable work to our readers," she affirmed, but it must be profitable for the editor as well. "Last year this was not the case," she lamented. Hale, who had spent considerable editorial energy convincing her readers to renounce frivolous luxuries, found that many readers still considered her magazine a luxury rather than a necessity: "It seems to be the opinion of many people that literature is a *luxury,* and if they must make any retrenchments, this luxury is the *first* to be dispensed with."[49] In this circumstance, she faced an interesting test of her formulation of a market culture based on good motives. Because production of the magazine was not based in luxury but governed by necessity and good motives, her readers ought not to treat it as a luxury. The conditions of their consumption must match the conditions of her production. The failure of her subscribers to understand the necessity of this parity caused Hale intellectual and financial distress. By July 1836, she was beseeching her subscribers to "act the friendly part" and pay their back debts.[50] In the December issue, she informed her readers that beginning with the January 1837 issue, she would merge her publication with Louis Godey's *Lady's Book.* In this final editorial, she decried not only the failure of her subscribers to act like friends and discharge their debts but also the fact that more women had not contributed their literary efforts to the magazine to "lighten the labors of the editor." Hale feared she had failed to achieve financial independence for herself and intellectual independence for her readers.

Despite her economic frankness, Hale worried that her readers would question her alliance with an explicitly commercial publication such as *Godey's Lady's Book.* Although she welcomed the relief from her monetary woes, she justified her association with Godey's commercial success by framing her new editorship in cultural terms. The new magazine, Hale argued, would benefit from the increase of profit brought in by a merger of the subscription lists. The larger pool of subscribers would offer a national audience for her championship of American literature, thus increasing the scope of moral profit as well. She did not want her former readers to think she had abandoned her principles.

Hale introduced her vision of the new incarnation of the magazine in a lead editorial, "The '*Conversazione.*'" She was particularly concerned with the tone of the conversation. "We shall not affect the learned, logical, or profound style; nor yet permit that air of *badinage* which usually resolves itself into satire or coarseness," Hale informed her readers. She promised to adopt the "tone of playful vivacity, intelligent observation, and refined taste, which predominates in the social *re-unions* of the good and the gifted." By defining the tone of the magazine, she also defined a readership already well acquainted with matters of literary taste and intellectual refinement. The "re-unions" she imagined inspired conversations in which "all that is lofty in genius, and holy in sentiment, flows out as naturally and beautifully as the flowers bloom in the light of a fair June morning."[51] These conversations mimicked those of the literary conversation clubs that were popular among both men and women in the 1820s and 1830s, especially in Boston.[52] Before the death of her husband, Hale had belonged to a literary club in New Hampshire called the Coterie, whose members gave dramatic performances and public readings. Drawing on this model, Hale was able to explicitly invite men to join her *Conversazione*, making an argument for the importance of the magazine in public culture as well as in private education.

Hale played up the important relationship between public and private conversation. She was very clear that it was an engagement rather than idle chitchat. Members of the *Conversazione* must procure a ticket, in the form of the magazine, and regular attendance was required. By framing the arrival of the magazine as a performance on a particular day, Hale conjured up the image of an audience gathered to enjoy the performance, a united community spread out across the national landscape. She invited "every lady in our land" to attend the *Conversazione*, melding a national agenda for cultural improvement with the hope of increased circulation of the magazine. The editorial staff of the magazine, which Hale proudly informed her readers included Lydia Sigourney, Hannah Gould, Elizabeth Ellet, Eliza Leslie, and Emma Willard, conducted the *Conversazione*. Subscribers were expected to foster an ongoing conversation among themselves. Part of their reading pleasure came from the knowledge that they were part of a community of readers united by the intellectual and aesthetic perspective that Hale, as editor of *Godey's Lady's Book*, promoted.[53]

Once she had set the scene for the monthly parlor production, Hale outlined its contents, delineating first the importance of fashion, the costumes for the drama at hand. She carefully noted that the fashion plates, and advice the magazine provided, were not intended to be blindly imitated; rather, she expected a reader to determine for herself what would be most appropriate. The "sacred beauty of Christian Character" that Hale hoped to instill in her readers was manifest in the fashion, poetry, literature, and art in the magazine.[54] In laying out the sentimental education she planned for her readers, Hale obliquely referred to the economic circumstances that had curtailed her first educational venue and closed her editorial by consoling herself and her readers that Louis Godey's *Lady's Book* offered a "broader field" to broadcast these ideas. Her own education about the trials of the sentimental marketplace is evident throughout this editorial. As editor of *Godey's*, she tried to create a world defined by good motives in which property and propriety were integrated rather than at odds. Having learned the hard way that professional modesty was not always rewarded, she wanted to fashion an arena in which it would be applauded. By teaching her readers to integrate public and private as part of the Christian Character she sought to inculcate, Hale saw the possibility for a Christian marketplace that united sentiment and profit.

Many second-generation Federalists were unable to transform their arguments about national culture to appeal to this broader audience. By refusing to engage with the pragmatic commercialism of American society, the contributors to the *North American Review* limited their ability to influence the development of market culture.[55] Although Hale shared their disdain for "unthinking" commercialism, she addressed the issue directly and proposed practical reform. Her economic philosophy had clear connections to the classical republicanism popular in Federalist New England, but it was tempered by her desire to find a harmonious balance between the self-interest and the common good.[56] Her own experiences in the market influenced the development of her ideas about market culture. The virtue of good motives remained paramount for Hale, but good motives could further the interest of an individual as long as it did not conflict with the larger social good. Self-interest governed by good motives could refine and reform market culture. It was permissible, Hale admitted, "to do well," as long as the profit came from activities that purported "to do good." With the help of Louis Godey, Hale reached a wider audience and expanded her vision of national culture to be compatible with a national market. She justified her move to *Godey's* by assuring her readers that it would provide a greater circulation for her ideas. In this way, she was more of a pragmatist than the editors of the *North American Review,* who resisted wider circulation in the name of elitist purity and effectively curtailed their own influence. This kind of engagement became increasingly important as the urban population grew in the 1830s. As the number of prosperous women and men began to increase, older models of deference, so dear to Federalists, began to lose what little persuasiveness they might have had in the early Republic.

Two

TELLING TALES

Narratives of a Moral Market

*I*n 1803, Samuel Miller, a prominent Presbyterian minister and author of *A Brief Retrospective of the Eighteenth Century,* bemoaned a decline in scholarly rigor that he attributed to superficial reading.[1] Readers were abandoning the moral lessons of sermons and the seriousness of philosophical texts and immersing themselves in the sprightly musings of literary magazines, the political arguments of newspapers, and the emotional palpitations of sentimental novels.[2] This new kind of reading, Miller remarked, prepared the reader for the new "commercial spirit" of the day. "Light, superficial, and miscellaneous reading" fit "men for the compting-house, and scene of enterprize [sic] and emolument, rather than the recondite investigations of the closet."[3] Mothers should not only fear the dangerous effects of novel reading on their daughters' virtue but also worry about the susceptibility of their sons to the seduction of commerce.

The novel troubled Miller because it represented a fundamental transformation in reading practices. Novels were qualitatively different from sermons.

Novelists looked to everyday life for their subject matter; characters in novels were ordinary men and women. Contemporary settings and compelling plots gave novels a special ability to affect the hearts and minds of readers. Novels, Miller had to admit, were well suited to "the practice of conveying certain principles on the subjects of morals, religion, and politics."[4] Like the parables Christ had used to communicate important truths, novels could "promote the cause of both knowledge and virtue."[5] The power of this pedagogy impressed Miller, but he worried about the proportion of good novels versus bad novels, which he estimated was one in a thousand.[6] A novel could just as easily be written by someone with a bad heart as with a good one, thus leading an unsuspecting reader into treacherous moral territory. "Corrupt opinions are put into the mouths of some favorable hero," Miller warned.[7] It was the responsibility of parents, therefore, not to reject novel reading, as they might have done in past generations, but to carefully monitor the reading habits of their children.

Miller also worried about reading habits, as novels, periodicals, and newspapers encouraged episodic reading that was not conducive to serious study. "Facts are stored," he grumbled, "not for the exercise of rational criticism, not for the deduction of important truth, but that they may be again distributed."[8] Casual reading prepared the reader for the circulation of information as a commodity, a fact exacerbated by the tendency of authors to rush books into print rather than craft them over years of rigorous examination. "Every contemptible scribbler has become an adventurer in this boundless field of enterprise," Miller exclaimed.[9] The superficial reading of superficial books and periodicals did not, in his opinion, bode well for the future of moral education in America. His discussion of the conundrum of novel reading demonstrates how reading practices were an important part of the formation of a national identity and a national culture from the earliest years of the Republic. The critique of the persuasive nature of fictional texts was subtle rather than reactionary. Critics like Miller tried to model a style of moral reading rather than simply condemn popular works.

The increase in available reading material in the early nineteenth century became an explosion by the 1820s.[10] As steamboat routes, canal networks, and railroad lines expanded and improved transportation between the states, commodities began to circulate more freely. Access to books and other printed material increased the number of readers in communities across America. Americans expected to purchase or borrow a large number of novels, periodicals, newspapers, pamphlets, advice manuals, and tracts. Whereas observers from the earliest years of the Republic had drawn connections between reading and the formation of a national identity, the improvements in transporting goods provided new ways to reach a growing national audience. Reading preferences also divided the nation, contributing to the social distinctions of class and gender as well as to the cultural distinctions of high and low culture. Leisure reading did not interest all who had been taught to read, but those who embraced reading invested books, magazines, and periodicals with a special kind of authority that shaped not only their personal interactions but also their understanding of social definitions.[11]

As the literacy rate rose, reading became an important precondition for a middle-class definition of virtuous citizenry and a central part of the childhood education for both boys and girls.[12] Some children learned to read in the newly formed public schools that opened across the country in the early years of the Republic. Others learned in Sunday schools founded in the first decades of the nineteenth century.[13] Mothers played an important role in teaching children to read, and reading as a family activity became an integral part of middle-class domestic life. In addition to the Bible, families read a wide variety of sermons, tracts, and denominational reports circulated by benevolent and reform organizations. Newspapers, magazines, gift books, novels, and children's literature also competed for readers' attention.[14] Religious tracts provided didactic models for children's fiction and contributed to the rising similarity between adult and child reading practices. Children's literature illustrated practical moral lessons of Christian faith through stories of everyday life and helped create an audience for didactic fiction.[15] Although these tales for children relied on the stark characterizations of good and evil that defined religious allegories, the tales' sentiments provided a new kind of realism for small readers, who came to rely throughout their lives on quotidian moral narratives for advice. By the 1830s, this generation had become enthusiastic producers and avid consumers of the didactic sentimental magazines, fiction, and advice books that flooded the market in the second quarter of the nineteenth century.

Religious Enterprise

Itinerant preachers of the Second Great Awakening traveled through cities, towns, and villages, stirring up demand for new forms of religious reading. They urged newly converted men and women to turn their faith to practical purposes through benevolent organizations.[16] Many who listened to their sermons craved additional spiritual instruction, and as a result, between 1790 and 1830 the number of religious texts circulating throughout the nation increased dramatically. In 1790, there were fourteen religious newspapers; by 1830 there were more than 600. Published from Vermont to Louisiana, these newspapers helped to expand the Christian population. The growing numbers of religious groups also competed for the attention of pious readers and potential converts.[17] Religious pluralism in antebellum America required creative solutions to the problem of gaining and holding the attention of potential worshipers. The most successful religious publishing organizations were the American Tract Society, the American Bible Society, located in New York City, the American Sunday School Union, and the Methodist Book Concern in Philadelphia. Members of these organizations were fundamentally concerned with shaping the reading practices of as many Americans as possible. All these societies depended on donations and, especially, the largesse of wealthy merchants, whose contributions made capital investment in state of the art printing technology possible. Successful both economically and spiritually, these societies revolutionized the production and circulation of religious texts. The American Tract Society was the most innovative of these publishing concerns, and other groups frequently adopted its practices.[18]

In 1824, the executive committee of the American Tract Society happily announced in its annual report that twenty-two new tracts had been published in the previous year, and a total of 770,000 tracts had been printed, one tract for every thirteen Americans. In the ten years since 1814, the society had published 4,217,500 tracts.[19] Although tracts were sold to raise money for the society, they often were distributed free of charge, and for the executive committee, these impressive numbers quantified moral progress. Despite this success, members of the society felt they had only begun to scratch the surface of the nation's spiritual needs. Reverend Lathrop of St. Augustine, Florida, who saw the nineteenth century as "this enlightened day of religious enterprise," wondered why "there should still remain fields of moral culture, and subjects of moral wretchedness, unnoticed and unpitied by the eye of Christian philanthropy?"[20] Reverend Lathrop wanted to expand the "Age of Benevolence" by spreading Christian doctrine to those in need. Other reformers echoed his sentiments. They saw the growth of national organizations such as the American Bible Society and the American Tract Society as a way to harness the power of the expanding market to print and circulate tracts.[21] The success of these organizations supported the growth of a national spiritual market through the centralized production of texts and the development of sophisticated methods of circulation.

In its crusade to bring religious reading material to a needy public, the American Tract Society saw the market revolution and spiritual revolution as complementary. The society celebrated its role as a religious enterprise that mobilized the forces of business in the name of moral and spiritual growth.[22] In 1824, the society's Boston and New York branches entered into a reciprocal relationship that allowed each branch to supply the other with tracts. They also built a new headquarters and publishing house for the combined societies on Nassau Street in New York. Wealthy philanthropists, such as the Tappan brothers, paid for the most current printing technology to meet the demands of the market, and the *American Tract Magazine*, the society's official publication, moved its office to New York, which became the hub of a growing organization with national ambitions.[23] A national organization offered an opportunity to coordinate the activities of the society, especially fund raising, the primary source of support for the publication of tracts. In 1826, for example, the *American Tract Magazine* called on its female readers to raise $5,000 to pay for the printing of tracts.[24] The consolidation of the society made it possible to print and distribute tracts at the lowest possible cost. Regional tract societies purchased tracts from the New York office and then distributed them to an ever-widening group of readers from all economic and social levels.

The circulation of tracts became interdependent with the growing networks of a national market.[25] Coordination of the distribution of tracts was one of the primary reasons for locating the main office in New York City. The growth of transportation networks—steamboats, the Erie canal, and later the railroad—made New York City an important hub in the circulation of goods and information. Moreover, tract societies considered steamboats an ideal place to leave their tracts. The long hours of travel, they reasoned, might induce an otherwise uninterested reader to pick up a tract and be converted.[26] The American Seaman's Friend Society and the American Bethel Society, primarily concerned with canal workers, found that the lack of reading material available on ships and canal barges made sailors and canal workers more interested in reading tracts—out of boredom if not from religious curiosity.[27] Merchants facilitated the distribution of tracts by agreeing to carry tracts with them to more remote parts. The willingness of merchants to assist in the circulation of tracts fostered an intellectual and pragmatic relationship between a spiritual and a commercial market. Indeed, the American Tract Society saw itself as an enterprise that God allowed to prosper.

Many prominent clergy representing a wide variety of theological positions were active members of the American Tract Society. Committed to an interdenominational approach, the society's Publishing Committee stipulated that the tracts must focus on doctrines that formed spiritual links between denominations.[28] The committee commissioned authors to write texts that instructed readers on the relationship between reading and salvation. Tracts were published in five major genres: religious classics, reprints of tracts from British tract societies, moral stories, moral stories for young readers in Sunday school, and didactic advice. The persuasiveness of these publications lay in their ability to turn stories of ordinary life into religious parables, to infuse religious teachings with the immediacy of familiar experience, and to animate theological discussions with emotionally accessible and entertaining narratives.[29] Each genre was considered appropriate for different groups of readers, although readers often read broadly across the available list. Because most tracts were written as allegory, readers of varying sophistication could find moral instruction in their pages.

In addition to the impressive statistics illustrating the number of tracts printed and circulated, the 1825 Executive Committee report included a section titled "Narratives: Illustrating the Usefulness of Religious Tracts." Following the format of a tract, this narrative made clear the beneficial relationship between merchants and clergymen and the circulation of goods and tracts.[30] The story is a conversion tale about a merchant who agrees to sell tracts at the request of a clergyman. He takes no interest in the sale of the tracts until he reads one, *The Shepherd of Salisbury Plain* by Hannah More, and experiences conversion himself. The merchant gives the tract to his business partner, who has the same experience. Together, they begin to distribute tracts in great numbers and join several benevolent institutions.[31] This tale illustrated the great faith society members had in the power of reading and the ability of a tract to inspire immediate conversion. The benefit for those who circulated the tracts was as important as the benefit for those who received them. Tracts often emphasized the virtues of reading and its power as a catalyst for moral behavior. Tract societies hoped they could capitalize on a palate developed by "cheap" reading, and that readers accustomed to having their emotions stimulated by fiction would be equally susceptible to the immediacy of redemptive reading. Religious conversion through reading could save the soul of an individual and prompt a person to pass on the tract to another, who might also use it to find God. Thus the circulation of tracts became the responsibility of those whose lives had been transformed by them.

For tract society members, this kind of conversion narrative emphasized the links between commerce and the religious ideas that defined Christian capitalism.[32] Once the merchants had been converted, the circulation of religious ideas became integral to their business. Before the merchant read the tract, he saw it as just another commodity to be sold for profit, and he assumed the clergyman would be the one to profit. After reading the tract, his notion of profit shifted and he saw that moral profit defined the value of circulating the tract. The stories not only taught moral lessons but also changed the commodity status of tracts by suggesting that the act of exchange was more than a commercial transaction. The American Tract Society prided itself on the ability to produce a ten-page tract for a penny, which made it possible to give tracts as gifts to those who could not afford even a nominal fee. Because tracts were usually free, readers willingly passed them along, increasing their potential influence exponentially. "And when we recollect how long a single Tract may be preserved, by how many individuals and families it may be read, and when read by them, to how many others it may be lent," the committee report noted, "it is difficult to conceive of a way in which more good can be accomplished by a very small amount of means."[33] Tracts had more than exchange value, they embodied the exchange of values.[34]

In the 1840s, the American Tract Society expanded its system of distribution by employing colporteurs, agents who distributed tracts to poor, rural men and women who were often only semiliterate. Colporteurs visited more than 150,000 families each year. They not only sold or gave tracts to the men and women they met but also engaged them in prayer, if they were willing.[35] Tract society members embraced the idea of colportage because they worried that the current methods of distribution did not extend widely enough or reach those in greatest need of spiritual guidance. Colporteurs confirmed that in rural areas of the West and South, beyond the range of the commercial networks essential to the distribution of tracts, the need for religious literature exceeded their ability to supply it.[36] Families "destitute of all religious books except the Bible, were each supplied with a book like Baxter's *Call* or *The Saints' Rest* gratuitously; and several thousand with the Bible or Testament by sale or gift."[37] Colporteurs readily sacrificed pecuniary profit in the name of moral profit. Some found that people insisted on paying for a book, some, fearing they would be asked to pay later, would only take the book as a loan, and others refused even a free book.[38]

The American Tract Society selected particular tracts for distribution by colporteurs. These tracts whetted readers' appetites for books, which were more expensive, usually priced at twelve and a half cents, although colporteurs sold them on a sliding scale or gave them to those who could not afford to buy them. The books were reprints of seventeenth- and eighteenth-century texts, emphasizing the timeless nature of the religious message even as the methods of disseminating it became increasingly "modern."[39] The interest in reprinting these older works supported a conservative religious and political agenda that strove to arrest independent religious behavior and define Christianity in traditional ways that supported the social and cultural hierarchy.[40]

Because tracts were short, they could be "read repeatedly with pleasure and profit" and appealed to readers who might not have the stamina to read an entire book. Their accessibility helped develop a readership for religious literature.[41] In addition to reprints of classic religious texts, the American Tract Society published tracts written exclusively for them, often by well-known authors and clergymen. The ability of the society to provide reading matter so cheaply made it possible for it to compete with other, more expensive forms of fiction.[42] Tracts adopted and adapted contemporary literary styles in the service of religious conversion with the intention of wooing readers away from more frivolous forms of reading.[43] Although colporteurs were usually concerned with poor readers, they also complained that the libraries of wealthier readers, who were willing to pay high prices for novels, contained little Christian reading, often only "a few Sunday School books, which their children had obtained as rewards."[44] The American Tract Society Publication Committee hoped that simple, moral stories would capture the imagination of potential converts who were accustomed to reading fiction of a more questionable nature.[45] Those who were committed to the mission of the society tried to redirect the appetites of all the readers they met in order to restrain the consumption of luxuries dangerous to individual moral health and national spiritual health.

The business tactics of the American Tract Society did not strictly conform to the dictates of an emerging capitalist economy. As with other sentimental enterprises, the society integrated the logic of a gift economy into the market economy by generating supply and assuming demand.[46] Its members believed that production based on good motives would generate an equal level of consumption. Because the tracts were given away rather than sold, the good motives of consumption could be effect rather than cause. The exchange of tracts was a continuous process that benefitted both giver and recipient. The indoctrination of another soul into Christian fellowship—through the giving of a gift—

was an important part of the gradualist millennialism that evangelical reformers espoused. Because the giving and receiving of tracts bound people together in a Christian community without erasing the hierarchy implicit in benevolence, the love of Christ could be extended without jeopardizing the social distinctions between giver and receiver. The gift was its own reward, and it offered no possibility for a reciprocity that could challenge the social hierarchy. To accept salvation as it was presented in these tracts was, at least implicitly, to accept the particular version of Christian life they presented.

The Shepherd of Salisbury Plain was one of the most widely circulated tracts. It was originally published in Britain in the 1790s, but many American imprints appeared after 1810, and new editions appeared regularly through the 1860s. More's tract was based on the story of Daniel Saunders, and several editions were published in the 1820s that included letters written by him. More's conservative philosophy resonated with American ideas about the relationship between moral virtue and economic opportunity. The story follows a gentleman of leisure. He is enjoying the beauty of nature when he meets a poor and pious shepherd. Despite poverty and his wife's crippling illness, the shepherd and his family live a clean, well-mended, and exemplary domestic and spiritual life. The gentleman, impressed by their ability to make so much of so little, secures a position as a Sunday school teacher for the shepherd, not to provide him with earthly riches but to allow him to use his "God-given talents" to provide his family with a home more suitable for their needs. *The Shepherd of Salisbury Plain* proposed an alternate market economy based on a Christian community. The story embraced a nostalgia for the past while reshaping that past to serve the interests of the present. We meet the shepherd because the gentleman, who becomes his benefactor, has come to experience nature in order to balance his worldly success. The natural world is not the gentleman's everyday experience, nor does he want it to be. Moreover, his solution to the shepherd's poverty is to remove him from nature rather than improve his lot in nature. The gentleman releases the shepherd from a life of manual labor by facilitating his transformation to a life of the mind as a Sunday school teacher. Yet the shepherd does not express any discontent with his life. The gentleman's sojourn in nature, therefore, succeeds not in bringing him back to the simpler life but in introducing the shepherd and his family to a life made possible by the market, for without the benevolent associations sponsored by the profits of the market, the paid position of Sunday school teacher would not exist.

The story reinforces the idea that the virtue of manual labor could be carried over into the world of mental work, a question of no small interest to middle-class readers.[47] The gentleman makes it clear that it is not his intent to make the shepherd wealthy. For middle-class American readers, this modest domesticity demonstrated that it was possible to inculcate the correct domestic sentiments and economy in the lives of the worthy poor without necessarily elevating them to the same level as the reformers. Readers could contemplate the ideal of social harmony without jeopardizing the social hierarchy.[48] By evoking a nostalgia for rural simplicity to examine questions of economic change and the possibilities for reform, the tract directly engages the issues of market culture, infusing the actions and locations of modern life with virtue. Tract writers employed the images and meanings of pastoral life in the service of the new market economy not by masking one with the other but by insisting that they could be mutually beneficial.[49] Some scholars have read the nostalgic pastoralism of this tale as a rejection of, or at least an ambivalence about, the market revolution. Although the tract does not explicitly engage the issues of artisanal labor or industrialization, neither does it ignore the central issues of the market revolution. The tract paints a pastoral vision of rural life that hoped to engage readers who did not personally experience the drudgery of such a life.

Another tract, *The Closet Companion; or a Help to Self-Examination*, engaged the questions of market behavior more directly and offered the reader a list of questions to promote virtuous Christian behavior. One of these questions—"Do I use the lawful means of procuring and furthering the wealth and outward estate of myself and others?"—explicitly addressed the importance of exhibiting virtuous behavior in commercial transactions. A subsequent question reminded the reader that he or she was also beholden to a higher law: "Am I strictly and conscientiously honest in all my dealings, not overreaching or defrauding any person, in any degree?"[50] This tract did not ask the reader to reject worldly success but to pursue it following the dictates of the Ten Commandments. It emphasized the importance of seeking out business partners and contacts who also conformed to these moral strictures, thus creating market networks of like-minded business men.[51]

Following this logic, tract writers appealed to their readers' economic pragmatism as a basis for moral reform. Rev. Austin Dickinson made an economic argument for temperance. He calculated that the overall sum of money spent on alcohol, assuming the consumption of a single glass daily at one cent a glass over a fifty-year period would amount to $1.8 billion.[52] Dickinson reminded his readers that this was a conservative estimate, as many drank more than a glass a day at considerably higher prices. Even the most conservative estimate, he wrote, would furnish enough money to pay for education—colleges, academies, and schools—in every part of the country. This windfall would be doubled, he argued, if one also took into account the time and resources squandered in the manufacturing and distribution of alcohol. Even the interest on this sum "would be sufficient to support the Christian ministry throughout the nation, to pay all our public taxes, and to carry on great national improvements."[53] Factoring in the "enormous expense of sickness, pauperism, crime and premature death" would further increase the amount of money to be saved by giving up spirits. Although Dickinson's suggestions for the use of the saved money had a specifically Christian character, the strength of his argument was economic first and moral second, a strategy that, even if it did not succeed in the magnitude of its proposal, must have resonated with an audience all too familiar with their own bottom line.

Other tracts employed the same strategy, imbuing the activities of everyday life with sacred meaning, offering advice to those unable to take advantage of the traditional sources of religious comfort. In one tract, *Advice to the Keeper of a Turnpike Gate together with Useful Hints to Travellers*, a gatekeeper is unable to attend church because of his responsibilities to his job. The tract addressed the reader directly. If you are "destitute of religious helps," it instructed, you should make it "your *daily business*" to infuse "*the very objects about you*" with religious meaning.[54] Investing daily activities and objects with

Christian significance held a particular emotional power for readers who wanted to find evidence of God's love in the world around them. The tract went on to declare that God had instructed man to improve "natural things" for our "spiritual profit." Jesus was praised for plain teaching: "He spoke in parables; by them he communicated, in the clearest and plainest manner, his heavenly doctrines and blessed precepts."[55] The tracts, like Christ's parables, had the power to convert by showing readers the grace of God in the world around them.

Although religious conversion was the primary goal of tract societies, the millennial vision of the members of these societies linked religious conversion to the improvement of the social and political aspects of national character. In a grand statement, the American Tract Society linked the fate of the nation to the virtue of its citizens: "This country is now in comparative infancy, *forming a character for ages,* and that the eyes of the true Friends of God and man throughout the civilized world are now directed here, that they may see *whether there can be* virtue enough in a people to support a free government."[56] Not surprisingly, the circulation of tracts was part of a vision that linked religious literature with commerce and politics in the common search for virtue in all aspects of national life. The desire to inculcate their particular vision of a Christian nation animated the members of the American Tract Society to make the most of this potential influence. For those who championed the idea of a Christian nation, there was no distinction between their religious beliefs and their vision of a moral market. For readers who were not reformers, the quotidian narratives of the tracts may have allowed them to imagine a more secular vision of moral economy, converting the religious message of the tracts into a vision of national identity more broadly understood.

Moral Tales

Adults were not the only audience tract societies hoped to influence. Many tracts were written for children. Inculcating moral and spiritual values in children promised a future nation of citizens imbued with Christian and republican virtue. Sunday school organizers saw children as more apt to be influenced by Christian teachings than adults and emphasized the importance of instilling and nurturing good Christian habits at an early age. Christian reading was not the least of these habits. Young Christian readers would grow up to be moral citizens who could then influence adults.[57] This return to God could lead to renewed efforts to support and nurture the family.

The Sunday school movement, which began in the 1790s, initially targeted poor children who were not able to attend school during the week. Compelling children to attend Sunday school classes also helped curtail the noisy games that disturbed church services. By the 1820s, Sunday schools had expanded to include the children of all parishioners, and the focus had shifted from basic literacy to Christian education.[58] Sunday schools introduced children to a wide range of Christian reading material, and the numbers of tracts written expressly for children increased dramatically. Like the American Tract Society, the American Sunday School Union played an important role in the development of children's tract literature. By encouraging the founding of a national network of Sunday schools, the managers hoped to contribute to the development of a Christian nation by shaping the reading practices of children. The American Sunday School Union wanted its members to think of themselves as part of a national community linked by evangelical concerns rather than as part of an individual church, an idea supported by the organizations's children's publications. Its distribution networks created a market for Christian children's literature, providing, by 1827, more than 50,000 books to Sunday schools across the country.[59] Children read these books and tracts during Sunday school, and teachers gave them as prizes for accomplishments. In addition to book prizes, library privileges were often granted to children who comported themselves well. Library privileges seem to have been as great an incentive as any prize to encourage children to attend Sunday school and learn its lessons.[60] Sunday schools strove to teach the pleasures of Christian reading and fuel the desire to possess a wide variety of Christian texts.

Tracts written expressly for children often focused on the love of books and reading to illustrate their morals, reminding young readers that the printing press had made it possible for every family to have a Bible. By the 1820s, tract writers had to compete with new forms of children's literature for the attention of young readers. They imbedded their moral messages in detailed fictional stories, thereby encouraging children to view religious instruction as both pleasant and profitable. The continual production of new Sunday School tracts made it possible for teachers to use "the impressive charm of novelty" to woo their young pupils.[61] Teachers used their pupils' enthusiasm for new stories to encourage them to embrace the lessons the stories told. They also awarded books as prizes for lessons well learned.[62] *Pretty Stories for Good Children* showed its readers the correlation between the beauty of the book and the worthiness of the reader. "Idle boys and girls do not deserve such a pretty book as this," the author lectured. Industrious boys and girls, however, did deserve pretty books, and good behavior could and should be rewarded as long as children did not covet pretty things for their own sake. In the hope that young readers would internalize the connection between moral virtue and moral commerce, one of the stories ended with a familiar reminder: "What shall man be profited, if he gain the whole world and lose his own soul?"[63]

The stories in *Pretty Stories for Good Children* address the lessons of good behavior and good motives from a variety of different perspectives. In "The Hymn Book," a story about Sunday school, Catherine Morris, a rich, vain, and selfish girl, learns humility. The teacher, Miss Stevens, has only five hymn books to distribute, and there are six children in the class. Catherine suggests that Eunice Edwards, a poor little girl in the class, is too plain to deserve such a pretty book. Miss Stevens gives the book to Eunice instead of Catherine to teach Catherine that it is inner rather than outer beauty that counts. Eunice, in a further illustration of Miss Stevens's point, lends Catherine her hymn book so that she will not be left out. Catherine is so impressed by Eunice's good example that she brings her a beautiful little Bible as a present the following week. This story illustrates the symbolic importance of Sunday school as a place to learn Christian charity not just from books, but from experience. Catherine learns from Eunice's example and she expresses her gratitude through the gift of a Bible, demonstrating that the awarding of prizes provided its own possibilities for moral education. Books were the vehicle of religious teaching and its reward.

Christians did not universally condone prize giving for Sunday school scholarship. In an 1842 editorial in *Godey's Lady's Book*, Sarah Hale sharply criticized the practice. Mothers must be ever vigilant, she warned, even in the seemingly safe haven of school. Rewards were "incitements to ambition" and contributed to a growing national obsession with wealth. "Let this besetting sin of our times be studiously watched by the Christian mother," Hale intoned. "Let her guard against this insidious influence of mammon. Let not *gold* be the standard value of everything." Children were particularly susceptible to misunderstanding the relationship between rewards and achievement. Hale warned that "when we offer *money* or anything which *represents* money, as the incentive to study, or the reward of good conduct," children are taught "to place a high value on the external motive which is presented to tempt his ambition or his appetite."[64] Hale feared the motivation to learn would become external rather than internal, and children would covet the prizes rather than treasure the lessons. The stridency of her editorial indicates just how widespread rewards had become—and recognizes the important influence childhood experiences have on adult behavior.

In the same editorial, Hale called on mothers to counteract the "cramping and debasing influence exerted by this systematic, absorbing pursuit after wealth." Motherhood, Hale reminded her readers, was an "awfully responsible office"; women must be "qualified for their station." If every woman who became a mother in the next twenty years faithfully performed her duties, she predicted, "a revolution would be wrought in the social and moral world!"[65] Hale articulated the important correlation between religious ideals and commercial behavior that defined a middle-class vision of a moral market. That she invoked a generation of mothers to educate a generation of children suggests both her belief that all citizens should receive a "correct" education about the market and her concern about the influence of books, as narratives and commodities, in that process of education.

Although the morals of Christian children's fiction were usually in harmony with Hale's ideals, the stories themselves often reveal how much the world of childhood confirmed Hale's fears. "Morning and Evening," another story from *Pretty Stories for Good Children*, teaches a little boy not to covet a friend's beautiful picture book and map puzzle. The lesson is a straightforward biblical one, but the details of the story, especially the detailed descriptions of the beautiful toys, suggest a host of new temptations in a changing world of childhood.[66] In "Dialogue between a Brother and Sister Concerning the Salvation of Christ," one of the most didactic stories, earthly desires are contrasted with the mercy of Christ. The story compares the gift of salvation with other kinds of inheritance. No one would refuse an inheritance, but many pass up the gift of salvation, which is much more precious and eternal. Despite this lesson, the worldly goods—dolls, books, and other toys—are lovingly described in this story too, alluding to the growing role of luxury items in everyday life and a child's interest in this kind of detail. The final story, "Reading the Bible," chastens its readers, "If you loved the Bible as you ought, you would read it a great deal more. You would like it better than your little story books; and you would try to do all that it commands."[67] The picture of childhood reading that emerges from these tales is not just a struggle against worldliness but also the creation of a Christian lens through which to view worldly goods.[68] Stories like these suggested a pragmatic acceptance that children were more likely to remember moral lessons that came in the form of pleasant tales.

The authors of children's fiction wanted to influence the development of morally self- sufficient citizens who could preserve the Republic.[69] These lessons encompassed an ever-increasing number of subjects as young readers became more voracious. By the 1820s and 1830s, for-profit publishers saw a market for children's gift books and annuals. Children who had enjoyed receiving tracts or books as gifts in Sunday school must also have looked forward to receiving gift books with beautiful gilt, embossed covers and lovely engravings.[70] Many gift books were miniatures, which made them desirable as beautiful objects. Children, who had been taught that industrious and virtuous little girls and boys deserved pretty books filled with entertaining and moral tales, could reconcile their desire for gift books with a Christian moral world view.

The popularity of gift books also created a receptive audience for children's magazines. Lydia Maria Child founded the *Juvenile Miscellany* in 1826, based on the success of her book *Evenings in New England* (1824), which adapted the style of British authors such as Anna Laetitia Barbauld and Maria Edgeworth to reflect American culture and history. She was explicit about her debt to these authors, and in turn other American authors of children's books were explicit about their debt to the *Juvenile Miscellany*.[71] Barbauld and Edgeworth championed literature for children as an essential method of crucial lessons about middle-class identity: success was based on merit, hard work, and talent animated by virtue. Child adapted the more traditional representation of class hierarchy to embrace American notions of republican equality and the possibility of social mobility to appeal to her American audience. The magazine was bimonthly, and children eagerly anticipated its arrival. Lucy Larcom, Caroline Healy Dall, Louisa May Alcott, and Thomas Wentworth Higginson all remarked on their childhood appreciation of Child's magazine and acknowledged the influence of the *Juvenile Miscellany* on their careers in literature and reform.[72] The magazine enjoyed critical and economic success until Child's abolitionist views, which she published in *Appeal in Favor of that Class of Americans Called Africans,* alienated the parents of her young readers and cost her many subscriptions.[73] Sarah Hale assumed the editorship of the magazine in 1834, but it never regained its former popularity and ceased publication in 1836. Despite its failure, the *Juvenile Miscellany* had helped create a market for children's magazines that continued to grow. By the end of the 1830s, children could choose among a wide range of books and magazines.

Contributors to gift books and children's magazines tried to capitalize on their popularity and build careers that focused on children's literature. The Peter Parley series, by Samuel Goodrich, and the Rollo books, written by Rev. Jacob Abbott, were among the most popular. Goodrich, like Child, was a pioneer in the field of commercially successful children's literature. He was profoundly influenced by More's *Shepherd of Salisbury Plain,* which was his favorite book and served as an inspiration for his own writing career.[74] Goodrich disapproved of the gruesome nature of fairy tales and the British perspective of many children's books. His first book, *The Tales of Peter Parley About America* (1827), was an attempt to provide a new American fiction for children and launched his successful series of books and a magazine.[75] Writing in the 1850s, Goodrich surveyed the progress of children's literature over the previous thirty years and remarked that the impressive number of books for children, which could be seen on the "teeming shelves" of a children's book-store like C. S. Francis in New York, provided a striking index of "the amazing advances made in everything which belongs to the comfort, the intelligence, the luxury of society."[76] Jacob Abbott, like Goodrich was influenced by reading religious tracts and had written some himself.[77] In the Rollo series, he tried to anticipate and answer the kinds of questions that young children, especially boys, would ask about the moral and practical challenges of life.[78] The Rollo titles included *Rollo at Play; or Safe Amusements* (1837), *Rollo at Work; or, The Way for a Boy to Learn to be Industrious* (1837), and *The Rollo Code of Morals; or, The Rules of Duty for Children. Arranged with Questions for the Use of Schools* (1841). These books offered common sense advice, infused with Christian morality, about everyday problems without being as explicitly didactic as the Sunday school tracts.[79]

As the spiritual marketplace grew, the American Tract Society began to publish its own magazine for children. Its editor made it clear that he wrote to the children instead of speaking for them.[80] The young readers of this magazine were encouraged to engage in their own form of colportage:

Work for Boys and Work for Girls
Has *The Child's Paper* any hands? Has it any feet? Has it any wings? No. It has a beautiful face, and a busy tongue, and a warm heart: and that's all. It is only a month old, and can't *go alone.* Children you have hands and feet. Now, lend them to introduce us to your playmates and neighbors. Will you?[81]

The editorial went so far as to pen a sales script for children:

You can say, "Here is a beautiful and good paper for us children. Every line is for *us.* If you and nine more will pay ten cents each, you can have it for a whole year. As fast as you can count, boys and girls will find the ten cents. Is it not an excellent way to do good?"[82]

Parents and teachers, the editorial also suggested, had their own responsibility for increasing the circulation of such a worthy periodical. Those who were able, should follow the example of one Brooklyn merchant and provide a subscription for every family on their block. This editorial employed the American Tract Society credo that the circulation of texts was a spiritual duty and directly linked this duty to an acceptable form of market behavior. Another editorial in the same issue urged boys to petition their parents to let them earn money to donate to charity or provide books and tracts to "log cabin Sabbath Schools."[83] As testimony to the success of their suggestion, in a subsequent issue, the editors published "The Little Paper Agent," demonstrating a little girl's success in collecting subscriptions. The "dear little girl" came into the magazine office "looking very much as if she had some *business* on hand." She had braved long distances, cold weather, and muddy roads, but despite these obstacles, "she *had* a *purpose*, nothing could stop her" from collecting ten subscriptions from her neighbors. She poured a little pile of coins on the table and announced, "*The Child's Paper* hasn't got feet; so it can't go alone, and no hands, so I thought I would do my part to help it along." The editors, clearly delighted with the girl's industry, remarked, "How much better was this than to play all the time. And how beautiful is it to see children planning and *carrying out their plans* to be useful in their own spheres."[84] This editorial helped reassure both parents and children that it was possible to carry out this plan successfully. The emphasis on industriousness and good motives softened the commercial activity of soliciting and collecting subscriptions. By actively circulating tracts, these children could contribute to evangelizing the nation and learn industrious habits at the same time. The early introduction to the relationship between market practices and domestic economy that children's fiction, both religious and secular, provided emphasized the importance of an integrated view of Christian life. The happiness of not only individuals but also the nation depended on the early inculcation of habits of moral and spiritual economy.

Preparation for the "compting house" began early in the lives of antebellum Americans. Children of affluent families were expected, as much as those who aspired to influence, to find the lessons in tracts as useful. These tracts also helped develop a market of readers with an appetite for sentimental and didactic narratives. As the generation of young readers who came of age in the 1830s started families of their own, they turned to domestic advice books and fiction for models of a Christian home. Their reading practices drew overt connections between spiritual and moral advancement and economic profit and encouraged the interdependent circulation of religious ideas and market practices in the development of a moral market culture.

Three

CENTS AND SENSIBILITY
The Language of Business in Godey's Lady's Book

*I*n the mid-nineteenth century, there were many different paths into publishing. Sarah Hale entered the magazine business out of financial necessity. The American Tract Society exploited the possibilities of new printing technology out of evangelical fervor. Louis Godey embarked on a career in magazine publishing as an entrepreneur. Entering the publishing world as a business man rather than a literary man greatly influenced his tastes and strategies. Both Godey and Hale began their careers in the magazine business the same year, but Godey, who was almost a generation younger than Hale, came from a different background. He was born in 1804 to French parents, Louis and Margaret Godey, who had fled to New York City during the Revolution. As a child, he received little formal education. He was employed in New York as a broker until he moved to Philadelphia in 1828 and became a clerk and editor for Charles Alexander, publisher of the *Saturday Evening Post*. In 1830, Godey and Alexander became co-proprietors of the *Lady's Book,* although Alexander's association with the magazine was brief.[1] (After

Figure 2. Louis A. Godey, portrait engraved for *Godey's Lady's Book*, 1850.

Alexander sold his interest in the magazine, Godey added his name to the title. Godey made slight alterations to the titles several times during its years of publication, but for the sake of consistency in this text I always refer to it as *Godey's Lady's Book*.) Godey married Maria Duke, a member of a wealthy Philadelphia family, in 1833, providing him with both domestic happiness and the capital necessary to sustain a magazine in the turbulent 1830s.

Godey was not a pioneer in the magazine business, but before 1830, no magazine had lasted more than a few years. Godey's success came from creating a skillful amalgam of past practices and current innovations. Although interest in women's magazines was on the rise, Godey found that in addition to building a national market for his magazine, he had to educate his women subscribers, particularly women, about how to conform to the business practices of market culture. Women were an important part of the growing market for luxury goods, and magazines depended on their patronage. The editorial discussions, penned by Godey and Sarah Hale (after she became literary editor in 1837), were more than the perfunctory reminders to delinquent subscribers so common in the magazine business. Godey and Hale crafted a sentimental language of business that reconciled the moral ideals of a middle-class readership with the demands of market economy.[2]

Every editor and publisher struggled with the problem of delinquent subscribers and alternately cajoled and berated readers to remit the money they owed.[3] Godey and Hale, however, mobilized editorial convention toward more ambitious ends: in addition to ensuring the financial health of their own enterprise, they wanted to shape market behavior. They presented their sentimental education about the market in terms of mutual benefit and mutual obligation. Paying for a subscription was not just an economic transaction, it created an ongoing relationship. Godey and Hale tried to teach readers how to recognize legitimate agents of the magazine, conduct business transactions, and honor their debts. They explained the relationship between aggregate cost and individual responsibility, and they introduced their readers to the idea of timely payment of debts. They congratulated their readers on their ability to recognize value and discern the difference between legitimate, virtuous consumption and frivolous, profligate waste. In short, they taught virtuous market behavior and provided a language to discuss it, all while ensuring a profit for their magazine.

Godey and Hale crafted an "imagined community" of subscribers drawn together not just by the advertised contents of the magazine but also by its market philosophy.[4] The successful balance of these two aspects helped the magazine succeed where other publishers had failed. *Godey's Lady's Book* was one of the first magazines that could boast a nationwide readership. Readers from the North, South, East, and West subscribed. Godey and Hale were careful to cater to regional interests without engaging in sectional politics.[5] The American Tract

Society and other Christian organizations that created national networks for the distribution of tracts could evoke shared Christian morals as the glue that bound the far-flung organization together. Godey and Hale had a more complicated argument to make. They hoped their readers shared their commitment to republican virtue and Christian morality, but they had to persuade their readers that the content of the magazine was worth the price of a subscription. In order to appeal to as many people as possible, Godey and Hale needed a more nuanced definition of their community. Godey's intention, as the title of his magazine made clear, was to create a national community of ladies. *Godey's Lady's Book* tempered the intellectual ambitions of Sarah Hale's *American Ladies' Magazine* with a wealth of fashion plates, sheet music, fancywork instructions, and other accouterments of genteel domesticity. The visual diversity of the magazine was made possible and affordable by new printing technology. Although the magazine championed the ideals of separate spheres, it also offered readers compromises and new tactics to negotiate the ever more complex relationship between home and market.[6] Godey and Hale presented their readers with specific strategies for behaving in the marketplace. These editorial discussions—blending the language of sentimentalism with the pragmatism of business—suggest that the links between the two were at the core of middle-class sensibility. The balance of home and market represented by the magazine is an important reminder of the crucial role played by Louis Godey in the business of the magazine. Godey was able to engage editorial and literary talent and exploit the new distribution networks provided by canals, steamboats, and railroads that made it practical to deliver the magazine to readers throughout the growing nation. In the 1850s, in the January advertisement for the new year's subscription, he often touted his magazine as the "Book of the Nation" and described it as "Devoted to American Enterprise, American Writers, and American Artists."[7] The popularity of *Godey's Lady's Book* suggests that these business strategies modeled a market philosophy that appealed to a wide range of nineteenth-century Americans.

Absent Friends

In December 1835, Louis Godey inaugurated his editorial page with a reminder to his readers to renew their subscriptions: "Many of the subscriptions commenced with the January number of 1835, will be discontinued with the December number. No offence must be taken at this proceeding, as it is done to prevent the error of continuing those who only ordered the work for one year."[8]

The financial panic of the previous winter had hit the publishing industry hard. Godey did not want to lose subscribers who were merely tardy with their payments, but he could not afford to assume that this was the case. This editorial also served as a reminder to some of his subscribers that although he had carried them a whole year without payment, he was not willing to continue this practice for another year: "It is seldom that we have to do that disagreeable thing, to dun, nor will we do it now—but merely suggest that we do not feed on the chameleon's dish, the air, but on the more substantial things of this earth."[9] Godey hoped the mere suggestion of a dun would be enough to prompt his delinquent subscribers to pay their debts. As gentle as his reminder was, he was unable to resist expressing at least a little of his frustration: "We can only suppose that it is that vile habit of procrastination on the part of our patrons that withholds from us 'that which enriches not them, but makes us poor indeed.'"[10]

The language of this editorial varies from a perfunctory reminder to a sentimental plea to a sharp rebuke, a technique common in the magazine business, in which all publishers struggled to make subscribers pay. Yearly accounts were customarily settled in January, and Godey was torn between the need to collect those debts and his desire to increase rather than diminish the number of subscribers. The circulation of the magazine, even to delinquent subscribers, was an excellent method of advertising it, but Godey did not want to operate a credit system for his subscribers. The practice of sending magazines before subscription money had been received played a large role in the failure of many early magazines. Godey's pressure on his subscribers to keep their payments current was indicative of a general change in business practices requiring debtors to pay in short order. As cash transactions became a more common form of exchange, the older traditions of restraint in debt collection began to change.[11] These tensions were a natural part of the growing pains of the new cash economy, but for Godey this was further exacerbated by the fact that his subscribers were women.

Magazines marketed directly to women were a new cultural product in the 1830s. For many women, a subscription to *Godey's* was their first experience buying this kind of product. Godey extolled the usefulness of his periodical, reminding his readers how many different kinds of education were available in its pages. Despite the enthusiasm for his magazine, Godey discovered, just as Sarah Hale and many other editors had, that in times of economic difficulty, a subscription was a luxury, not a necessity. Godey frequently reminded his readers that it would be more costly to purchase separately the engravings, sheet music, fancywork instructions, and other regular features of the magazine—items, he implied, that were necessities of genteel life rather than luxuries. From this perspective, the magazine was not only a bargain, but a requirement. Although Godey made much of the fact that his magazine was designed for women, he knew that it was often a male member of the household who was responsible for paying the bills. With this in mind, his editorials suggested ways for women to broach the subject of business with their husbands or fathers.

Once he had initiated a conversation with his readers, Godey began to address them with some frequency. At first he confined his discussion to practical matters that focused on circulation. The monthly arrival of the magazine later encouraged the idea of an ongoing editorial dialogue with readers about the state of affairs at the magazine. In 1836, Godey launched a new phase of these dialogues by addressing "the Patrons of the Ladies Book" directly:

> My very kind friends! No doubt you will be surprised, though I trust not offended, at this unusual mode of addressing you; but, as I have a favor to ask, I thought it best to lay aside the stiffness of editorial intercourse, and apply to you familiarly, in my own proper person. I am about to engage in a new enter-prize [*sic*], and I want your assistance.[12]

Godey changed to a more familiar mode of editorial address in order to engage his readers as "business partners." His new enterprise was another publishing venture, the *Saturday News,* and the favor he asked was an additional subscription. By framing his advertisement as an invitation to render assistance, Godey alluded to the fact that most capital for business ventures came from private sources. In this instance, he solicited cultural rather than monetary capital.[13] By linking business and friendship in this overture, Godey was, in effect, inviting his female subscribers to participate in the camaraderie of male business partnership. Because he actively solicited women as both producers and consumers of his magazine, he had to rethink the role of women in the market and acknowledge the connections between domestic economy and business economy. Godey's success encouraged other publishers to see value in a women's market.[14]

Soon after boldly claiming his subscribers as friends, however, he took some to task for their failure to live up to the terms of friendship: "Not withstanding our 'Mild as moonbeams' hint to some of our *absent* friends, we have again had cause to charge our man of the Quill to make out sundry accounts and send by mail to those who 'Although forgetting are not forgot.'"[15] By using the term "absent friends," Godey implied that the failure to remit had been an oversight, not a conscious choice. Above all, he wanted to avoid unpleasantness in this most unpleasant task, but he could not mask his irritation at being placed in such a position. "Nobody will thank us, but that revered gentleman, so often mentioned, 'My Uncle Samuel,'" he wrote. "His treasury will feel the benefit of it, as all our duns are sent by mail. Why cause this disagreeable task—our aversion!"[16] By calling attention to the potential profits for the US Post Office, he could reassert the common interests of publisher and subscriber. By displacing the question of profit onto the Post Office, Godey underscored the fact that these appeals for money were equally disagreeable for him. This made him a different kind of business man. He wanted the *Lady's Book* to be a new kind of business, governed by a sentimental style of market relations.

Although Godey was unfailingly polite in his business correspondence, his letters on subscription issues were much more businesslike. He assumed his male subscribers were accustomed to a more formal language of business, and he omitted the flowery language and metaphors of the more public magazine editorials, concentrating instead on practical matters:

Mr. Burke & Mr Langston Esqr
Cincinnati, Ohio

Yours duly rec'd covering ten dollars ordering Lady's Book for S. D. Black, Montgomery, Ohio. The January nos has been sent to him—

One copy to Mr Richard Burke, Cincinnati, Ohio. Mr—— has been a subscriber since Jan 1836 and owes in the year 1840 which this remittance would pay—

Miss Cynthia Langston will have credit for the money remitted and $1.50
on a/c of Phillips—

Your own subscription commenced Jan of 1836 and you have paid $12 pre-
vious to this—1840 is therefore due, which this remittance pays.

Very respt yours,

L. A. Godey

Phila Jan 5/40

If I am in error will of course cheerfully correct.[17]

Unlike the public rhetoric, which stressed morality and a community of subscribers, in the privacy of his business correspondence, Godey confined his
discussion to dollars and cents. The prosaic nature of his private correspondence indicates how much Godey was able to shape the public rhetoric of his
editorial correspondence to create a business language that would appeal to
his female subscribers. He intentionally addressed pragmatic business issues
through sentimental rhetoric.

Godey suspected that one of the reasons his female subscribers did not
pay their bills in a timely fashion was their lack of knowledge about business
practices. Aggregate cost, he believed, was an important business lesson to
teach his readers. He approached this lesson from two angles. First, he made
clear the benefits of aggregate cost by championing his ability to provide
engravings, sheet music, and other benefits that would cost more purchased
separately. He also noted his ability to pay writers well and that profits were
lavishly reinvested in the magazine itself.[18] The other side of this equation,
however, was the cost incurred by Godey. In one reminder to delinquent subscribers, he provided a brief lesson in economics. If 10,000 subscribers sent
their subscription payment postage due, Godey instructed his readers, the cost
of postage for each subscriber would have been only fifty cents, but the cost
to him would be $5,000. "There is a difference," he noted, "and we need hardly
add, a very great one."[19] This graphic illustration of aggregate cost, Godey
hoped, would demonstrate the importance of keeping strict accounts. If

women understood their role in maintaining the financial health of the enterprise, they would be more likely to honor the reciprocal terms of business.

Sentimental Swindlers

Although most of the discussion of subscriptions was designed to cajole delinquent subscribers or woo new subscribers, in one instance Godey beseeched his subscribers not to pay. As the circulation of his magazine increased, Godey experienced a new kind of subscription problem. In 1837, several men posing as subscription agents traveled around New England and New York collecting money. As soon as this was brought to his attention, Godey placed advertisements in the local papers warning subscribers to beware of these false agents. The discussion of this problem in the editorial pages of the magazine was more than just a warning. Godey wanted to educate readers, who were unfamiliar with this kind of market transaction, about what to expect from a traveling agent.

In the early years of the magazine, Godey used traveling agents to solicit and collect subscriptions. He published the names of his agents on the cover of the magazine and provided them with letters of introduction. This method of identification became particularly important when confidence men began to take advantage of people's inexperience and pass themselves off as agents. As the subscription list grew, so did the potential for fraud. Although Godey referred to his subscribers as friends, they were, in fact, strangers, vulnerable to the wiles of a world of strangers. Confidence men were a particular problem for subscribers who lived in cities: "City subscribers are respectfully requested not to pay any money to persons that are not able to produce a written authority from the publisher to collect."[20] But potential subscribers in the countryside were also vulnerable. Confidence men took advantage of the growing interest in *Godey's* and traveled through villages and small towns in New York and New England collecting subscription money.[21] Godey scolded his readers for not being more careful in their business dealings. "What surprises us, is the fact, that not one of the persons who have been deceived in New York State can tell the name of the fellow who has imposed on them, so that we are unable to advertise him," he wrote.[22]

The failure to ascertain the legitimacy of an agent before handing over money exposed the naïveté of rural subscribers and revealed the artfulness of these swindlers, who probably distracted their potential customers from asking their names by focusing on the name of the magazine itself. Godey was amazed by the failure of people to follow even the most basic practices of sensible consumption. That persons should pay money to an individual showing no authority, is singular," he noted, "and that they should not take a receipt, is still more strange."[23] This lack of common sense about business dealings confirmed Godey's hunch that his subscribers needed to be educated about the market. This was not the first time he had described how to pay subscription agents; he regularly included a list of agents and the proper method of payment on the cover of the magazine. But the success of these swindlers reinforced the importance of clarifying the responsibilities of subscribers. Buying a magazine subscription required a new kind of knowledge about market transactions. As Godey's comments indicate, many women did not know to ask for a written authorization from the publisher, and they did not think to ask for a receipt.[24] In short, they were operating on the terms of a more familiar kind of market transaction, usually carried on between those who knew each other, in which oral agreements were as binding as written agreements.

Rural consumers were accustomed to the sharp dealing of peddlers, but as subscribers to *Godey's Lady's Book,* they were purchasing an abstract commodity, a form of futures. Purchasing a subscription from an agent was a different kind of consumption from the usual exchange with a peddler in which the goods were received at the time of exchange. The publisher wanted the money in advance. The subscriber wanted to pay after the service was rendered. Subscription agents were middlemen. As advocates for the publisher, they made the transaction of purchasing a subscription tangible, but they were also selling a commodity that could not be exchanged at that moment.

The success of the confidence men depended on the transportation networks used to distribute *Godey's Lady's Book.* One swindler, James Garland, traveled along the highways of New England and the Erie Canal.[25] Even as print capitalism made the circulation of knowledge ever more rapid, there were plenty of places where news of these confidence men did not precede them or, as in the case of the Erie Canal, they could travel as fast or faster than news of their chicanery. Godey's only recourse was to advertise Garland in local papers throughout New England and New York in order to warn unsuspecting subscribers. Garland had collected subscriptions from Brattleboro, Vermont, to Bristol, Rhode Island, in New England and from Syracuse to Lockport in New York. The rural towns of New England were rapidly becoming part of the commercial networks of market culture, and the development of a rural middle class meant new markets for goods and new territory for swindlers. New York State offered the same combination of rural simplicity and consumer appetite, as the new towns that flourished along the Erie Canal sustained a growing middle class.[26] For small town and rural subscribers, their encounter with a subscription agent was one way market culture was becoming a part of their daily life. For some, it was their introduction to a new method of exchange.[27] More than anything, the subscription problems highlighted the contradictions of the marketing strategies of sentimental magazines. Although editors worked hard to convince their readers that a magazine provided a community of like-minded friends, in cases like these, the boundaries of the community were hard to delimit because they were defined by market transactions rather than geography or kinship.

Confidence men succeeded because they were able to participate in a new market economy while appealing to old market practices such as barter. The willingness of fraudulent agents to take less than full payment for the magazine—a subscription cost three dollars a year, but swindlers took as little as one dollar—contributed to their success.[28] Subscribers were not suspicious of the discount because they were accustomed to negotiating prices. Since he did not have to provide a product, a fraudulent agent could accept any sum as a full subscription. It was often a subscriber's propensity to strike a bargain that closed the deal for the swindler.[29] The enthusiasm for a bargain worked to the advantage of a man like Garland, and he proved to be difficult to apprehend. "We have not yet been successful in arresting the self constituted agent of the Lady's Book, Mr. Garland," Godey had to admit. "This fellow," he went on to say, "has caused us great uneasiness" because of his ability to collect "a large amount of money, and an immense number of subscribers." His success "has caused some dissatisfaction among those who were deceived by him," and to make matters worse, "another fellow has gone to work in New York state."[30] It was not the erosion of society that concerned Godey here, but the erosion of his profits. In his eyes this was not a social problem, it was a business problem. His goal was to educate his subscribers about the new market, which was based on paper authority rather than oral tradition.

The irony of these confidence men's success was that they found not only new subscribers but also conscientious ones who paid in advance. Many of the would-be subscribers who had paid their money to Garland still expected to receive their subscription. The phrase "some dissatisfaction" was an indication of Godey's attempt at diplomacy. Garland's success as a swindler meant that someone, subscriber or publisher, had to absorb the loss. From Godey's perspective, it was clearly the subscriber who had failed—either to ask to see written confirmation of the collector's authority or to ask for a receipt. Godey was a pragmatic businessman. Although he tried to appear sympathetic, he could not let his business practices be dictated by these sentiments. For some of his readers this was a rude introduction to the new terms of market participation. Nevertheless, Godey tried to turn Garland's success into advertising. He used his reports of fraud to call attention to the growth of the magazine's popularity and the geographical breadth of its readership:

> Such is the popularity of the Lady's Book, that rogues who solicit subscribers on their own account, are springing up in all parts of the country, and continue to do a pretty good business. Our cover will show the names of a few of these worthies. All agents authorized by the publisher, have a written commission to act as such.[31]

Godey, like his contemporary, P. T. Barnum, was adept at turning negative publicity into advertising.[32] As swindlers cut into Godey's profits, they also provided "objective" evidence of the growing popularity of the magazine. And as they attempted to take advantage of *Godey's* growing popularity, the magazine redoubled its efforts to create an educated community of subscribers.

A Select Circle of Friends

After Sarah Josepha Hale joined Godey on the masthead of *Godey's Lady's Book*, she shouldered some of the responsibility for petitioning delinquent subscribers. Hale focused less on the dollars and cents of the magazine business, choosing instead a narrative style that played on subscribers' sentiments. This went beyond editors' customary badgering and became a concrete representation of Godey and Hale's conviction that their method of conducting business was dictated by good motives. They insisted that subscribers were obligated to conduct their business based on the same rules of propriety. Hale expanded the metaphors and responsibilities of friendship to reflect that bond. She appealed "TO THE HEART AND CONSCIENCE OF THE DELINQUENT SUBSCRIBERS OF THE LADY'S BOOK" by claiming that a "Dun" was "unbefitting the character of the Lady's Book."[33] This appeal to the heart drew on religious metaphors and tempered the apparent harshness of the business world.[34] Once Hale captured her readers' attention by appealing to their sentiments, she could return to a more pragmatic discussion of money: "Yet no person acquainted with the generous forbearance practiced by Mr. Godey, even to his own great loss of property, would at all blame him, though he did send out a *severe dun*. The amount due him on account of the Lady's Book, is so large, that we do not like to name the sum lest it should be thought incredible."[35] Like Godey's discussion of James Garland, Hale's editorial turned an economic problem into an opportunity to discuss the success of the magazine. She must have calculated that her readers would be curious about the large dun, which suggested both the wide circulation of the magazine and Godey's considerable wealth. In light of Godey's generous treatment of both his contributors and subscribers, Hale implied that a delinquent subscriber, who had any moral compass, could not help but be moved to settle her account.

After tempting her reader with hints of unmentionable wealth and debt, Hale returned to the prosaic reality of paying bills. The recent "'pressure' in the money market," she conceded, had made it difficult for "southern and western friends" to obtain money to pay bills, even though Godey did accept banknotes from solvent banks within a reasonable geographical distance. Happily, Hale reminded her readers, the economic climate had improved, and it was possible to honor outstanding debts.[36] Hale offered forgiveness for delinquency in exchange for an immediate remittance.[37] By acknowledging the practical problems inherent in settling accounts, Hale comforted her readers, once again calling attention to the wide networks of the magazine's subscription list. Her strategy worked, and in editorial pages two months later, she congratulated the "noble-minded patrons" who had paid their bills.[38] By alluding to a flood of virtuous correspondence, Hale hoped to prick the consciences of tardy subscribers who were as yet unmoved. For those who had sent money, she offered a vision of the rewards of the reciprocity of good motives. Proper market behavior was not only honorable, Hale noted, but also gave "pleasure to our kind hearted friends, who, with their fair hands have penned apologies for the long delay." Once the money had been received, Hale could redefine the terms of her plea by insisting that "kind wishes" were the most valuable thing, not the money.[39] Her editorial attempted to reconstitute a community of friends threatened by economic irregularities. The reference to the "fair hands" suggests that Godey and Hale held women responsible for conducting their own business. At the end of the editorial, Hale invoked a biblical proverb to remind her readers of their obligation to keep their subscriptions in good standing: "These things come over our anxious path like the blessing of reviving showers after a long drought. The DUN, which we trembled to put forth, has proved a 'word fitly spoken,' and will, we trust, continue to be 'like apples of gold in pictures of silver.'"[40] By using Solomon's words (Proverbs 25:11) to pronounce the appeal for money as "a word fitly spoken," Hale evoked both the informality of business conducted between friends and the Christian underpinnings of moral market culture.

When appeals to friendship failed, Godey and Hale again resorted to chastising their subscribers. This time around, they emphasized how guilty a delinquent subscriber must feel: "The publisher returns his sincere thanks to those who take and have *paid* for the work—*they* must read it with pleasure; but what must be the horror of the person who every month receives a mute dun in the shape of the Book. Can he or she peruse it with any satisfaction? It is to be presumed not."[41] Hale reminded her readers that unless their habits of consumption were prompted by good motives, they transgressed the boundaries of moral market behavior. By reinventing the magazine as its own form of dun, she was able to mobilize the social scrutiny of the real community in the service of the imagined community. It was difficult to hold *Godey's* imagined community to the same scrutiny members of a real community would have experienced. "Fair ladies who would die upon the mere suspicion of owing their milliner," were, Hale noted, "allowing their accounts to stand from year to year insensible to our repeated, and at this time earnest request for a remittance."[42] By calling attention to other business relationships in women's lives, Hale was able to put the publisher-subscriber relationship in a familiar context. She assured her readers that the publisher's ledgers were confidential, but she sowed the seeds of suspicion by suggesting that not all who could display the magazine on their center tables deserved to do so.[43] By hinting at the possibility of discovery, she hoped that watchful eyes would monitor the private transactions of the imagined community. As a public object in the parlor, the magazine was a marker of not only taste but also market behavior. In another attempt to generate revenue, Hale proposed a competition. "We have a strong inclination," she announced, "to offer one of the handsomest shawls that our stores can furnish to the Lady who will make us the largest remittance in the next three months, either for past or coming subscriptions." And as if to convince herself of the propriety of such a plan, she reiterated the suggestion: "We will do it. It is an offer—let us see who will win it."[44] If she could not appeal to a woman's better nature, she could capitalize on her weakness with a gentle bribe.

The readers of *Godey's* grappled with another community problem. Godey frequently published letters from subscribers who complained about the inconvenience caused by neighbors who borrowed their copy of the magazine. When and if the copy was returned, one writer grumbled, it was so dirty, torn, and stained that it was "no longer fit to occupy its place on the center table or in the library."[45] This letter and many others Godey published suggested that borrowers belonged to a class of women whose economic behavior was not defined by good motives. The topic of borrowing, in fact, became the subject of running commentary. In the 1850s, the editorial pages included a section called the Borrower's Department in which Godey reprinted the correspondence he received from subscribers and local newspaper editors about this issue.[46] These women, the letters implied, needed the kind of instruction on economic behavior that the magazine provided. Godey agreed.

Godey usually advised his subscribers to refuse to lend their magazine, arguing that a borrower's deprivation would prompt her to pay for her own subscription—although women were not the only culprits and much of the discussion on borrowing centered on the unwillingness of a father to pay for a subscription and his capitulation only after his reading of the magazine was disrupted when it was no longer possible to borrow the magazine.[47] In an 1840 editorial, Hale proposed a solution to this problem that struck a balance between the financial constraints of the magazine's readers and her desire for a larger subscription base. After expressing regret that she and Godey were unable to give the magazine as a present to poor families unable to subscribe, she proposed that three or four families subscribe jointly: "The expense, for each family would be but trifling; and they would secure the privilege of an independent perusal of the work, which should be of no small importance to an American."[48] Hale presented *Godey's* not just as required reading for those who aspired to a genteel style of living but also as a prerequisite for virtuous citizenship. Her emphasis on independent perusal was more than a nod to the complaints about messy borrowers, it was an assertion of the importance of economic independence for consumption based on good motives.

Subscription clubs also offered a way for women who were unable to afford a subscription to earn their subscription in kind. By organizing a group of five or more subscribers, a woman could secure a free subscription for herself and a reduced rate for those in the club. The rates for clubs were advertised on the cover of the magazine, and club subscribers were encouraged to organize early in the year to assure prompt delivery. By the 1850s, subscription clubs had become a sustaining force in the growing circulation of the magazine.[49] Subscription clubs, which capitalized on the idea of magazine readers as a community, made the imagined national community visible in local terms. Hale noted that the clubs were "increasing all over the land," and she predicted that *Godey's* would "soon have a select circle of friends in every village and town."[50] Although the financial incentives for these clubs were clear for both publisher and subscriber, Hale defined their significance in terms of moral profit. The clubs brought "the minds and hearts of our readers towards each other and toward the same moral truths." Indeed, Hale went on to suggest that the clubs were "strengthening the bonds of our national Union, which, next to our faith in God, should be our most cherished sentiment."[51] Hale's editorial linked the sentiments of nationalism and religion to the moral truths expressed in the magazine, using the successful marketing of the magazine as an index of moral success. By putting the bonds between *Godey's* ladies on par with those of church and state, Godey and Hale stressed that the sentiments that formed the foundation of religious and national feeling defined the sphere of the magazine. Godey and Hale often blurred the difference between political identity and market identity. If America were a perfect Republic, "in humble imitation of Plato," Hale opined, "the subscription for a lady's periodical [would] always be paid *in advance.*" Subscriptions were debts of honor, she lectured her readers, and should be "binding on the consciences of those who have voluntarily contracted for the work."[52] Godey and Hale merged the ideals of community and individual honor with their desire for a national market of virtuous consumers. Their vision of the market, they argued, was synonymous with national identity.

By 1850, the tone of the editorials regarding delinquent subscriptions began to shift. As the subscriber list grew and the magazine's financial health became more secure, Godey and Hale focused on the longevity of the friend/subscriber relationship, offering more gentle reminders of accounts past due. In earlier reminders, Hale had worried that subscribers might not heed her requests, but now she could assert, "We feel sure they will accompany us through the coming seasons, and therefore to none of these friends do we say farewell." She continued in a "whisper" to subscribers "who have apparently forgotten that friends have reciprocal duties—'We do wish each and all who have not *paid* for the 'Lady's Book' would transmit the amount due before the opening of the new year.'"[53] Her whisper replaced the stridency of the earlier reminders. Although she had offered the external "pressure" in the market as an excuse in the 1838 editorial, in this passage Hale implied that neglecting to pay a subscription was a social and moral failure, the betrayal of a friendship as much as a lapsed business obligation.

Building on that same theme, Godey called attention to the lost possibilities for altruism in two editorials titled "The Publisher's Dream." In them, he "recounts" dreams in which all of his delinquent subscribers remit their debts. In the first dream, subscribers are swayed by Godey's rousing speech. Although he awakes before he can direct his clerks to record the credits in his account books, he heralds the dream as a portent.[54] In the second dream, a subscriber gives the speech. After introducing himself as Godey's oldest and largest debtor, he not only clears his balance but also congratulates Godey on the many contributions his magazine has made to national literary culture. He is particularly impressed by Godey's intention—if he could collect the "inconceivable amount of money" still owed him in overdue subscriptions— "to erect a most splendid home for all such heart-broken or superannuated editors, publishers, and writers" whose financial penury has been caused by the "negligence" of delinquent subscribers.[55] This benevolent plan touches the hearts of all his subscribers and they begin to pay their accounts in full, but the sound of the money piling up beside him shatters the vision, and Godey awakens to find it has only been a dream. He assures his readers, however, if such a thing were to happen. he would gladly put the money toward such a good cause. Godey often used metaphorical examples of altruism to convince his readers that his discussion of business did not revolve around personal gain but the perpetuation of literary culture. He was always quick to mention the generous sums he paid for submissions to the magazine, suggesting that a subscription was a way of supporting the growth of American literature, explicitly linking his vision of a national market with Hale's vision of a national literature.

With this goal in mind, increasing the subscription list was as important as ensuring payment from current subscribers. All the pleas for remittance appealed to the "hearts and consciences" of the subscribers, but none more than an appeal for new subscribers in 1850, when the magazine was compared to a lost child. Hale worried, she told her readers, that they always felt anxious "sending one paper away" on a "lonely and uncertain journey." She turned the magazine into a lost child, an irresistible image in sentimental culture. Without companions, she sighed, "these little fellows, in their seeming insignificance, may probably be kicked into some corner, or miss their way and be lost among the hills and hollows." Subscribers should take pity on these poor little magazines, "solitary and alone," Hale pleaded. "Give them company, and they will travel swiftly and reach their destination more surely!"[56] This vignette offered a comfortable and humorous way to talk about the activities of the market. Hale transformed an anonymous act into a personal interaction that evoked the bonds of maternal care.

Godey gave up the practice of traveling agents in the 1850s and continually reminded his readers that the only reliable way to subscribe was to send their money directly to him.[57] He also made payment in advance part of the criteria for new and continuing subscriptions. With 150,000 subscribers in 1860, Godey was less dependent on the patronage of any one person. By 1853, Godey was congratulating his subscribers on their reliability. He reprinted an editorial from another magazine that celebrated "Lady Subscribers" who are "prompt to pay their subscription bills, and won't suffer themselves to get in arrears with the publisher." Moreover, Godey's readers "appreciate his efforts to cater for their amusement and instruction, and have ever a kind word and approving smile to cheer and encourage him in the arduous duties which lie before him." The editor ended wistfully: "Commend us to lady subscribers. How we envy Godey, who deals with ladies almost exclusively! No wonder he has prospered."[58] Godey still appealed to husbands and sweethearts to pay for subscriptions, but women had become more visible as independent actors in the market. In the 1860s, Godey once again changed his marketing strategy when the discussion of subscriptions took on a more impersonal tone. Anecdotes were replaced with a standard list called "Some Hints," which outlined common mistakes to avoid when remitting subscription money.[59] Wooing subscribers was no longer necessary.

Godey saw a national market in terms of circulation: post offices, shipping routes, railroad lines, and subscription agents. Hale saw the cultural possibilities that these networks created in conjunction with new education possibilities, especially for women. Together they framed a national identity that was distinctly linked to what historians have come to identify as a middle-class sensibility, but by characterizing it in national terms, Godey and Hale avoided defining their imagined community of subscribers in class terms, emphasizing a set of discursive practices and national sentiments that were not defined by economic distinction.[60] They offered a national identity that reconciled moral imperatives with market imperatives. *Godey's Lady's Book* clearly articulated middle-class mores and a language of nationalism that encompassed both the virtue of the private sphere and a sphere of virtuous commerce. The magazine translated republican values into the new imperatives of market culture.[61] The language of sentimental pragmatism that underpinned the relationship between publisher and subscriber was useful in shaping the amorphous networks of an emerging middle-class culture. What began as a merger of commercial desire and cultural strategy, provided a series of imagined and, in the case of the ladies's subscription clubs, actual communities of like-minded people. The sentimental education about the market that *Godey's* offered its readers provided an acceptable way for a growing middle class to reconcile the overlaps between the private world of the home and the public world of the market. The imagined affinities between subscribers that Godey and Hale played on so effectively created a larger set of national associations that helped soften the image of America as a voracious market into an America defined by a vision of virtuous commerce.

$\mathcal{F}our$

∞

The Economy of
Domestic Happiness

$\mathcal{B}$y the end of the 1820s, a generation of girls who had grown up in prosperous families that subscribed to the new definitions of domestic life found themselves in the position of managing their own households and contending with the challenges of market culture.[1] The common complaint that girls were brought up in idleness and spent all their time reading novels at the expense of practical education was largely an exaggeration, but this perception helped justify a growing market for advice books about practical domestic matters. This advice literature illustrates the complexity of antebellum definitions of domesticity and the importance of domestic economy to the success of domesticity. Indeed, domestic economy was much more than cooking and cleaning, and its recurrence as a theme in antebellum popular fiction and advice manuals demonstrates how important it was to the market philosophy of sentimental pragmatism.

Lydia Maria Child, the daughter of a prosperous baker and wife of an idealistic and economically unreliable lawyer, knew from personal experience, despite a considerable income from her literary work, how tenuous the financial solvency of a middle-class family could be. In 1828, she published *The Frugal Housewife*, and despite a rather tart review by Sarah Hale, the book sold well and went through twelve editions by 1833. "It is the character of true economy," Child wrote, "to be as comfortable and genteel with a little, as others can be with much."[2] Child addressed her book to "the poor," although this audience included women who needed washing instructions for silk and daughters who had grown up without any practical domestic education. Child's readers were, therefore, a particular kind of poor: women who aspired to a domestic life of genteel elegance on a limited budget. This suggestion of aspiration was, in part, what prompted Hale's criticism of Child's work. Hale did not like the idea that women whose circumstances were improving would aspire to wealth, or that those whose circumstances were diminished would pretend wealth. Child refined her definition of her audience in the preface to *The Mother's Book* (1831), in which she described *The Frugal Housewife* as "suited to the wants of the middling class in our own country." Although some booksellers had not seen the profit in another cookery book, Child astutely observed that the sale of 6,000 copies in one year confirmed there was no book that targeted this particular audience.[3]

Subscribing to the dictates of true economy could not guarantee financial stability, Child conceded, but the education of women was an important stabilizing factor. "There is no subject so much connected with individual happiness and national prosperity as the education of daughters," she proclaimed.[4] A well-educated mind, Child reminded her readers, was not a luxury but a necessity, given the vicissitudes of the economy: "A mind full of piety and knowledge is always rich; it is a bank that never fails; it yields a perpetual dividend of happiness."[5] She advocated a comprehensive education that encompassed intellectual and practical achievements. Nothing threatened family prosperity more, Child lectured her readers, than the failure to be pragmatic about domestic economy.

Child instructed an aspiring middle class through the faults of an established one. Rather than encouraging her readers to embrace the activities and attitudes of genteel life, she cautioned against taking up leisure activities and travel simply because they were "cheap." Instead, she exposed the real costs of leisure, particularly the cost of educating children only in genteel pastimes at the expense of practical knowledge. A wife without domestic accomplishments was of little help in times of hardship and could, in fact, contribute to her husband's financial woes. Waiting to marry for money only postponed the problem: "But who that marries for money, in this land of precarious fortunes, can tell how soon they will lose the glittering temptation, to which they have been willing to sacrifice so much?"[6] In short, Child's advice demonstrates that for her, middle-class status was as much defined by a pragmatic understanding of the relationship of domesticity and domestic economy as by genteel practices. The ability to distinguish oneself from the lower class and to protect oneself from the vagaries of a turbulent economy was as important as the ability to emulate the upper class.[7]

The process of setting up a household was as important as the system of domestic management employed to run it. Child warned her readers against exorbitant spending on home furnishings. "There is nothing in which the extravagance of the present day strikes me so forcibly," she grumbled, "as the manner in which young people of moderate fortune furnish their houses."[8] This kind of emulative behavior, she noted, more often than not threatened the ability of a young couple to establish the kind of genteel household they aped. Often, she observed, as did other authors who wrote on this topic, newly married couples spent so much money on domestic niceties that they did not have enough money for practical necessities such as bedding and kitchen utensils. This lack of private comfort undermined the illusion of gentility that fashionable parlor suites were designed to represent. Even for those who could fashionably furnish a house without cutting corners, the instantaneous domesticity of these new households fell short of the genteel model in other ways. As Nathaniel P. Willis archly remarked in 1855, "The proprietor of almost any house in New York might wake up in thousands of other homes and not recognize for a half hour that he was not at home."[9] The American habit of decorating created respectable anonymity, but it lacked the coziness and sense of history that Willis found so charming in English homes. He admired (and romanticized) the English practice of carefully collecting each piece of furniture to serve a particular purpose, rather than just to fill up space. In either case, the priorities of new prosperity could easily be read through domestic furnishings.[10]

Although Catharine Sedgwick did not write didactic manuals, she devoted considerable energy to illustrating the principles of domestic economy. Her didactic novel *Home* (1835) presented, in explicit terms, how the material world of the home could represent a moral, Christian world view.[11] *Home* traces the life history of the Barclay family, but it is first and foremost a handbook to educate readers about furnishing their homes, conducting their domestic lives, and realizing the ideals of domestic happiness through the practical application of domestic economy. Although its protagonist, William Barclay, is a merchant, Sedgwick dedicated the book to "Farmers and Mechanics," suggesting that home life rather than work life offered the possibility for common experience. She hoped her vision of domestic life would have a broad appeal to residents of both the country and the city. Her dedication also suggests the importance of a male readership for books about domestic economy. As Mr. and Mrs. Barclay set up housekeeping, Sedgwick outlines their choices and philosophy in detail. Mr. Barclay chooses the contents of their new household very carefully, opting for plain, serviceable furniture rather than ornamental things. He saves the balance of their money for a book fund and substantially increases their library.[12] William Barclay developed his theories about domestic order and happiness as child, when he and his widowed mother were obliged to depend on the kindness of friends. These households gave him the opportunity to study many different modes of domestic economy:

> Few persons, probably, have thought so much as William Barclay of the economy of domestic happiness. He had lived in various families and seen much waste and neglect of the means of virtue and happiness which Providence supplies through the social relations.[13]

Barclay's early education in the pitfalls of household management inspired him to make "a chart for his future conduct, by which he hoped to escape at least some of the shoals and quicksands on which others made shipwreck." His experience convinced him that "a household, governed in obedience to the Christian social law, would present as perfect an image of heaven, as the infirmity of human nature, and the imperfections in the constitution of human affairs would admit."[14]

The well-being of the Barclay family is manifested through the orderliness of their household, their thoughtful child-rearing practices, their charitable actions, and their spiritual acceptance of personal tragedy. At every turn, Sedgwick holds up the Barclay family as a mirror through which the reader can see the failings of the other families presented in the book. Although these failings are often personal or spiritual, they almost always have attendant economic consequences. Only by balancing moral and economic decisions could a family succeed, Sedgwick argued.[15] A person's actions at home and in the world must be in accord with Christian social law, Sedgwick contended, and the environment of the home was the most important influence on the success or failure of a family's life.[16]

The economic upheavals of the late 1830s prompted authors to advise those unfortunate readers who were in retrenchment and to caution those who were careless of their prosperity. In a review of Hannah F. Lee's *Three Experiments in Living* (1837), Sarah Hale pronounced, "This little Book is one of the most successful *experiments* of popularizing domestic economy which has ever been made."[17] Demand for the book was so great that the publisher issued several editions in the first few weeks after publication. By 1846, the book had gone through twenty-one editions, and Hale praised it as "one of the most celebrated and useful books every published in this country."[18] The popularity of the novel prompted the publisher to initiate a monthly series on domestic economy. Hale predicted that these moral tales would have more influence than lectures, essays, or even sermons on the same subject. *Three Experiments,* like *Home,* traces the vicissitudes of a family economy. As the Fulton family's fortunes improve, however, the virtue of their family economy suffers. Lee focuses on the dangers of emulative behavior without the restraint of "true economy." Aspiring to wealth, she argues, is poor economy; instead, she champions the middling condition. Samuel Colman, the editor and publisher of the volume, states this clearly in the preface: "We daily see abundant reason for believing, that, as a practical rule of conduct, we cannot do better than to follow the emphatic advice of the stern and uncompromising Junius: 'Let all your views in life be directed to a solid, however moderate, independence; without it, no man can be happy, or even *honest.*'"[19]

The first section of the novel, "Living Within the Means," tells of the exemplary behavior of the newly wed Fultons, who have only the promise of Dr. Fulton's medical career to support them. Despite their limited means, Frank and Jane Fulton manage to build a happy home and charitable medical practice. Their ability to be benevolent despite their limited income is contrasted with the failure of wealthier acquaintances to do the same. When Jane puzzles over the discrepancies between the lavish homes and clothing of her wealthy friends and their laments about being unable to contribute to benevolent causes, Frank reminds her that the appearance of wealth is not always an indication of true wealth. Often those whose homes and wardrobes are the most lavish are what he calls the "poor rich"—people who live so far beyond their means that they are always short of funds. The Fultons congratulate themselves on their ability to feel rich even without a large income, but they soon begin to forget this lesson. The second section, "Living Up to the Means," traces their gradual abandonment of their virtuous habits of domestic economy. Jane is tempted by the habits of her wealthy friends, and as Dr. Fulton's practice grows, neither of them is as careful as they had been on a smaller income. Both are still mindful of economy, but only enough to balance their budget and not enough to save as they had before. In the book's final section, "Living Beyond the Means," the Fultons succumb to all the bad habits illustrated in the first section. Instead of allowing their income to dictate their style of life, they allow their sense of entitlement to justify incurring debt. Husband and wife no longer communicate on economic matters, and reckless extravagance combined with the desire to provide their children with a fashionable life ultimately ruins them. This section illustrates the dangers of unchecked emulative behavior, and in the case of their indulgence of their children, a misunderstanding of the meaning of "good motives."

The popularity and influence of this novel stem from more than just its engaging writing style and topical subject matter. The ruin of the Fulton family is a tale about the amnesia of prosperity. Lee reminds her readers that anyone could be drawn into behavior perilous to family fortunes. Her advice would have resonated with those who found themselves in economic straits, and those whose own amnesia was revealed by the Fultons' example. Domestic economy was the concern of men and women of all walks of life, Lee argued. In a particularly poignant passage of the book, a poor woman talks to Jane Fulton about the difficulties working women had collecting money from rich women, even those involved in benevolent organizations. The failure of these wealthy women to practice domestic economy meant that they did not understand the value of time and the importance of prompt payment, no matter how small the sum.[20] Their failure, in turn, interfered with the ability of poor women to practice good domestic economy and threatened not only the individual's livelihood but also the prosperity of the nation.

Readers who enjoyed fiction on domestic economy were also a prime audience for practical manuals. In 1839, Sarah Hale published the first of several domestic manuals that established her as an authority on practical household matters. In the preface to *The Good Housekeeper; or, The Way to Live Well and be Well While We Live,* she informed her readers that her book was more than just another collection of recipes: "Such rational and Christian views of domestic economy have never before been enforced in a treatise on housekeeping; and, the writer flatters herself that this will be well received."[21] The first edition sold out in less than a month. In the preface to the second edition, Hale, who was adept at marketing, commented on this. One of the main lessons she hoped to teach her readers was the difference between true economy and frugality. Although she acknowledged Child as founder of the household advice genre, she returned to her old criticism of Child's emphasis on "cheapness," preferring to define the audience for economy in different terms. Like Sedgwick and Lee, Hale distinguished between the miserable poor, those whose vices prevented them from achieving prosperity, and the luxurious poor, who lived on credit or speculation. Neither group, Hale insisted, would be interested in recipes that used inexpensive ingredients, but the great majority of the rest of the population would: "The rich, who intend to continue so, the thriving who mean to be rich, the sensible and industrious who love comfort and independence, the benevolent who wish to do good—These classes all practice economy and will not despise 'cheap dishes.'"[22] In other words, economy was not just a necessary evil but a positive good. Hale's recipes for Indian pudding and other inexpensive but tasty dishes illustrated the lessons of Sedgwick and Lee's fiction in the most concrete terms.[23] Hale dedicated her book to "Every American Woman who wishes to promote the Health, Comfort and Prosperity of her family." By including prosperity in this list, she envisioned a prosperity that came from the good motives of domestic economy rather than the suspicious motives of speculation.

In an 1840 editorial, Sarah Hale condemned "speculation" as a word with magical power, like the genie in Aladdin's lamp, and the ability to make or break fortunes on a whim; but "economy," she noted, was "the real cabalistic word of Americans."[24] Economy was a word "useful on all occasions" and "used by all classes," she fretted. Politicians promised attention to the national economy, business men whispered that it was the secret of their success, farmers and mechanics attributed their prosperity to the "successful practice of economy," and even women proclaimed themselves economists. Hale took issue with women's false sense of economy. To save a small amount of money at a washerwoman's expense and squander a large amount of money on "elegant superfluities" was not true economy. She contrasted complaints about the cost of a girl's education with the insistence that the most fashionable milliner and dressmaker must be employed to make her wardrobe. She attempted to recover the word "economy" from its petty and parsimonious associations and called upon all "American ladies" to practice true economy, suggesting that in this moment of economic turmoil, women must rise to the occasion as they had done during the Revolutionary War. "The great mass of our people, for the last ten years," she argued, "have lived beyond their incomes; they have dressed too fine, and each family has aimed at being thought richer than its neighbor."[25]

The epidemic of economic carelessness was due largely to "the facility with which credit was granted," Hale chided. "Every body could run in debt, and it was such good economy to purchase things when you could get them cheap and be trusted for them besides!"[26] True economy required a system that both recorded expenses and regulated them judiciously. With a proper education about the deceptive nature of economy, women could help men resist speculation and reinvigorate a national economy burdened with foreign debt. True economy was based on an integrated system in which all forms of economy operated in harmony. Saving a few cents on the wages of a washerwoman disrupted the whole system. A woman's domestic economy played an important part in not only the management of her own household but also the prosperity of her husband's business and the health of the national economy. Although this editorial explicitly linked the political economy and domestic economy, as Hale had done many times before, it also insisted on a necessary harmony of production and consumption to regulate the terms of economy.

Catharine Beecher, one of the most influential writers on the subject of domestic economy, agreed in principle with many of the ideas put forth in fiction and popular manuals, but she considered this kind of education inadequate. She argued that domestic economy must be systematically taught as a science rather than anecdotally taught by example. Her *Treatise on Domestic Economy for Use of Young Ladies at Home and at School* (1841) was written as a textbook for female schools, and she wrote a companion volume, *Miss Beecher's Domestic Receipt-Book,* to complement the course of study outlined in *Treatise.*[27] Only when domestic economy was treated as a subject on a par with political economy and moral science, Beecher insisted, would women, and the "great moral enterprise" of the nation, benefit from the systems of habit and order based on Christian morality that defined domestic economy. The scientific teaching of domestic economy was essential for two reasons. First, serious instruction was the only way to convey to parents the importance of this knowledge in the education of all girls. The science of domestic economy must not replace the study of literature, history, and moral philosophy, but it must be taught with the same rigor. Second, mothers were not able to offer their daughters a proper education on this topic. Their own knowledge, largely gained through experience rather than study, was not scientific. Implicit in this criticism of the educational ability of mothers was the suggestion that the education of most mothers had either been ignored by their own mothers or, in a world of social mobility, had been the wrong kind of domestic education for middle-class domesticity. The future of the nation should not be left in the hands of mothers unable to approach this educational mandate with the appropriate rigor and training. Teaching domestic economy in school ensured that the greatest number of girls would receive a comprehensive education on this topic.[28] Beecher's emphasis on the importance of organization and rational thinking was, in part, a response to the economic chaos of the moment. Her approach to the practicalities of domestic management emphasized that the sentiments of family life and Christian nurture were rooted in an economy of domestic life every bit as structured as the economy of the market. The doctrines of Christianity gave order to the chaos of everyday life, and this in turn gave order to the chaos of the market.

Beecher devoted a lifetime to developing a moral philosophy that balanced the spiritual and economic imperatives of middle-class life. In 1838, as a response to the theological controversies that divided the Presbyterian Church, and in an attempt to reconcile other doctrinal differences under the umbrella of common moral laws, Beecher published *The Moral Instructor for Schools and Families: Containing Lessons on the Duties of Life, Arranged for Study and Recitation, Also Designed as a Reading Book for Schools.* In this text, she presented a moral framework designed to reconcile economic success with religious virtue. Beecher explained and justified the possibilities for a virtuous life amid democratized prosperity.[29] She organized her system around the justification of social hierarchy and the ethic of hard work, which the capricious success of the new market economy seemed to erode. Worldly success, she reminded her readers, was often temporary. Moral virtue and the work ethic, therefore, remained the only assurance of a happy life both here on earth and in heaven. The sons and daughters of the wealthy must be taught the skills to survive economic adversity and learn to resist the temptations that wealth placed before them.

Beecher's focus on restraint supported her argument about the moral superiority of the successful. Superiority was not measured by worldly success, which was available to anyone willing to pursue it. Moral superiority, and by extension social position, was based on the ability to resist the temptations material success offered. The most important lesson parents could teach children was the virtue of self-restraint, which would benefit them in their own economic exploits and preserve the virtue of their homes if they were successful enough to be released from the toil of everyday business. By framing free will in terms of restraint, Beecher emphasized the importance of self-sacrifice as opposed to self-indulgence and the resonance of ideas about free will with the imperatives of free enterprise.[30]

Whereas Beecher argued for the serious study of domestic economy by girls and women, T. S. Arthur, a popular magazine author, argued for the study of domestic economy by men. Arthur tempered the moralism of his economic fiction with an engaging pragmatism about the fluctuations of the market. He began his career in Baltimore, in the mid-1830s, as the editor of the *Athenaeum and Young Men's Paper,* but when the demand for his fictional contributions to *Godey's, Graham's,* and the *Saturday Courier* increased, he moved to Philadelphia, where his literary career flourished. He remained a constant contributor to *Godey's* until the mid-1850s, when the success of his own literary magazine, *Arthur's Home Magazine,* demanded all of his energy. He also published numerous volumes of his collected stories as well as his best-known work, *Ten Nights in a Barroom and What I Saw There* (1854).[31] As editor of the *Athenaeum,* Arthur was accustomed to writing for a male audience, which colored his perspective on issues of domestic economy, even after he became a regular contributor to ladies' magazines such as *Godey's.* Although clearly men and women read both the *Athenaeum* and *Godey's,* the assumed audience defined an author's perspective. Male and female authors both insisted that the economies of home and market must be kept in balance, but women approached this balance from the point of view of domestic economy, whereas male writers, such as Arthur, focused on the political economy of the business world and the ways it could be reformed by the logic of domestic economy.

Whereas Sedgwick and Lee had examined the problems of domestic economy that began with marriage, Arthur's fiction often explored the question from a male perspective in order to assess when marriage made economic sense. Arthur devoted particular attention to the problems of housekeeping on a salary of $1,000 a year, the minimum amount he considered viable for a genteel household.[32] It was the "matter-of-fact" side of marriage and the economic underpinnings of domesticity that interested him.[33] His discussion of marriage did not dwell on the kindling of love or the duties of women but the importance of the reciprocal duties of husband and wife. The discussion of women's duties, Arthur noted, was ubiquitous: "in books of domestic economy, in tales, essays, newspaper paragraphs, and in current conversation do we hear iterated and reiterated the lesson of woman's duties to her husband and her household." Many writers contributed to the image of ideal feminine domesticity, but "who writes and talks of the husband's duties?"[34] In his fiction, Arthur attempted to fill this gap, emphasizing the importance of cooperation between husband and wife in economic matters and the dependence of successful business economy on rigorous domestic economy.

Although many of his stories are told from a man's point of view, it is often the female character who possesses the economic sensibility. In "The Clerk's Marriage," Henry Adrian, distressed by a friend's pronouncement that marriage on $1,000 a year is folly, prepares to call off his engagement.[35] Rosa, Adrian's fiancée, outlines a plan that will make marriage possible. Although she is from a wealthy family, her education has included practical domestic skills as well as female accomplishments that provide her with marketable skills. She offers to contribute to their joint income. Henry, concerned about the loss of social status, protests, but Rosa is able to see how to turn $1,000 a year into "a sum large enough to supply the real wants of two persons who have independence enough not to be enslaved by a mere love of appearances."[36] She is a true economist, practicing economy without jeopardizing their class status. They save money by foregoing a bridal tour, and they rent a house instead of boarding. Arthur describes in detail the simplicity and taste of their furnishings. Rosa's skills in domestic management and her ability to give music lessons make middle-class domesticity possible. They live a happy, simple life, much to the envy of Henry's bachelor friend, who had warned him that his income was too small. Stories like this reassured male readers that the benefits of marriage were greater than its financial obligations.

Arthur frequently illustrated the difference between economizing and true economy. In "Is It Economy?: The Experience of Mr. John Jones," the Jones family moves from a boardinghouse to their own house, a move that requires them to purchase furniture. Both husband and wife agree that they must be modest in their purchases, but there are significant differences in their approach to this problem. Mr. Jones makes his decisions based on price, even though Mrs. Jones has urged him to buy "good" things: "'I don't want anything very extra, Mr. Jones,' returned my wife, a little uneasily. 'Though what I do have, I would like good. It's no economy, in the end to buy cheap things.'" Mr. Jones does not like the implication that he is cheap, but he misses his wife's point: well-made furniture lasts longer and is cheaper in the long run. Instead of heeding his wife's suggestions, however, Mr. Jones buys a houseful of cheap furniture. Arthur provides a wealth of details about the prices and kinds of furniture and rugs purchased, offering concrete points of comparison for his readers. Despite his cheap purchases, Mr. Jones finds that he has still overspent his budget by $100. After only three months, the furniture begins to show wear and has to be mended. Mr. Jones discovers, much to his chagrin, that his economizing is not economical. Cheap furniture is cheap in craftsmanship as well as price. After three years, the furniture is worn and shabby, if not broken, and the cost and inconvenience of repairs have been substantial. Finally, Mr. Jones accepts his wife's original assertion that well-made furniture is more economical than cheap furniture and has a cabinet-maker make new furniture to replace the old. Years pass without a repair, and Mr. Jones admits to his wife that this furniture is much better, to which she replies, "Cheap furniture is dearest in the end. Every housekeeper ought to know this in the beginning. If we had known it, see what we would have saved."[37] At the end of the story, Mr. Jones acknowledges that he was the one who needed to learn that lesson. His wife, although she does not hold the purse strings, is the one who understands domestic economy.

In "Can't Get Along," Arthur addressed the importance of strict accounts and prompt bill paying to restore the equilibrium of domestic economy.[38] Felix and Harriet Hall cannot understand why they struggle so hard to make ends meet, when Felix's co-worker Hawkins lives well on the same salary. Harriet discovers that Felix is the problem; he spends money on trifles that add up to a significant sum, and he is especially soft-hearted when it comes to presents for the children. They agree that Harriet will manage the finances. Felix will stick to an allowance, polish his own boots, and shave himself. At first these tasks seem like terrible privations, but Felix quickly learns that he can do them better than anyone he previously had hired, and he enjoys the sense of independence his industry provides. After a year of strict economy, Harriet has paid their debts and saved some money. Although they have denied themselves a few luxuries, Felix admits his wife has changed their spending habits without changing the quality of their life. Impressed by her ability, he leaves all further money matters to her, and they live comfortably on his salary. The lessons of economy were simple, Arthur taught his readers, and must be practiced by both men and women. A man's failure to see domestic spending in economic rather than sentimental terms disrupted domestic economy, just as a woman's isolation from the matters of business could cause financial strain.[39]

Arthur did not confine his championship of women's business acumen to the domestic sphere. In "Tell Your Wife," Aaron Little, a businessman in financial difficulty, reads a newspaper article "in which the writer suggested to business men in trouble, the propriety of consulting their wives."[40] Although Little scoffs at the article, it plants the idea in his head, and despite his initial skepticism, he talks to his wife about his business troubles. He tells her that he is going to ask Mr. Lawrence to be a partner. His wife, knowing the state of Mrs. Lawrence's domestic economy, advises against it. The Lawrences, she informs her husband, are too extravagant to be a real source of capital. Instead, she offers to help her husband. She sells their furniture to raise the necessary capital and moves the family to a boardinghouse, which relieves her of her domestic responsibilities. Her younger sister comes to care for her children, and she works in her husband's business as his chief clerk. By contracting out her domestic labor, Aaron Little's wife finds a solution that later became the basis of Charlotte Perkins Gilman's ideas in *Women and Economics* (1898) for household reform based on the division of domestic labor.[41] Arthur demonstrates that domestic economy depends on a well-integrated system of domestic management, not necessarily on the labor of one woman.

Mrs. Little is a better manager than the previous clerk, and she discovers her predecessor embezzled money. Under her careful management, her husband spends less time trying to borrow money and devotes more time to his business. Soon their fortunes improve. Mrs. Little's skills in domestic economy easily translate into the business world. A business and a home are run by the same management principles, she observes. Aaron Little is impressed with his wife's ability to manage the business, and they remain successful business partners. Mrs. Little's sojourn in the world of business is not cut short by her husband's return to solvency. Because she entered the world of business in the name of familial duty, she is not compelled to return to the domestic sphere once the crisis is over.

Arthur's fiction made visible the reciprocal connections between the work of the home and the market. The economic partnerships of women and men complemented their emotional partnerships. His stories emphasize the interdependence of the business and domestic spheres rather than their separation. Husbands and wives were partners in both spheres. Domestic production became the production of capital that resulted from savings. With careful management and restrained consumption, many families could aspire to a comfortable domestic life that had been restricted to the wealthy. Arthur's fiction suggests that women, rather than men, were responsible for the successful balance of home and market. Women had a sentimental vision of economy, one that combined reason and feeling. They saw the relationship between home and market as an integrated economy rather than as two separate spheres. Arthur advocated a form of business partnership that crossed the lines of home and market in both directions. He highlighted men's domestic responsibilities and recognized women's domestic duties as work. He stopped short of recommending that men should do housework, but he did suggest that it was a man's obligation to provide his wife with domestic help if she needed it.

The economic vision Arthur presented depended on the partnership between husband and wife, but women entering the market independently were subject to greater constraints, and the translation of the home into a business was another matter. Arthur's story "Taking Boarders" (1851) paints a sobering portrait of Mrs. Darlington's financial difficulties after her husband's death.[42] Mr. Darlington had been a wealthy and successful lawyer but had suffered heavy losses from unwise speculation. In struggling to recover what he had lost, he squandered the remainder of his fortune, and his failure brought on his death. Mrs. Darlington knew nothing of these financial losses until after the funeral. The story begins as she contemplates the future. She is left with the household possessions and $1,000 to support herself and her five children. Although she has no business experience, she decides that taking in boarders is the best way to generate income. Despite her oldest daughter's protestations about the "dreadful exposure" such a plan promises, Mrs. Darlington can think of no other acceptable alternatives. Taking in boarders appears to be a "genteel" business, one for which they have been trained by their own domestic experience.[43] Most important, Mrs. Darlington believes that it will preserve at least the outward appearance of their old way of life. Her first concern is to conceal her insolvency, to avoid the exposure that public participation in the market would bring. She discovers, however, that concealment is not good economy.

Her friends agree that taking boarders is the least conspicuous way to support the family, but her brother, Hiram Ellis, opposes it. He disputes her assertion that her domestic training as a hostess will provide the necessary skills for running a profitable boardinghouse. "It takes a woman of shrewdness, caution and knowledge of the world, and one thoroughly versed in household economy, to get along in this pursuit," he argues.[44] Hiram removes the genteel veneer from the proposed enterprise, distinguishing between domesticity and the business of domesticity. Mrs. Darlington does not understand this distinction. She rejects his suggestion to open a school, because she is afraid of the scrutiny of her peers. A school would reveal the family's insolvency to their circle of friends and require her daughters to work. A boardinghouse, she believes, will only require her own invisible management.

Mrs. Darlington's boardinghouse is a disaster. Paying guests do not behave in the same manner as invited guests. Mrs. Darlington is not a good economist; she breaks all the rules of business. Because she feels insecure about having empty rooms, she lets them for less than her own cost of maintaining them. One unsavory family of boarders refuses to pay, and another ruins furniture and wallpaper. One woman is abandoned by her husband, and Mrs. Darlington, who sympathizes with her predicament, allows her to stay on for free, seriously depleting her own income. Her son, who had been a virtuous law student, is corrupted by several dissipated young boarders who turn him into a gambler. As the final straw, a confidence man convinces her youngest daughter, Miriam, to elope with him by offering to support her family. Hiram rescues Miriam at the last minute—revealing that her would-be seducer is a notorious gambler and bigamist—and lectures her on the folly of keeping boarders:

> Hundreds of women resort to keeping boarders as a means of supporting their families, when they might do it more easily, with less exposure, and greater certainty, in teaching, if qualified, fine needlework, or even in the keeping of a store for the sale of fancy and useful articles.[45]

Unlike the options Ellis outlines, taking boarders does not maintain the balance of home and market. The crass behavior of Mrs. Darlington's tenants is evidence of market behavior that is not dictated by good motives.

With Miriam's safe return, Mrs. Darlington resolves to undertake a new enterprise, and the family regains its privacy. She and her daughters swallow their pride and open a school. It is truly a family business, for Ellis helps make up the deficit until the school can support them. Many of their friends are happy to send their children to a school run by such accomplished young ladies. This network of friendship obviates the need for interaction with and exposure to strangers, and the school rapidly becomes a success. Although their enterprise is still located in their home, it does not disrupt the circle of domesticity and they are better able to choose their clientele. At the end of the day, they are free to be a family and shut out the world.[46]

By opening their home to the market, the Darlingtons exposed themselves to the dangers of the public sphere: vulgarity, dissipation, abandonment, dishonesty, gambling, and seduction. In short, Arthur touched on every image of middle-class anxiety about the complicated relationship between cultural and economic definitions of class status that separated the genteel from the crass.[47] Class status, he admonished, was tenuous and must be carefully guarded. A woman must choose her approach to the market carefully. Although the home may be opened to the market, it must be closed in the evening to maintain a balance between public and private because the parameters of the moral market were observed within class lines, not across them. Mrs. Darlington thought that keeping borders was an enterprise governed by the sympathy of exchange among friends, and as a form of hospitality, boarding could be defined in terms of a gift economy. Her gift of hospitality to the destitute woman, who had no way to reciprocate, having dropped below the lower boundary of the middle class, jeopardized her own family's well-being. It is only when she returns to an exchange relationship within her own class that her market life can be governed by the principles of gift exchange. Although money is exchanged, the relationship between the Darlingtons and the families whose children attend their school includes a mutual recognition of gentility. The Darlington girls give their students the gift of an accomplished and genteel education in exchange for the gift of maintaining their social status.[48]

Arthur's economic fiction continued to be popular, and he regularly published collections of it, sometimes several volumes in one year. The light tone and cheerful moralism of his stories helped move this kind of economic advice away from the religious focus of the earlier generation of women writers. The pragmatic approach to the relationship of the home and the market helped make moral market behavior seem like common sense. In spite of its moderate approach, fiction like that written by Arthur worried the conservative proponents of domestic economy. In 1869, Catharine Beecher published a revised edition of her *Treatise on Domestic Economy*, coauthored with her sister Harriet Beecher Stowe and renamed *The American Woman's Home*.[49] Harriet Beecher Stowe had published her own book of domestic advice, *House and Home Papers* (1865), a few years earlier, and based on this, Harriet contributed chapters on gardening and decorating that extended Catharine's argument about the unified Christian home.[50] Catharine Beecher's system was based on her faith in a rational science of home economy. Like T. S. Arthur, she emphasized the importance of accounts in management of the home. She encouraged her readers to calculate the time and money they spent on necessary and ornamental things, and on intellectual and benevolent purposes, so that they might balance their accounts in accordance with their Christian beliefs.[51] She devoted an entire chapter to "Economy of Time and Expenses" in which she emphasized that "true economy" was constituted by "the *right apportionment* of time."[52] This new edition, Beecher noted in her introduction, would offer guidance to women who might be confused by the "crude speculations as to women's rights and duties" proposed by feminists. Beecher strongly disapproved of the movement for women's rights, which she saw as a degradation of women's most important social influence in the Christian home. Women's rights were a distraction from the proper respect and training for women's true profession. Beecher even suggested that her model Christian home could be run entirely by women, not only rejecting the public male sphere targeted by women's rights activists but also isolating men in the public sphere, away from the center of society, the home.[53] Although *The American Woman's Home* was popular, for its sensible advice as well as the celebrity of its authors, the advice it offered was tied to an earlier era. A new generation of brides wished for advice that sounded more like Arthur than Beecher.

Mary Virginia Terhune, known to her readers as Marion Harland, was well aware that young brides could easily be baffled by the plethora of advice on domestic matters available at their local bookseller. In order to distinguish her book from the many other choices, she called her domestic manual *Common Sense in the Household* (1871). Terhune addressed her readers in a friendly tone, assuring them that all women new to housekeeping needed advice. She encouraged her readers, for example, to start with simple recipes and build up a repertoire rather than threaten domestic harmony by producing culinary disasters. Building on the popularity of her manual and expanding her domestic advice, Terhune published a fictional version of her ideas about domestic economy in *Godey's* the following year.[54] "Stumbling Blocks" traces Mrs. Letsome's business day in the "family firm." The story begins with Dr. and Mrs. Andrew Letsome at the breakfast table, reading the newspaper. Both husband and wife read their own paper, and they share the news with each other and their children, who listen attentively. In a discussion of the issue of woman suffrage, Mrs. Letsome rejects the political model of equality for a model of business equality in which each partner attends to separate business. She calls this the "co-partnership" of marriage.

Mrs. Letsome is an interpreter of domestic ideology, not an advocate for radical reform. Terhune's use of business analogies to describe both Mrs. Letsome's marriage and the domestic economy of her home offered a vocabulary for her readers to use with their own husbands.[55] Terhune, Catharine Beecher, Sarah Hale, and other antisuffrage feminists saw a power in their visions of domesticity equivalent to the political power of the public sphere. Economic opportunity, based in domestic economy, was more influential, they believed, than politics. Rational domesticity was necessary for sentimental domesticity. The variety of the work included in these domestic systems indicates that first Beecher and then Terhune expanded the boundaries of the domestic sphere by emphasizing the common sense of their systems, which, for Terhune, included the right of women to continue earning money after marriage.

In Terhune's story, Mrs. Letsome has developed a rigorous system to organize her daily activities. Despite this, she fears she is a "bad economist of time." She frets, "My achievements are not commensurable with my ability, never equal my expectations."[56] Her carefully organized day is constantly interrupted by women who do not manage their time as well as she does. One woman, who interrupts her schedule for more than an hour by telling long and tedious stories, delivers a speech, unconsciously parodying herself: "'We women of business know one another's trials so well that we cannot be too considerate in respecting the time and engagements of our sister-workers in the hive where there are so many drones,' she said creamily."[57] She finishes her soliloquy by complaining that women "fritter away their time—and time is money, and more than money, for a minute lost is never regained—is absolutely deplorable."[58] Although Mrs. Letsome is too polite to express her exasperation, Terhune hoped her readers would sympathize. Time is Mrs. Letsome's most precious commodity; it is the only thing she cannot make.

Because other women do not run their homes and charitable activities in a businesslike fashion, Mrs. Letsome's system is forever in jeopardy. The root of this problem, as she sees it, is the lack of serious business training for women. Although many women engaged in business of some kind before they married, they generally viewed it as only a "temporary expedient" and did not devote their skills and energy to mastering the business. Letsome's idea of "co-partnership" depends on the maintenance and use of these skills *after* marriage as well as before. A young bookkeeper would learn her profession that much more carefully, Letsome insists, if she knew that "her proficiency can be made the sources of profit to herself and her husband."[59]

Young families would be much more prosperous, Mrs. Letsome asserts, if milliners and dressmakers were not ashamed to practice their former professions on an occasional basis to augment their husbands' income. Terhune contended that although the public and private spheres should remain separate, the market should not be separated from the home. The lack of industry for profit in the home jeopardized the harmonious domesticity of the middle-class more than its presence. The leisure of marriage was artificial. Women who knew the value of money and contributed to the family income were less likely to succumb to the desire for luxuries. Women's contributions to the family income were a constant in middle-class life, Terhune declared, and women must learn to respect the value of time and follow a domestic system. Terhune, like T. S. Arthur, insisted that the symbiosis of women's business and domestic roles represented an improvement in domestic life rather. Women's work could contribute to social mobility. "Don't you see," she beseeched her readers, "how quickly the whole face of society would be altered?"[60]

Mrs. Letsome's system of time management allows her to pursue a writing career without jeopardizing her other responsibilities. She uses the time she would have spent doing plain sewing to write, and the income she earns from one month of writing provides more than enough money to pay for three months of plain sewing. The opportunity cost of plain sewing is too high to make economic sense.[61] She portrays her literary efforts as part of the larger business of domestic economy: "For ten years past [her writing] had brought her money with reputation. The first article for which she asked or received payment was written under the stress of earnest desire, almost agony, to aid her husband in his early struggles upward."[62] By insisting that her husband's aspirations provided the impetus for her writing career, and that her profits were for his benefit, Mrs. Letsome absolves herself of any selfish motive. Yet although

Terhune asserts that Mrs. Letsome's career is secondary to that of her husband, the continuation of her career after the early struggles were won, and her description of it as a "profession," gave it a prominence in the family economy that sentimental descriptions could not belie.[63] Terhune used the language of business in an attempt to make women's work visible, to call it work rather than duty. Unlike her husband, who can use his work to excuse himself from social duties, Mrs. Letsome has no excuse. The parlor is the site of both production and leisure. Her female friends do not respect the division of her day into a productive morning and a social afternoon, and because she does not have a separate work place, she is required by duty or love to interrupt her work whenever anyone comes to call. Middle-class conventions of sociability required that she conceal the work that underpins her leisure.

In the eyes of women who do not manage their time, the time Mrs. Letsome spends on fancywork obscures the other work she does. Because fancywork filled the idle hours of young, unmarried women who did not bear full responsibility for the domestic burden, Mrs. Letsome is criticized by her peers for the intricacy of her fancywork. The crimson stripe in an afghan she gives to a friend is condemned as "red with the blood of murdered *time!*"[64] Mrs. Letsome defends herself by explaining the role fancywork plays in her larger domestic system. It is a form of transition work to be done at the end of the day while she talks with her children. The products of her labor were gifts of love; her attention to her children was a gift of time. Her fancywork serves an additional purpose. "Those married ladies who are addicted to the failing of crochet and other light fancy-work," Mrs Letsome muses, "are often influenced by the dislike to appear overwrought by the regular duties of the household when their husbands are at home."[65] The parlor, a workshop during the day, must be transformed into a sphere of leisure in the evening. Fancywork is the work of leisure, an artificial boundary drawn at the end of the day to return the parlor to a leisure space. The only person for whom the home is strictly a sphere of leisure is her husband, who leaves his work behind when he steps through the front door. "Coming home" Terhune instructs her readers, "is [a man's] recreation and we would not have it seem like an exchange of workshops."[66] Although the leisure of the domestic sphere is usually characterized by historians as female, and the labor that produced the leisure is usually characterized as male, this story reveals the parlor as a "workshop." At the end of the day, when the parlor becomes the site of male leisure, women must create the appearance of leisure. The maintenance of the home as a sphere separate from the market was an investment in male leisure as well as female leisure.

The balance of business and domesticity that Terhune's description of Mrs. Letsome's career represents is at the heart of the reform she proposes. Remembering the presentation of her first check to her husband, Letsome exclaims, "Talk to me after that, of the sweetness of utter dependence upon the one beloved!" Her husband's grateful acceptance of the money brought them closer together. "It is time such tawdry tarletane of sentiment went out of fashion," she insisted. "This is the age of workers, not droning dreamers!"[67] The economic and sentimental relations of marriage were not at odds. By organizing home and marriage like a business, Terhune complemented the efforts of other women to domesticate the market. Born in 1830, Terhune grew up in a world where the work of middle-class women was increasingly visible. Two generations younger than Hale and her contemporaries, Terhune benefited not just from their advice about domestic economy but also from the example of their own market behavior. By 1870, even from a conservative perspective, the possibilities of domestic economy had greatly expanded. Despite her forthright use of business metaphors, Terhune's crusade was not to unleash women into the public sphere but to call attention to the true nature of their activities in the private sphere. Although this was less radical than the crusade for woman suffrage, it had a lasting impact in its own right. Domestic economists struggled to make the extent of the domestic sphere visible, calling attention to the veiled activities of middle-class women and showing how they were consistent with, rather than in opposition to, domestic ideology. The cultural work performed by conservative women such as Terhune contributed to the success of radical causes in ways that even Terhune could not have anticipated. By advocating a woman's right to earn money without shame, she contributed to the transformation that occurred in the acceptance of all kinds of women's work.

Terhune's emphasis on common sense resonated with women and men alike. In 1878, Edwin T. Freedley, an author of nonfiction business advice, published as part of the Business Library Series *Home Comforts; or, Things Worth Knowing in Every Household; Being a Digest of Facts Established by Science, Observation and Practical Experience, Respecting the Important Art of Living Well and Cheaply, Preserving Health and Prolonging Life.* Freedley dedicated his book to "Every Young Woman Who Aspires to be a Good Wife and Good Housekeeper, and Who Believes that True Wisdom Consists in Knowing What is Best Worth Knowing . . . In the Hope and Belief that it Contains for Her Words Fitly Spoken, Which Solomon Compared to '*Apples of gold in pictures of silver.*'" Freedley compiled his book as a companion to his *Common Sense in Business,* emphasizing the interdependence of these two subjects in the preface. "The success or failure of men in business," Freedley reminded his readers, "is often so intimately dependent upon the influences that surround them in their homes."[68] Freedley saw himself as a collector of "the crude and undigested mass of suggestions" about domestic advice. He drew on all the major authors, including Catharine Beecher, Harriet Beecher Stowe, and Mary Virginia Terhune, as well as numerous male authorities. He incorporated all of the familiar advice on domestic economy that had fueled forty years of advice manuals and even devoted an entire chapter to "The Art of House-Furnishing," in which he emphasized the correlation between taste and practical economy, the hallmark of middle-class discussions of domestic commodities. Freedley and his predecessors in the market for domestic advice all agreed that the way to achieve a balance of domestic happiness and business success was to integrate the two economies.

By 1885, the American Economic Association had turned its attention toward a vision of economics that incorporated Christian moralism. Ethical economists such as Richard T. Ely, John Bates Clark, and Henry Carter Adams argued that solving the social problems made so stark by the unhappy nature of labor relations required attention to the moral consequences of political economy. Although ethical economists did not cite Sarah Hale, Lydia Maria Child, Catharine Beecher, or Edwin Freedley, they made similar arguments about the importance of integrating political economy and domestic economy. Like the domestic economists of the antebellum period, ethical economists argued that the only way to keep the spheres separate was to promote a vision of moral economy that resonated in both home and market.[69] Although they presented this as a new vision of the economy, these men, born in the late 1840s and early 1850s, had grown up surrounded by similar arguments made in advice manuals and fiction that laid the ground work for their vision of a moral economy. The extension of this vision of moral economy to define the economic lives of working-class men and women was new. This shift was testimony to both the success of writers such as Hale, Child, and Beecher, who helped make these ideas common sense, and the changing nature of class definition in the post–Civil War period.

Five

THIS LAND OF PRECARIOUS FORTUNES

Economic Advice for Women

*I*n an antebellum home, a parlor was a new space for most men and women. The parlor, with a suite of formal furniture, was an important tangible representation of gentility, but its uses were subject to invention, change, and scrutiny by members of the family and those who came to visit them. Even in the late 1860s, when the parlor had become a more common domestic space, the environment of the parlor often failed to ensure genteel behavior. S. Annie Frost, the author of *The Laws and By-Laws of American Society* (1869), an etiquette manual, instructed her readers about the appropriate garb and behavior for a polite visit to a friend or acquaintance. "It is a sign of low-breeding," she cautioned, "to fidget with the hat, cane, or parasol during a call." These fashionable accouterments were "signs that the caller is in walking dress, and are not intended, the hat to be whirled round the top of the cane, the cane to be employed in tracing the pattern of the carpet, or the parasol to be tapped on the teeth, or worse still, sucked."[1] This tidbit of advice conjures up a striking image of just how awkward social relations in

the parlor could be, given the economic fluctuations of the nineteenth-century economy and the constant introduction of "newly genteel" visitors to the
parlor. Visitors, like the women who received them, were not always as comfortable or sure of themselves as their fictional counterparts. Frost's advice
about the dangers of parasol sucking and tooth tapping suggests that even if
the behavior of the newly prosperous was defined, in part, by the emulation
of elite behavior, it was a difficult process to school oneself in genteel practices.[2] Even as late as 1869, and with the help of such useful volumes as *The
Laws and By-Laws of American Society,* the growth of a middle class was far
from a seamless rise to gentility. Aspiration to taste and refinement was easier than its performance, and acquisition of the accouterments of gentility did
not mean that people knew what to do with them, nor did the correct possessions and behavior guard against the boredom attendant on the performance of social niceties. From a historical point of view, these fractures reveal
as much about the process of class formation as do the moments of success.[3]

Maintaining middle-class status was another kind of work that went on
in the parlor. As a stage for the performance of middle-class morals and manners, in many homes, however, the productions of the parlor went far beyond
the tableaux vivants and amateur theatricals popular at midcentury.[4] The parlor housed the activities of both the leisure and labor of women who frequently struggled to maintain genteel appearances. Often, parlor productions
were cottage industries that sustained families during hard times. In many
cases, as traditional forms of domestic production decreased, they were
replaced by a new kind of domestic production that tied the home to the market in significant ways and appropriated rhetoric about women's leisure in the
name of economic solvency. For many middle-class women the parlor was a
place of production for profit—sometimes this was for the moral profit of the
charity fair, but often it was for personal profit, to augment or replace the
income of a husband or father.

Although these parlor activities did not conform to the strictest interpretations of middle-class domesticity, they were by no means secret or shame-
ful. The popular press published many articles and manuals that addressed
the proper integration of leisure and labor within the parlor. The parlor had

many uses, and the furniture and decorations of a nicely appointed parlor served both useful and symbolic functions. Larger houses had a front and back parlor, effectively screening the private family sociability from its public sociability, but in many houses a single parlor served both purposes. This meant that family members had to distinguish between the public and private uses of the parlor, reserving private activities for times when visitors would not be expected. The many uses of the parlor meant that it leant itself well as a metaphor for the activities of "middle-class" life. A suite of furniture, which included armchairs specifically designed for men or women, represented the social aspirations of a family. A center table held a lamp for reading and provided a place to display books and magazines that were testimony to intellectual achievement; a separate work table was devoted to sewing and fancywork. Shelves to hold additional books and objets d'art confirmed a family's commitment to aesthetic sensibility, as did the paintings and engravings that decorated the walls. Families who could not afford to purchase all of these furnishings found ingenious ways to make them.[5]

The labor of genteel self-fashioning, and the importance of an appropriate domestic space in this work, was a subject of particular interest to Louis Godey as he inaugurated his *Lady's Book*. He introduced himself and the magazine to his readers in an editorial about the transformation of a private space into a public forum for both pleasure and profit, and he laid out the role of the *Lady's Book* as a guide in this process. In January 1831, six months after he launched the magazine, Godey published an editorial vignette about the origins of the *Lady's Book* in which he proclaimed that a lady's boudoir had been his model.[6] "The Cabinet Council" begins as the author is ushered into the boudoir by Prudence, the bower-woman, whose existence suggests the wealth of the inhabitants of this boudoir. The author greets his cousins, Penelope and Miss Mary, and his Aunt Elinor, "the very pearl of the ancient sisterhood of spinsters," who are assembled in Miss Mary's "brilliant boudoir."[7] Aunt Elinor makes the "mysterious announcement" that the visitor wishes to take one more look at the boudoir "to see if anything has escaped his notice." The mystery behind the announcement is revealed when the visitor confesses to Miss Mary that he has chosen her boudoir as the model for his new publication, thus suggesting that Godey is the visitor. Aunt Elinor, in her role as chaperon, sanctions the scrutiny of the author's investigation of this private room and lends her endorsement to the translation of a private vision into a public commodity.

Miss Mary is flattered by her cousin's attention, and she compares her boudoir to a fine painting, acknowledging not only its beauty and her skill in its decoration but also its integrated aesthetic impact. The boudoir is a profusion of antiques, plants, fossils, flowers, books, and other objects that signal taste, education, and breeding. A creeping plant ties together the diverse contents by growing around and over them. Godey identifies specific objects that represent the range of topics his magazine will address: a painting of a charming landscape signifies the importance of visual images in sentimental culture; an antique looking glass, which had been the property of Miss Mary's grandmother, represents tradition; a fossil represents science; an exotic plant demonstrates botanical knowledge; and a Greek vase symbolizes erudition. These objects read like the physical manifestation of the curriculum for a girl's education.

The careful arrangement of "rich and profuse negligence" that highlights Miss Mary's taste and refinement is contrasted with the prim, mathematical neatness of Penelope's boudoir. Both boudoirs are symbols of their inhabitant's taste, the author concedes, but it is Mary's boudoir he chooses as the model for his magazine.[8] In Penelope's boudoir, the individual details are too visible; they betray the labor used "to drill her little squadron of embellishments."[9] Yet the casual elegance of the disarray in Mary's boudoir, Penelope observes, cost her three times as much effort. Mary concedes, but she qualifies Penelope's observation. "That is true enough, Penelope," she said, while a slight blush tinged her cheek, "but the toil you speak of is not apparent."[10] The boudoir gives the appearance of being "the work of the moment": the finished room renders her work invisible. This mode of production was as important to Godey as the "index" that the contents of the boudoir provided for his magazine. By defining the genesis of his magazine in these terms, Godey claimed a place for it in a refined boudoir or parlor and suggested to his readers that the magazine was the product of a similar kind of inconspicious production, which inherently conveyed taste and gentility to those who consumed it.

In order to emphasize the important and interdependent relationship between these forms of production and consumption, Godey calls attention to the very labor he sought to erase. He uses Miss Mary's description of the contents of her boudoir and her methods of decoration to lay out the logic behind inconspicuous production in several ways. Not only did the excessive neatness of Penelope's boudoir reveal the pains she had taken to arrange it, a realization that was "disagreeable" to any visitor, but by describing the decor of her boudoir as a "squadron of embellishments," Godey conjured up images of uniformity and the suggestion that these embellishments had been purchased rather than collected. Although some items in Mary's boudoir had been purchased, most were found, made, or inherited; it was not her buying power that was being applauded by Godey, but her ability to create an aesthetic unity between the old and the new.[11] The combination of objects, old and new, rare and whimsical, natural and artistic, that fill Miss Mary's boudoir erased the market even as they signified wealth and taste.

The catalog of objects in Mary's boudoir was not intended as a checklist for potential decorators, although it may have been used that way. The description of the boudoir commodified the aura of gentility and was designed to prompt aspiration as much as recognition in readers of the magazine.[12] The collection of objects collapsed and contained the past in a way that made it accessible to "new" ladies at the beginning of their own history of gentility.[13] Godey used the boudoir to stand in for the acquisitions of those in a newly prosperous middle class who felt conspicuous about consumption in both positive and negative ways. He wanted his magazine to represent both old and new, established tradition and contemporary ideas.

Although Godey chose Miss Mary's boudoir as the model for his magazine explicitly because the labor of its creation was hidden, the amount of labor remained important. His vignette celebrates the additional work of inconspicuous production: despite its appearance of spontaneity, it was an art of production rather than painful labor. Once he had introduced the desirability of this kind of work, Godey drew attention to the fact that the magazine itself had been two years in the making and that his own production conformed to these standards. The contrast between the visible and invisible labor of decorating the boudoirs was central to the aesthetic understanding of the relationship between production and consumption. For Godey's readers, the aesthetics of production were as important as the propriety of consumption. Godey used the vignette to define the core of the sentimental education about economics that his magazine would provide for the next fifty years. The kind of production as well as the manner of production was crucial to situating a commodity in a virtuous marketplace.

Miss Mary and Penelope christen the magazine "The Lady's Book," capitalizing on the new democratic usage of "lady," which combined inclusion and refinement.[14] The boudoir was a space increasingly attainable by women who aspired to be ladies. In naming his magazine the *Lady's Book*, Godey was doing more than just describing its contents; he was defining his subscribers: a nation of ladies. His definition of "lady" was subtle; he never conveyed the impression that everyone *was* a lady, merely that everyone *could be* a lady. He wanted the magazine to be the arbiter of both personal and national taste. By inviting "every lady in the land" to subscribe, he signaled his interest in cultivating a national market. This was an ambition increasingly possible in the 1830s, as transportation networks made circulation more practical and printing technology made high-speed production affordable. Godey also hoped to translate growing national sentiments into commercial success for his magazine.

Godey frequently reminded his readers about the usefulness of his magazine as a source for practical advice. Although the aesthetics of domestic space and female conduct dominated the pages of his magazine, he was well aware of the ways the pressing concerns of domestic and political economy affected his women readers. Godey regularly included articles that incorporated issues of political economy, reviews of books on political economy, and biographical sketches of prominent intellectuals such as Jean Baptiste Say interspersed between the fiction, fashion plates, recipes, and fancywork patterns that made up the bulk of the magazine.[15] In 1830, William Sullivan, a Harvard-educated lawyer, wrote *The Political Class Book*, which became a popular source on political and economic issues, going through numerous editions during the 1830s. Louis Godey praised it and quoted Sullivan at length, concurring that it was "one of the most striking defects in our system of education, that females are so generally uninstructed in the substance and form of business." It was equally important, Sullivan asserted, for women "to know well the nature of contracts, and the forms in which they should appear, and to be able to keep accounts accurately . . . as to be able to speak Italian or French; to paint flowers and landscapes; or converse well on the comparative merits of poets and novelists."[16] Godey's vision for his readership acknowledged both the labor and leisure of middle-class life.

In *The Mother's Book,* which offered advice on all aspects of parental responsibilities, Lydia Maria Child informed her readers that "every young person ought to be well acquainted with the contents of Sullivan's Political Class Book."[17] Both Godey and Child referred to the turbulence, uncertain economy stability as the prime reason for women's education about business matters. Women had long been important contributors to family finances, but the number of women who searched for ways to make money increased in the antebellum period. Advice women had traditionally given to one another became a commodity that one woman could sell to others in the hope that she could make money from that advice. Such advice appeared in magazines, novels, and books on domestic economy. By the 1850s, there was a greater demand for appropriate employment for women, and conduct manuals began to include chapters that directly addressed economic matters. It was not until after the Civil War, however, that books entirely devoted to economic advice for women became popular. These books stressed the importance of correct market sentiments in framing the economic behavior of both women and men. The availability of these books offers an interesting window into the activities of the parlor where this economic advice was read. A more careful look through the lace curtains and between the velvet drapes reveals a substantial amount of labor alongside the leisure.

As a steadily increasing number of women without independent financial means chose spinsterhood over the obligations of marriage and the dangers of childbirth, the issue of women's economic preparedness and opportunities became an important topic in the discussion of a woman's sphere.[18] This issue was of as much interest to conservative women as to women's rights activists. Conservative writers, female and male, championed the importance of practical economic education long before women's rights advocates linked economic issues to the question of political equality. In some cases, these writers framed their advocacy of women's economic issues, especially domestic ones, almost as a rebuke to a vision of women's rights centered around politics. In the early 1850s, the issue of women's employment became a popular topic of discussion. Despite the success of Sarah Hale, Emma Willard, and others as advocates for women's education, and the growing number of women teachers, there were never enough teaching positions to provide employment for all the women who desired it. Sewing was traditionally seen as a way for women to augment their income, but the health effects of constant sewing combined with inadequate wages galvanized women and some men to call for new economic opportunities for single women and widows. These advocates framed their arguments largely in terms of humanitarian concerns. They used this issue to challenge the call for women's rights made by their more radical sisters, often contrasting the more pressing needs of economic support with the personal vanity of politics. The efforts of women's rights advocates, conservative women argued, muddied the waters of woman's sphere and attempted to extend women's public activities into inappropriate areas that jeopardized women's access to appropriate economic activities. There were many things women could do in public, they noted, as long as they conducted themselves discreetly and remained true to their natural callings: the nurture and education of children. In these circumstances, many forms of employment could be made open to women if men would relax their objections to this expansion of opportunities. Advocating for suffrage and political rights, conservative women cautioned, raised more obstacles to the success of the crusade for women's employment than it removed.

For conservative women, authorship offered a way for women to speak out on women's issues and participate in the market from an acceptable, private position. Having claimed the privilege of that privacy, conservative women authors did not hesitate to actively participate in the expanding literary market. A significant number of women who were published authors of fiction augmented their incomes by writing popular manuals and advice books. Frequently, these women justified their forays into the world of popular publishing by stating their intentions in a short preface that reminded their readers of their virtuous motives for proffering such publication. These prefaces offered an opportunity for authors to justify their appearance before the public and to create an image for themselves. In the case of prolific authors such as Sarah Hale, the preface was a chance to instruct her readers on the proper use of her works. Hale justified her production of fashionable literary texts as part of her crusade for education by translating the trifles of sentimental culture into a form of education. Just as she repeatedly reminded her magazine readers that her writing was not a luxury but a necessity, she insisted that they share the seriousness of her approach to any topic, no matter how trifling it might appear. Her assertion in the preface that her work was important was more than just an intellectual justification for her pursuit of a popular topic. She often used the preface to remind her readers of her economic interest in these works. Although she was not as forthright about these issues in print as she was in her private correspondence, Hale laid intellectual and economic claim to her work in no uncertain terms.

In 1859, in a letter to George W. Childs of the Philadelphia publishing firm Childs and Peterson, Hale reminded Childs of their earlier conversation about publishing a flower dictionary. Although Hale had refrained from suggesting a new edition of her own dictionary during their conversation, she did not hesitate promote the idea in her letter. The formal nature of the letter allowed her to state, with a directness that conversation might not have permitted, that *Flora's Interpreter* remained unsurpassed and Childs should publish a new and expanded edition. Hale insisted her work still had "the best selections of poetry and the most perfect arrangement of the Flower language which have ever been prepared." She maintained that it could not be superseded unless "some plagiarist should appropriate my whole plan." She ended by speculating that if it were attempted, "my publishers would, I hope, guard the rights of my heirs as well as their own to this valuable work."[19] Hale linked her claim to literary superiority to her claim on the profits of her work, softening the stridency of her assertion by linking it back to responsibility for the well-being of her children.

Flora's Interpreter was one of her most successful publications.[20] She wrote three sets of introductory remarks for this book over its thirty-year life-span, addressing the perfection of its arrangement, the problem of plagiarism, and the ways in which she increased the book's value with each new edition. She positioned her dictionary at the center of the crusade for the development of American literature and defined her project in patriotic terms: "I think it is time our people should express their own feelings in the sentiments and idioms of America."[21] As new editions appeared, the expanding canon of American poetry provided her with an easy way to "give novelty as well as increased value" to those editions.[22] Her loyalty to American poetry had, she asserted, made her work more popular in Europe. In later editions she complained that plagiarists had poached on her championship of American poetry and stolen her profits. She described her own acts of borrowing in gentler terms: "Making a book (*not writing it*) is somewhat like preparing a dinner; the ingredients must be collected from many places, and these are usually so disguised by the preparation, that little of the original flavor remains."[23] Writing as cooking was an extension of the household economy; the domestic metaphor disguised both her own market production and the fact that her ingredients were literary works, which she briefly listed, "tender[ing] [her] sincere thanks to their amiable authors." Although it was common practice to republish the works of other authors without regard to copyright, it is interesting to compare Hale's "cookery" to her thoughts on the use of her own work as an ingredient. "The beauty, variety, and excellence of these gems of thought, fancy, feeling, and passion, can never be equaled in any work of this kind," she announced in the preface to the 1848 edition, "unless, indeed, our imitators take our selections bodily from Flora's Interpreter, as some of them have already done to an extent which is very obvious." Hale elaborated on this accusation in a footnote in which she stated that "all the poetic selections here designated as 'anonymous,' were written by Mrs. Hale, expressly for Flora's Interpreter. Those who use these will know from whom they borrow."[24] Hale did not object to the use of her poetry by others, as this could only augment her reputation, but she was torn between the decorous conventions of anonymous authorship and the profitable imperatives of sentimental enterprise. If she could not prevent plagiarism of her work, she was determined to profit from it, if only in the form of her reputation. She monitored the use of her poetry in anthologies closely. In one case, she insisted that a publisher replace the poem he had chosen with one she preferred. Hale acknowledged that replacing the poem would increase the cost to the publisher, who had already sent her the proof, and offered to pay the difference.[25]

In the 1848 edition of *Flora's Interpreter,* Hale added a new section, *Flora Fortuna,* which used the sentiments of the first section to tell fortunes and create elaborate floral messages. This was not a compilation but an original creation, and Hale did not mince words in staking her claim to the profits: "But we trust that in the part now added—FLORA FORTUNA—no one will thus interfere, for some years at least, to take from us the profits of projecting and preparing a work that has cost us so much time and research.."[26] Hale's discussion of profit made the entrepreneurial nature of her work visible. Time and research were her means of production.

Hale used her position as literary editor of *Godey's* to promote women writers; she did not shy away from reviewing her own productions, especially her compilations of poems. In a review of the *Ladies' Wreath,* a literary annual, she noted that she felt no compunction in recommending the work, which she had edited, because it contained "the choice productions of the genius of women." If anyone should doubt this characterization of the poetry in the *Ladies' Wreath,* she hoped that they would "have the opportunity of examining this volume, and judging whether we over-rate the genius of our poetesses."[27] Because this work was an anthology, she could recommend its contents without seeming to promote herself. Her hope that the entire readership of *Godey's* would examine the book was an overt piece of marketing, however, as any profits generated by the sale of the book would belong to her. Hale's review appeared during her first month as literary editor for *Godey's Lady's Book,* but her self-promotion was not unusual, as Godey often used the editorial pages to promote his other enterprises. In this same issue, in fact, there is a substantial puff piece for the *Philadelphia Saturday News and Literary Gazette,* Godey's newest publishing venture.

Although Hale was a strong advocate for domestic roles for women, she recognized that the security of middle-class status was tenuous and that practical skills were an indispensable part of a girl's education. Women, Hale and her contemporaries argued, could not afford to be ignorant about business matters. The "fear of falling" underpinned middle-class self-definition. Lydia Maria Child summed up this perspective in *The Little Girl's Own Book* (1837): "In this land of precarious fortunes, every girl should learn how to be *useful.*" She went on to emphasize that "in this country it is peculiarly necessary that daughters should be so educated as to enable them to fulfil the duties of a humble station, or to dignify and adorn the highest.[28] The links between domestic felicity and business success were too close to be ignored. *Godey's Lady's Book* offered a form of bankruptcy insurance. Hale, like Child, cautioned parents that their daughters should not be educated simply as a marker of status; they needed marketable skills in the event of financial catastrophe.

Hale wrote numerous essays and editorials on the subject of women's employment, and in 1859, she proposed a volume of "Words to Women" to her publisher, George Childs, who had remarked on "the many *letters* and applications of distressed ladies in search of employment." Hale reminded him that this was a subject she frequently addressed in her editorials and noted that she had received many letters of thanks from women who had benefitted from her advice. She proposed a book that could include "'stories' (short ones) Essays or 'Editorials' rather, and 'Hints' on almost every subject of concern, complaint or congratulation which my sex consider important"and ended her letter with the familiar query, "Will you publish it?"[29] The suggested title was sufficiently ambiguous to protect the reader from unwanted attention; no woman wanted her financial embarrassment advertised. Advice stories, essays, and hints were the standard format for education about the market in *Godey's;* stories provided an opportunity for sympathy as well as education, essays addressed the more abstract principles of economy, and hints took the form of an etiquette manual, offering concrete advice.[30] Despite Hale's urging, the volume was never published.

Hale was not the only author who wrote for *Godey's* on the topic of women's employment. Throughout the 1850s, there were frequent essays, stories, or editorials that addressed the need for an expanded sphere of employment for women. In 1852, Alice B. Neal contributed a series of articles titled "Employment of Women in Cities." Neal began her series by noting, "Public opinion would seem to have decided that but two classes of employment are legitimate to our sex, teaching and the needle." These two avenues of employment, she insisted, could not possibly satisfy the needs of all women who found themselves thrown on the mercy of the marketplace. It was a disservice to all women, she argued, that the arbiters of public opinion satisfied themselves with pronouncing the natural dependence of women, pitying those who must labor on their own behalf and congratulating society that the avenues of teaching and needlework were available to women who must labor. Having pronounced these things, Neal noted archly, "public opinion turns to the discussion of some new theme, with folded hands and a satisfied conscience."[31] The purpose of her series, Neal informed her readers, was to call attention to not only the many women who must support themselves but also the ways that public opinion "has shut out all choice and variety," crippling women's ability to achieve modest independence in times of financial need. Neal clearly differentiated herself from more radical advocates for women's rights, refusing to "soil [her] lips with the war-cry for 'female emancipation.'" She argued that the crusade for economic opportunities for women in need should not be confused with the public appearances of women's rights activists. Instead, throughout her series of articles she implied that expanding the economic avenues open to women would curtail interest in the arguments made in the name of "female emancipation." Those women most susceptible to the arguments of women's rights were those whose needs were most difficult to meet. Women who had been raised in comfort and lost their support through the death of a father or a husband were usually the least well equipped to support themselves. Often, Neal argued, they had wasted their education, focusing on social accomplishments rather than serious study, and were not qualified to teach or did not have the physical stamina for sewing. Society had to provide for them but also recognize their ability to be useful in a wider range of occupations.

Neal introduced three new avenues of employment open to women that demonstrated, she argued, the success of allowing women to participate in new kinds of employment. In her first article, she visited the Philadelphia mint. Although women played no role in the more labor-intensive process of melting the metal and stamping the coins, they were almost entirely responsible for ensuring that the newly minted coins were the correct weight. Neal described the work room as light and airy and filled with the cheerful sound of female voices and laughter. She was "struck with the ease and propriety of the employment, the neat and cheerful aspect of the room." It is "so much pleasanter," she remarked, "than if the same number of men and boys had been at work." The employment of women at the mint was an experiment initiated by Franklin Peale, the chief coiner at the mint, two years earlier. Peale noted that he now considered women better suited to this work than men; the experiment had been a great success for the mint and the women themselves. More than 600 women applicants had been turned away for lack of available positions, emphasizing, Neal noted, the need for more employment opportunities for women.[32]

For her second article, she visited the Philadelphia School of Design. She reminded her readers that the all beautiful objects they examined in their shopping expeditions had been designed by someone, and who better than women, who understood design from both a practical and aesthetic standpoint? Because manufacturers had been accustomed to depending on European designs, Neal noted, the introduction of design schools for women did not displace a traditional male work force. It was essential to overcome the prejudice against design schools for women, she argued, because schools such as the Philadelphia School of Design would provide the means for "honest independence" and a "wide sphere of employment" for "educated, intelligent women" as well as free American manufacturers from dependence on foreign designs: "If English manufactures are not content to be under the control of foreign influence, our countrymen can never be."[33]

Her final article, on shopkeeping, picks up the same theme of the natural relationship between women's understanding of the value and aesthetics of goods as the purchaser and their understanding of these things as designers or shopgirls. Women make better attendants in department stores, Neal notes, because they understand the psychology of their customers. A skilled shopgirl is a "physiognomist" and can read her customer's taste. This saves both the customer and the shopgirl needless labor, because she knows which goods will satisfy each customer. Unlike a shopman, with his "cringing servility," a female attendant used her good breeding and ability to share the "good sense and right feeling" of her customers to "quietly [attend] to her business to the best of her capacity." Her serious and professional demeanor obviated the question of inferiority. Shopkeeping, Neal proposed, was an excellent occupation for women who found themselves in reduced circumstances, because they could use the knowledge they had gained as customers to serve new customers while supporting themselves at a level of reasonable comfort.[34] Far from being "unwomanly," shopkeeping was a natural occupation for women, she argued. Like teaching, it allowed her to extend her skills from the domestic sphere into the market rather than creating a public role that was at odds with her private role.

In an editorial in the same issue as the last in Neal's series, Hale echoed her sentiments, stating categorically, "Yes, women need a wider sphere of employments for their tastes, talents and the affections. Then they would not invent delusions." Like Neal, Hale presented her advocacy of the expansion of women's economic sphere as a rebuke to women's rights activists, but her editorial was also a rebuke to her male contemporaries, whose "ostrich in the sand" approach to the problem frustrated her. Despite her unceasing advocacy for women's education, Hale was quick to condemn the idea of a life of pure intellect for women. Instead, she argued, a woman's first responsibility was to God, and her faith, rather than her ego, must dictate the use of her education. She mustered this argument to support her call for women's employment. Many women spent a significant part of their adult life unmarried, Hale noted, and "God, who has created nothing in vain," had a plan for them. "God has not implanted an impulse in the hearts of women," she insisted, "without preparing a way for them to obey it."[35] Women should not be prevented from finding public ways balanced with their private roles, to be useful, for that drove women to embrace delusions such as the call for political rights, which to Hale seemed much more dangerous than economic independence.

In another editorial, Hale had proposed that women might be "employed to great advantage" as colporteurs. Not only would this give a woman a concrete way to act on her faith, but the smaller stipend that a woman would require would save tract societies money and increase the number of available colporteurs, as these societies were always anxious to employ more.

Women would not be able to "penetrate the wild places of our land," Hale conceded, but they would be the most effective agents in the "settled portion." "The talents of pious women," she asserted, "now allowed to be wasted on trifles, would be employed in the cause of moral improvement." Rather than placing women in direct competition with men, the increase of women colporteurs would allow pious men who had shouldered the burden of colportage out of duty, "often at great pecuniary sacrifice," to "enter on other pursuits more beneficial to themselves and society." The beauty of this proposal, Hale insisted, was that it was not at odds with women's domestic duties, which were "the most sacred, the most happy, the most honorable she can perform." Instead, important employment, like colportage, would draw women away from novel reading and other frivolous pursuits that encouraged them to waste their time in unproductive and even dangerous behavior. Until men provided "suitable employments for the talents and time of their daughters as well as their sons," Hale chided, daughters would "fall into indolence or frivolity." She ended her editorial with an appeal: "Try the experiment, Christian men, you who have to power to order and arrange. We believe that success, almost beyond calculation, would crown the enterprise."[36] For all her evocation of Christian duty, Hale never lost sight of the economic importance of the enterprise.

Catharine Beecher also weighed in on the issue of women's employment, addressing the question of professional respect and training. Even in the profession of teaching, women were discriminated against because of the expense of a liberal education and the inability of parents to devote sufficient resources to the thorough education of their daughters. Because men had superior educations, they were able to compete for teaching jobs on unequal terms. As a result, women often lost "posts of honor and emolument" to men, even when the pupils were female. This competition denied women economic opportunity and had a depressing effect on women in general, who had little incentive to strive for high achievement given the constraints of their future profession. What would be the effect on young men, Beecher queried, if all the liberal professions were taken from them and only those available to women were made open to young men? The effects would be devastating, she argued. If teaching positions of "honor and emolument" were open to women, they would approach their training with the same energy and rigor as their brothers. Many women could fruitfully occupy themselves in the years between the end of their own schooling and marriage. This would strengthen rather than threaten their roles as wife and mother and be a "rich blessing to their country and the world." But without the honor and respect afforded to male teachers, even the finest women teachers would be forced to relinquish their posts from the exhaustion of overwork.

In the early 1850s, advice about business for women also began to play a more prominent role in etiquette manuals. Mrs. L. G. Abell included in her *Woman in Her Various Relations* (1851) a chapter on "Success in Business."[37] The general tenor of her advice was conservative; she advocated the domestic role as the most important, but she offered advice on how to balance the other demands placed on women. The section on business is short, and its prose, unlike the direct prose in rest of the book, is convoluted. Abell alternates between addressing the reader directly as "you" and talking more abstractly about behavior that contributes to "a man's success." She was, it appears, uncomfortable discussing women's business directly and tried to use men's business as a model for women to follow. She gave the usual advice about honesty, integrity, agreeable manners, and punctuality and warned against being too credulous and confiding. This advice was general enough to apply to men or women, but there was one piece of advice she addressed directly to her female readers: "Judge of men by what they *do*, not by what they *say*, notice what they do in unguarded moments."[38] Mrs. R. P. Clarke, a woman of business interviewed by Caroline Dall in 1864, furnished a similar piece of advice: "I want my life written because I want women to know that they can manage their own affairs, if they will only use their wits. Let them do as I did, look at men and see what they do with their own money and then do the same. Follow the advice they give each other not what they give to women."[39] By the winter of 1864–65, when Dall conducted this interview, Clarke was at the end of a long and successful career in real estate and money lending that started when she took in boarders after her husband's factory burned down.[40] Abell was not as outspoken as Clarke, but she encouraged the same kind of industry and ingenuity that had made Clarke successful in her enterprises. Careful management of time, Abell informed her readers, would allow them to fulfill their domestic duties and still have time for other pursuits. As long as she fulfilled her duties as wife and mother, a woman would find that "doors of usefulness and profit [were] everywhere open to woman, suited to her sphere and her character."[41] Abell advocated a balance of woman's various relations, not a choice among them and indicated that women's economic activity could be sanctioned by conservatives as well as radicals.

Eliza Leslie, a frequent contributor to *Godey's* and a successful writer on household issues, addressed the problems of balancing domestic responsibilities and literary aspirations in *Miss Leslie's Behavior Book* (1853).[42] She included two chapters on literary issues, one on how to behave toward women authors, whom she termed "lady authoresses," the other on the business aspects of a literary career, outlining professional conduct and offering practical advice. Leslie based her advice on her own experiences as an author. As a teenage girl, she had written *The Young Ladies Mentor; or, Extracts in Prose and Verse for the Promotion of Virtue and Morality* (1803), but she did not appear in print again until 1827, when she published *Seventy-Five Receipts for Pastry, Cakes and Sweetmeats*, the first in a series of successful cookbooks and manuals for domestic economy. In addition to her cookbooks, she made her literary reputation in the early years of her career by writing stories and advice for children and editing gift books. After she won a prize from *Godey's Lady's Book* for her story "Mrs. Washington Potts," she became a regular contributor to the magazine. She briefly edited her own magazine, *Miss Leslie's Magazine* (1843), published in conjunction with T. S. Arthur and backed by Louis Godey, but she resigned the editorship after a year, and the magazine continued under the direction of T. S. Arthur under a new name.

Eliza Leslie made clear the difficulties women who wrote for a living faced in distinguishing their workplace within the domestic sphere. For literary women, the parlor was also the office, and household items were tools of the trade. She chastised women who dropped in on writers, interrupting them at their labors: "Recollect that to a woman who gets her living by her pen, 'time is money,' as it is to an artist. Therefore, encroaching on her time is lessening her income."[43] Leslie evoked Benjamin Franklin's advice to young tradesmen to stress the economic underpinnings of sentimental authorship.

Before her literary career took off in the United States, Eliza Leslie enlisted her brother Charles, a well-known painter living in London, to help find a publisher and a readership for her children's fiction. Charles, who peddled Eliza's stories to a number of London publishers, regretfully informed her that the market for children's fiction was no better in England than in the United States. The primary problem, he noted, was that "many ladies of fortune, who are fond of seeing themselves in print, write books of that class and give them away to the publishers."[44] This practice put authors who wrote for income at a great disadvantage. A literary acquaintance of Charles suggested that Eliza write for annuals, either British or American, a piece of advice she followed with considerable success. Brother and sister also corresponded on the nature of children's literature, Charles frequently asserting his agreement with Eliza's criticism of the overt didacticism of children's literature. Charles admitted to a fondness for these tales in his youth, but he noted, "Now that I have grown older and know more of the world, it seems to me to be a great mistake of their well-meaning authors to deceive mankind into virtue." He encouraged Eliza to "describe characters *as they are,* and not as . . . *they ought to be,* or ought not to be."[45] Charles reiterated his position in another letter the following year. He complimented his sister on her stories but suggested they would be even better if they did not rely on didactic moral conventions. Children's authors, he noted, strayed too far from depicting human nature as it is, preferring instead to "make a nature of their own, in which little monsters of virtue, sense, and fine sentiments, are contrasted with caricatures of folly."[46] Static pictures of good and evil, Charles cautioned, were not the most effective teachers. He rejected the "trash that is now published in the rage for universal improvement" and championed works of fiction that were "built on the rock—nature." He compared his view on literature to his method of painting, remarking that he did not like to be influenced by contemporary styles of landscape painting but preferred to "look only at nature and the best of the old masters." He noted that when Constable began a sketch for a painting, "he endeavor[ed] to forget that he has ever seen a picture."[47] This was excellent advice for writers, too, he surmised, as this practice would have saved even great writers such as Sir Walter Scott from the flaws in his novels. Eliza Leslie must have valued her brother's advice, for when she won a prize from *Godey's* for her story "Mrs. Washington Potts," the reviews praised her ability to draw such lifelike characters and still convey a moral message.

In *Miss Leslie's Behavior Book*, Eliza devoted considerable attention to the appropriate behavior surrounding a literary career. For instance, she admonished her readers not to ask an author for free copies or the loan of her books, nor should they ask to borrow pens, ink, or paper: "There is a spice of meanness in requesting from [a lady authoress], as a gift, any portion of her stock in trade." She provided detailed information about the kind of paper, ink, paper cutters, and other materials appropriate to commercial writing, and she emphasized the importance of a clear, legible hand and a neat final product. Aspiring authors, she cautioned, should not to confuse the fashionable calligraphy of letters and album verses with the penmanship of literary business.[48] The privacy of the parlor allowed women writers to claim that although they participated in the market, they were not *of* the market, but this claim also denied them the ability to claim time and respect for their work. Because labor looked like leisure, women who wrote for profit appeared to be part of a gift economy rather than a business economy.

Most of the advice she offered was to those who might make the acquaintance of an author such as herself. Although most of her instructions were general, she offered one very specific piece of advice addressed directly to women authors. Strangers would not hesitate to ask impertinent questions about profits, but it was imperative to "reply concisely that these things are secrets between yourself and your publishers." If an author answered such question directly, she was bound to invite incredulous responses: "'Why, really—you must be coining money. I think I'll write books myself! There can't be a better trade,' &c." The pragmatism with which Leslie addressed literary careers stood in direct contrast to the romantic image of the artist associated with great writers. She emphasized that "ignorant people always suppose that popular writers are wonderfully well paid—and must be making rapid fortunes—because they neither starve in garrets, nor wear rags—at least in America."[49]

Another chapter cataloged every aspect of the preparation of a manuscript from the first purchase of a ream of paper, for the sake of economy, to the final binding of the finished document. With each step, she emphasized the importance of quality materials, careful workmanship, and attention to detail; she focused on the craft of writing and revision that underpinned the expression of literary genius, dispelling the notion that inspiration alone was the basis of literary success. She recommended that strict accounts be kept of the money spent on materials and the time spent on each piece, the literary equivalent of a business ledger. She instructed her readers that as with any business enterprise, a balance must be kept between time spent, pages produced, and accounts received.[50] Periodicals paid by the page, and this allowed an author to gage how much she could earn.[51] For Miss Leslie, the business aspects of authorship were as important as the inspiration to write.

Because it was not possible for all women who needed to make money to pursue literary careers, in 1863 Virginia Penny published *The Employments of Women: A Cyclopedia of Woman's Work.* Her intent was to furnish women with information that would encourage them to seek employment beyond the seven professions outlined by Harriet Martineau in the 1830s.[52] These professions, Penny observed, were already too full, and women needed practical advice to aid them in their search for other work. Because she did not camouflage her advice about women's market activities with the usual domestic advice, she could not interest a publisher in her work and published it at her own expense. In the preface, she observed that books on the "'Sphere of Woman,' 'The Mission of Woman,' and 'The Influence of Woman'" were easy to find, but a reader who no longer had "the comforts of life," needed more practical advice and how to find a way to "earn a respectable livelihood." Above all other considerations, she concluded, "it is the great want of the day."[53] Penny addressed a readership of both working-class and middle-class women. Her book could be used by philanthropists a resource for suggesting new kinds employment to needy women.[54] It could also, she noted, save women of leisure from a life that was "aimless and profitless." She used "profit" in both of its senses: women could benefit morally from engaging in productive activities and could earn money behind the guise of worthy activity.

Employments of Women was published at the height of the Civil War, a time, Penny observed, when increasing numbers of middle-class women found themselves in need of a profitable enterprise. Her book was not a financial success until it was republished in 1870 as *How Women Can Make Money: Married or Single.* The new title promised answers to a question that haunted many women. The text of the new edition remained unchanged, but the publisher included illustrations of several employments outlined in the book. Some illustrations depicted uncorseted women of the working class, others showed elaborately dressed middle-class women. The engravings reinforced the distinctions made in the text itself. Although Penny stated in her introduction that she "used the words girl and woman indiscriminately," she did not use the term "lady" indiscriminately.[55] Throughout the text, certain employments were discussed as suitable for ladies. Penny acknowledged that women "in reduced circumstances" needed to earn a living as much as women who had never known the privileges of money. The inclusiveness of her work sidestepped the issue of class difference, but the distinctions of the text made it clear that only certain kinds of employment could maintain the status of middle-class women. The new edition used the illustrations to assure an uncertain middle-class audience that this book was suitable for their needs.

Unlike Hale's carefully composed discussions of women's market opportunities and the pragmatic advice of Mrs. Abell and Eliza Leslie, Virginia Penny's book did not use the sentimental language of business that *Godey's Lady's Book* had popularized. Rather, she placed the economic activities suggested by sentimental texts in the larger context of the world of women's work which was part of a subtle but cumulative change in the portrayal of women's relationship to the market after the war.

Penny's book demonstrates the increased interest in appropriate economic venues for women and the growing success of the genre of economic advice genre for women. In 1869, Charles Barnard, a Boston journalist, published a series of fictional economic confessions under the pseudonym "Mrs. Maria Gilman." The subject of these texts was market gardening—Barnard had been a florist before he began his career as a journalist—and their formula was a familiar one: a didactic tale of penurious widowhood and subsequent entrepreneurial success. Like many women advice writers before him, Barnard wove a compelling domestic tale through detailed business advice about market gardening. At the end of *My Ten-Rod Farm, or How I Became a Florist*, Barnard, speaking as Gilman, positioned his book among other practical best-sellers: "Mrs. Warren's charming 'Home Manuals,' for house management, 'Our Farm of Ten Acres,' 'The Garden

That Paid the Rent,' 'Ten Acres Enough,' 'How to Farm Profitably,' are all eagerly sought after. May not the same good fortune be awarded to My Ten-rod Farm, or How I Became a Florist."[56] Authors often asked readers to recommend their books to friends, but what made Barnard's efforts interesting were his choice to adopt a female pseudonym to lend authority to his work and his explicit the connection between the strategies of household economy and market economy. Although women still did well to heed Mrs. Clarke's advice and follow a man's advice to other men, the perception that women understood the economic needs of other women better than men did and could offer authoritative advice marked a new understanding of women's work.

The success of Barnard's economic advice fiction launched his journalism career, and he continued to write, under his own name, on economic topics, although less frequently in the guise of fiction. In 1881, he published under his own name *Co-operation as a Business,* a revised version of a series of articles he had written for *Scribner's Monthly Magazine,* the *New York Spectator,* and the *Independent,* combined with a paper he had delivered at the American Social Science Association.[57] In practical terms, he discussed the advantages of cooperative savings and loan associations, building associations, and insurance associations, arguing that cooperation between men and women with small capital made possible personal and national prosperity through the "mutual benefit of capital, labor and the consumer."[58] Cooperative business should not be confused with "Socialism, Communism or other vicious fancies," he insisted: "It simply [meant] business."[59] Most of Barnard's examples were from Britain, and he conceded that cooperative business had a substantial history of failure in the United States, but he traced the blame for this to investors' impatience for quick profits rather than the patience and commitment necessary to long-term success and respectable profit. Cooperation as a business also taught habits of saving and restraint and encouraged both men and women to take a long view of their economic health rather than be seduced by the illusive potential of speculation. It represented the "good of all as opposed to the gain of the few" by substituting "mutuality, helpfulness, justice, convenience, and cheapness for competition, selfishness, and useless expense and wastefulness."[60] In answering the critics of cooperation as a business, Barnard reassured his readers that "however much people may combine in associations for their mutual commercial advantage, there will always be freedom and room enough for individual talents, enterprise, and ability." The family would not disappear, nor would infants be nursed in "gigantic kindergartens." Only the relations of commerce would be modified, but those changes would bring significant social and moral advantages for society as a whole.[61] Barnard argued that teaching the average man and woman to understand the language of investment and to take a "wider view of the market and the world" would draw them out of their selfish concerns and make them "more thoughtful and considerate." Cooperation as a business made it possible for ordinary people to earn dividends and interest while gaining "prudence, economy, good fellowship, and justice for all." More than just good business sense, cooperation was "practical Christianity," the perfect combination of economic sentiments and moral sentiments.[62] Barnard's popular economics demonstrates the currency that the ideas of sentimental pragmatism had in the growing field of professional economic theory. As popular and professional writers on economics began to call for a modification of the conflict between capital and labor, they drew on the common sense of sentimental pragmatism, which emphasized the integration of domestic and political economy. The source of this popular wisdom was rarely acknowledged, but the parallels between the rhetoric of balance employed in economic advice for women and the new advice that economic theorists proposed for working men and working women was striking.[63]

By the 1890s, economic advice for women had taken on a more active tone, as the title of Mrs. M. L. Rayne's *What Can a Woman Do; or, Her Position in the Business and Literary World* (1893) suggests. In her prefatory remarks, Rayne referred to Harriet Martineau's discussion of women's work in *Society in America* (1837) more than fifty years earlier and happily reported that the field had considerably widened since Martineau's day:

In the State of Massachusetts, which was the scene of Miss Martineau's reputed observation, it is now announced that there are more than three hundred occupations open to women, instead of seven, and that 300,000 women are earning their own living in these occupations, receiving from $150 to $3,000 every year.

This computation does not include amateurs, or mothers and daughters in the household, and of course excludes domestic service.[64]

Rayne's approach to women and work had much in common with that of her predecessors. What distinguished it was the number of women she could catalog in each of the professions she discussed. She cited examples from seventy-five years of women's work. In 1893, the home was still the paramount organizing force in women's roles, public and private, just as it had been when Sarah Hale had entered the literary world three-quarters of a century earlier. The presence of Hale and all the other women Rayne included in her brief histories of the professions indicated that the metaphors of domestic economy could be continually reinvented in the service of a new era of women's work.

Six

FANCY THAT

The Pleasure and Profit of Fancywork

$\mathcal{T}$he image of a nineteenth-century parlor as a room of whatnots filled with knick-knacks, marble tables crowded with wax flowers under glass domes, velvet sofas draped in antimacassars, and gewgaws cluttering every surface remains both compelling and repulsive to the modern imagination. It conjures up sentimental nostalgia for an elegant, genteel era or caustic musings on the psychological implications of *horror vacui*. In both visions, however, the decorations of the parlor are objects of fascination through which a modern eye can read an encapsulated history of nineteenth-century middle-class culture. Despite the fascination with the image of the Victorian parlor, the production of these decorations, fancywork in particular, has received little scholarly attention. Although collectors and crafts people have lavished attention on the accouterments of sentimentalism, historians have only recently begun to explore the material culture of the nineteenth-century middle class as more than just the mis-en-scène for cultural history.[1] The critique that proponents of the Arts and Crafts movement leveled against fancywork in the late nineteenth century remained substantially unchallenged in intellectual circles until the late twentieth century. The penchant in fancywork for using materials such as fish scales and human hair contributed to its aesthetic condemnation.[2] Most discussions of fancywork examine it as the product of private female leisure.[3] The growth of the market for fancywork manuals and the careers of fancywork "experts" in the mid-nineteenth century, however, suggests a more complicated definition of domestic leisure and the many ways in which the parlor was the site of production. The popularity of fancywork instruction, and the sale of fancywork (discussed in the next chapter), demonstrate the active and independent involvement of middle-class women as producers and consumers in a developing market culture.

"Fancywork" describes not only fancy sewing, such as embroidery and tatting, but also parlor crafts such as wax flowers and hair jewelry. As a display of genteel industry, fancywork was a social investment in the appearance of leisure. The word itself contained a dichotomy between pleasure and profit that was at the heart of middle-class market culture. *Fancy* was the opposite of utilitarian. It implied leisure, aesthetic taste, and gentility but had overtones of frivolity. *Work* tempered this impression of flightiness and linked fancywork to the virtue associated with production.[4] As a labor of leisure, fancywork embodied the dilemma that faced middle-class women: their leisure was an important and visible marker of class, but their idleness raised anxieties about the dissipation of the rich. To balance these conflicting imperatives, middle-class women had to find a way to portray their labors as *fancy* work and their leisure as fancy *work*. Because fancywork was, by definition, both leisure and work, it carried the cachet of feminine accomplishment and deflected accusations of idleness. Fancywork provided the opportunity for both moral improvement and pecuniary gain, a dualism that appeared in the instruction manuals for fancywork as the pairing of pleasure and profit. The leisure time required to make fancywork was part of what gave it value; making fancywork was a profitable way to spend time.[5]

Fancywork replaced other forms of domestic production as a supplementary income source for urban women, and like literary work, it became a new form of domestic production.[6] Both rural and urban households relied on an influx of capital generated by women's labor. Home industries such as plaiting oat-straw or palm-leaf hats became common among eastern farm women in the first quarter of the nineteenth century. By 1827, the "Report of the Harrisburg Convention in the Interests of Domestic Industry" estimated that 25,000 people, primarily women, were employed in this industry. Wages for straw bonnet production could be as much fifty cents a day for the most talented women, but the average was twenty-five cents a day. Manufacturing buttons was also a popular form of home work for women in New England.[7] They offered women a flexible way to increase family capital or pay off debts. Often, however, women were paid in goods by the merchants who hired them. This did not increase the amount of cash brought into the household, but it allowed women to buy a greater quantity of manufactured goods for household use.[8]

The proliferation of fancywork manuals from 1850 to 1880 was part of a revival of interest in fancywork, an attempt to recover the "lost" arts of gentility and balance the profitable interest in fancywork with its cultured pleasures. The histories of fancywork included in the introductions to the manuals portrayed fancywork as an ancient tradition that modern practitioners could perpetuate. Nostalgia for the medieval roots of fancywork created a connection to a noble past for a generation of readers who felt that their mothers had neglected, or been unable, to teach them the arts of fine sewing. The Bayeux Tapestry—the mention of which invoked romantic images of Matilda, the consort of William the Conqueror, recording his triumphs in exquisite embroidery—was often cited as evidence of the aristocratic tradition of fancywork Matilda's noble deed was proof of the importance that could be attached to fine needlework.[9] Florence Hartley, author of *The Lady's Hand Book of Fancy and Ornamental Work* (1859), emphasized the European roots of needlework.[10] She compiled her volume from English, French, and German sources and included as the frontispiece a woodcut of a medieval lady embroidering a coat of arms on a standard. The medieval origins of fancywork that these manuals celebrated linked newly prosperous women to a genteel tradition they could call their own. The noble history of needlework, on which Hartley and other manual writers insisted, was an attempt to distinguish the leisurely work of fancy sewing from the drudgery of the seamstress's work. Needlework, according to Hartley, was a "source of unalloyed happiness"; those who "scorn[ed] the needle as a badge of drudgery, [sought] in vain for quiet pleasure, and [were] consumed with *ennui* and listlessness."[11] In an expanding world of leisure time and activities, fancywork was only one of many choices.

Even before the invention of the sewing machine in 1850, the role of sewing in middle-class women's lives had changed.[12] Many advice writers reminded mothers of the importance of teaching their daughters the skills of sewing even if they had the means to pay someone to do the work for them. Good sewing skills, they argued, were essential for a woman in any station of life. *Godey's Lady's Book* and *Peterson's Magazine* assumed the task of educating young women about the virtues of both plain and fancy sewing. A sewing work box was an important part of a middle-class woman's possessions, as the gifts Ellen Montgomery receives from her mother at the beginning of Susan Warner's *Wide, Wide, World* (1851) suggest. Prior to Ellen's sojourn with Aunt Fortune, her mother gives her a Bible, a writing desk, a dressing box, and a work box. Although Ellen had helped her mother choose the contents for her writing desk, the work box is a surprise, and she opens the package "with fingers trembling with eagerness." She is so entranced by the beautiful work box of "satinwood, beautifully finished, and lined with crimson silk" that she "almost screamed" with delight when she saw it.[13] Her mother provided the box for a practical purpose, but it demonstrated that utility did not preclude beauty. These gifts represent Ellen's rite of passage to womanhood, albeit at an earlier age than most girls. Her enthusiasm for the work box was a gentle reminder to Warner's readers that the pleasure of the writing table should be balanced by the pleasure of sewing.

Sewing, as a leisure activity, had stiff competition from novels and other new forms of leisure that enticed middle-class women and girls. Advice writers chided young ladies who spent too much time reading and not enough time engaging in other genteel pastimes, but they also worried that girls who spent too much time doing fancywork would not devote enough time to serious study. Florence Hartley championed the importance of needlework in the education of all women.[14] She was afraid that women no longer recognized the benefits of sewing skills and insisted that women in the "middle station of life" as well as their sisters of "humble" origin could use their needles "*with skill* . . . to promote the well being and comfort of [their families], and to gain and preserve that peace of mind which results from the consciousness of being useful."[15] The leisure hours of wealthy women, she noted, could be passed "not only with profit, but with pleasure." Needlework was not merely domestic drudgery, but an escape from the boredom that often was the price of leisure. Consumption of luxuries without at least some knowledge of their production was enervating, fancywork authors fretted, and threatened the cultural health of the nation.

After carefully defending the importance of needlework to all classes of women, Hartley stated, "Fortunately for all American ladies, the use of the needle in this country is fashionable in all the wealth of life; and those who are ignorant of it, whether they are aware of the fact or not, are condemned by the public sentiment of society."[16] This little barb reminded readers of the important links Hartley saw between domestic accomplishments and virtue, not only in personal terms but also as a reflection of national virtue. Despite her medieval frontispiece, Hartley declared that the impetus for her volume was patriotism and demurely asked to be rewarded for it: "The writer feels that she is doing good service to the commonwealth; and she trusts that her labours will be rewarded with that indulgent kindness which the American public never withholds from those who are sincerely engaged in the promotion of a good cause."[17] The good motives that prompted Hartley to publish this book, she implied, demonstrated that despite the personal profits this might bring her, her first responsibility was to the public good.

Hartley offered her middle-class readers an education that had once been the purview of the wealthy. As early as 1748, Mrs. Abigail Hiller made her living by teaching "Wax-Work, Transparency and Filigree, Painting upon Glass, Japanning, Quill Work, Feather Work, and Embroidery with Gold and Silver" to the daughters of Boston's elite families.[18] Fancywork, especially japanning and découpage, was popular in Ladies' Seminaries in the mid-eighteenth century.[19] Fancywork continued to be a standard part of a young woman's formal education at schools such as Mrs. Susannah Rowson's Academy in Boston, Miss Mary Balch's Academy in Providence, Rhode Island, and Mrs. Saunders's and Miss Beaches's Academy in Dorchester, Massachusetts, until the early nineteenth century.[20] As women's education, under the tutelage of Sarah Hale, Emma Willard, Catharine Beecher, and Mary Lyon, became more scholarly, fancywork was replaced in the curriculum of women's seminaries by academic subjects.

As fancywork played a smaller role in the curriculum of girls' schools, independent fancywork teachers catered to a growing number of interested pupils. By the 1850s, fancywork education had become a commercial enterprise. Virginia Penny included fancywork teachers in her *Employments of Women* (1863), noting that accomplished teachers could command a high price for their lessons. Madame D. in New York charged twenty-five cents an hour for lessons in crochet work and embroidery, whereas Madame N. charged fifty cents an hour and estimated that an able student could learn one stitch in an hour. At these rates, a fancywork teacher could earn between ten and twenty dollars a week, an income that exceeded the earning possibilities of most work available to women. Madame N. also employed women to make fancywork. These women worked out of their homes and could make as much as four dollars a week. In Madame N.'s opinion, there was plenty of work for anyone who wanted it.[21] In Philadelphia, the Misses H. ran a more comprehensive fancywork school: five lessons in leather work cost six dollars; lessons in wax fruit and flowers, paper, and rice-paper flowers were only one dollar a lesson. They also offered instruction in embroidery, hair flowers, bead work, and the arrangement of shells with mosses and grasses. The detail with which Penny describes these enterprises conveys a sense of how broad the spectrum of fancywork was and how specific a business it could be. A few teachers published manuals based on their lessons. For example, Sarah E. Herman, a wax flower entrepreneur, published *Instructions in Madame Herman's New Method of Making Wax Flowers* and promised the same results to pupils of her books as to pupils of her classes.[22]

Virginia Penny included a section on the human hair trade, which she described as work "nicely adapted to the nimble fingers of women, whether engaged in it for pastime or profit."[23] She listed artists, dressers, dyers, growers, manufacturers, and merchants. Despite its profound sentimental value, hair had a double life as a raw material when it was harvested for making wigs. Unlike sentimental locks of hair, which where rendered priceless by the circumstances of exchange, hair sold to be made into wigs was subject to a strict price index

Figure 3. Wax flower arrangement, courtesy of the Smithsonian Institution.

by which its physical characteristics determined its value. A lock of hair was unique. The waterfalls, coils, and curls that became essential elements in a woman's fashionable hairstyle were designed to be anonymous, to disappear into the hair of the wearer.[24] Women who were hair dressers and stylists often made hair jewelry on the side. Hair designers were the most highly paid of these stylists, commanding as much as fifty dollars for a design.[25] Teaching hair work, Penny observed, was another way to extend income. An ornamental hair worker could charge fifty cents a lesson. There were also regional opportunities in hair work. Penny related the story of one woman who took hair-jewelry lessons before she moved to Louisiana with her husband, who was a jeweler. Hair jewelry commanded a high price in the South, Penny noted, "for Southerners have had all such work done in the North."[26]

Magazines and manuals gave detailed instructions for a wide range of techniques for producing hair jewelry. Wooden forms that looked like a small version of a darning egg were used to give the hair shape as it was being woven or knotted. Then the wooden form was slipped out and a piece of jewelry the same shape was slipped in so that the hair creation formed a net around the pendant, earring, or brooch. Other forms of jewelry were made from ropes of hair that derived both strength and beauty from their intricate patterns. Instructions for hair work encouraged a practitioner to work on a special silk or satin pillow, so that the hair would slide easily and not get tangled.[27] The sensual nature of hair placed a premium on the personal manufacture of the jewelry to "protect" the hair from the "wanton" behavior of hair workers.[28] Although the authors of fancywork manuals acknowledged that jewelers could provide a more perfect specimen of hair work, manuals for hair jewelry cautioned against this practice:

> When we take into consideration the liability of having the hair of some other person substituted for that of own cherished friend, or that careless hands have idly drawn through their fingers the tresses which it appears almost sacrilegious to have even looked upon with a cold glance, the thought is repugnant.[29]

Hair work was a labor of love that produced the quintessence of sentimental value. The hair worker's callous behavior, however, drew attention to the problem of hair's sentimental value: the workers treated hair like a material, handling it roughly and substituting other hair when it was more convenient, with complete disregard for the feelings of the person who had commissioned the piece of jewelry. The hair workers provided a service in the name of sentiment but they did not perform it in a sentimental manner. As hair jewelry became more common and more elaborate, ready-made hair jewelry became available. In 1876, one jeweler boasted that the "Best Holiday Presents that a lady or gentleman can present are Hair Jewelry."[30] His advertisement invited customers to bring their own hair to made into jewelry or choose one of the lovely pieces already made up. By the 1870s, hair jewelry was as much a fashion as a sentimental souvenir of a deceased loved one.

Fancywork manuals also taught techniques for making wreaths out of human hair. Wreaths of hair were treasured objects of family sentiment, often combining the hair of all members of the family, both living and dead. Fancywork manuals recommended these wreaths as a way to organize locks of hair. A wreath could incorporate hair from many members of a family, "preserved in a form not only pleasing and appropriate, but so lasting, as well." Once a wreath had been made, it could be "handed down from generation to generation as one of those "heirlooms" always valued, a "'*memento mori*' of those gone before."[31] The technique for making a hair wreath involved wrapping individual strands of hair around wire forms shaped like flowers and leaves. A wreath might contain more than ten different kinds of flowers and their foliage. Some flowers were copies of recognizable blossoms, others were fantastic. The wreaths were mounted on a velvet or silk background and enclosed in a box with a glass lid, which was usually hung on the wall of the parlor. The wreaths were large, sometimes more than a foot in diameter and as much as six inches deep. They imitated the shape and style of funerary wreaths, but like other types of artificial flowers that were also popular forms of fancywork, they offered a permanent beauty that fresh flowers could not.[32] The wreaths took the abstraction of hair one step further by removing the hair from life and placing it behind glass so it could only be gazed upon and not touched. Some of the wreaths were so intricate that they did not look like hair. Although wreaths were much more elaborate than the simple forms of hair jewelry that just encased the hair behind glass, they invited a similar kind of gaze. But the woven hair jewelry was more sensual; it could be caressed, and the hair itself could be worn next to the skin.[33]

The popularity of fancywork created a demand for special materials. Mesdames Martin and Thomas, fancywork proprietors in New York, received a warm endorsement in *Godey's Lady's Book:* "We would suggest to all lovers of fancywork to pay them a visit as they are so obliging, and do their utmost to give satisfaction."[34] Their stock of patterns was continually updated; they

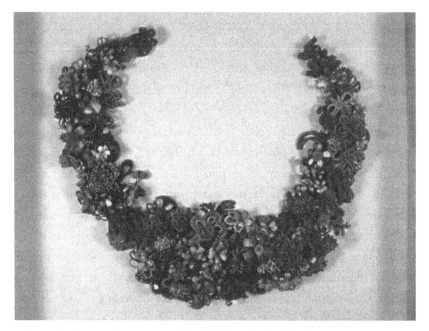

Figure 4. Hair wreath, courtesy of the Smithsonian Institution.

gave instruction on many varieties of fancywork, and they filled orders promptly. Their obliging nature and business acumen were further illustrated by the announcement that they had opened a summer "depot" in Newport, Rhode Island, that would be "invaluable to the lady visitors of that celebrated resort." Virginia Penny recommended fancywork-material stores as a good business for women.[35] In England and France, she noted, women were more frequently involved in such mercantile activities. A fancy store, she argued, could not only be a genteel enterprise but also help elevate the "taste of the community." By providing beautiful and tasteful items for sale, a proprietress could gently influence the consumption choices of the ladies who frequented her store. Penny offered advice about how to distinguish a genteel shop from an ordinary one. "The taste of the best keepers of dry-goods and fancy stores, millinery establishments, and embroidery shops," she observed, "will be displayed in the dress of their patrons."[36] A store for fancy goods was an appropriate enterprise for a lady as long as she conducted it in a decorous way. A woman could maintain her own gentility by extending her cultural influence through the tastefulness of her goods and her mode of conducting business.[37]

Penny's discussion of shopkeepers is reminiscent of Nathaniel Hawthorne's characterization of Phoebe Pyncheon's abilities in *The House of Seven Gables* (1851).[38] Phoebe transforms Hepzibah's little shop with her sunny personality and natural gentility, although her natural skill at business also contributes to her success.[39] Hepzibah, on the other hand, could hardly bring herself to open the shop. She is ill suited in every way to run a business: she cringes at the scrutiny and scowls at her customers, she does not know what kind of merchandise to carry, and she cannot make change. Shopkeeping mortifies her sense of herself as a lady. Phoebe, however, takes easily to shopkeeping because she has been trained in the practical matters of life. In addition to her marketing experience, Phoebe cites her successes at fancy fairs as evidence of her business sensibility. Her skills come from her mother, who is not a Pyncheon, nor, in Hepzibah's eyes, a lady, but Hawthorne saw Phoebe as a new kind of woman who combined both domestic and market sensibilities:

> Instead of discussing her claim to rank among ladies, it would be preferable to regard Phoebe as the example of feminine grace and availability combined, in a state of society, if there were any such, where ladies did not exist. There it should be woman's office to move in the midst of practical affairs, and to gild them all, the very homeliest—were it even the scouring of pots and kettles—with an atmosphere of loveliness and joy. . . . Such was the sphere of Phoebe.[40]

For Hawthorne, Phoebe was perfect balance between the sentimental and the pragmatic. Although historians usually place Hawthorne at the other end of the quill from Sarah Hale and her "damned mob," they all attempted to infuse market relations with a form of genteel restraint.

Godey's Lady's Book began to include patterns and instructions for fancywork in the early 1830s. From 1831 to 1832, *Godey's* contained a regular section, the "Ornamental Artist," which included instructions for fancywork, particularly the construction of ornamental boxes and baskets made from pasteboard and glass. The section outlined techniques for "Chinese painting" and suggested work boxes, screens, and small ornamental tables as appropriate media for this mode of transfer painting. Readers were instructed to purchase items to paint and books with images to trace from a fancy shop.[41] *Godey's* published excerpts from the fancywork instructions in Eliza Leslie's *American Girl's Book*.[42] These projects were mostly pin cushions, needle books, and reticules, which were easy and useful. Sometimes other aspects of the magazine reappeared as fancywork: "SINCE publishing 'The Secret' in our December, 1849, [issue] we have seen the same plate reproduced in every style. We have seen it on lampshades, on colored glass, on copper, tops of fancy tables, etc. The painter little dreamed of the immortality we have given to his picture."[43] *Godey's* congratulated its readers on their ingenuous use of the plate and relished the free advertisement.

Instructions for fancywork appeared periodically throughout the 1840s. In 1846, *Godey's* introduced crochet, which had been popular in England since 1838.[44] Fancywork instructions became a regular feature of the magazine in the late 1840s with the introduction of the "Work Table." The instructions for a fancywork technique in *Godey's Lady's Book* were often described in a series that lasted several months. Each month the technique was refined and more complicated patterns were suggested. One series on rice-shell work began with simple hair ornaments and built up to an elaborate basket. The author was quick to differentiate the delicate shell work described in the article from shell work available as souvenirs: "Those gay and sometimes gaudy, but often very striking groups of brightly-tinted shell-flowers, which we meet with at most watering places. These certainly form showy ornaments for table or mantle-piece, but are scarcely adapted for ladies' work."[45] Ladies who wished to undertake rice-shell work were not obliged to collect their own shells. They could be purchased from a shell dealer.[46] The wreaths and sprays were made by attaching individual shells, which resembled grains of rice in size and color, to silver wire. The shells could be made to resemble flowers or sheaves of wheat. Rice-shell work was also incorporated into more complex fancywork designs for parlor decoration. Hair ornaments, another suggested use for shell flowers, was complicated. It required specific materials and careful attention to instructions and patterns. Not all fancywork was as detailed as shell work, though, as not all women had the time or patience for something so elaborate.[47]

Figure 5. Shell-work cross, courtesy of the Smithsonian Institution.

Sometimes fancywork patterns were included in a *Godey's* series called "Everyday Actualities" that described everything from the manufacture of fancy items like artificial flowers to technological innovations in paper making. The series placed commercial forms of production in the context of the reader's own forms of production. An article on artificial flowers contained elaborate descriptions of the work environment and techniques practiced by French manufacturers that had been exhibited in 1851 at the Crystal Palace in

London.[48] The tools and machinery used were illustrated in detail, but there were no instructions for the amateur artist. The women who made the flowers were described as "workwomen," distinguishing them from *Godey's* readership. The following month, this series offered instructions for painting on velvet. The primary virtue of painting on velvet, the author of the article noted, was the speed with which a picture could be produced. Whereas a piece of embroidery could take a month, painting on velvet took only a few hours. This kind of fancywork represented a compromise of aesthetics and industry. Unlike the elaborate and painstaking processes of embroidery or the artificial flower making described in the previous issue, painting on velvet was a true parlor occupation. It did not require elaborate machinery or complicated technique, and it was possible to produce beautiful results in a reasonable time. This appealed to women with limited leisure time.[49]

Godey's was often explicit about the profitable nature of fancywork. *Carrie Lee's Talisman,* originally published as a story in the magazine and later circulated as an advertising pamphlet, was explicit in its instructions for a new kind of domestic production.[50] The story begins with the death of Carrie's parents. The only piece of property remaining after debts were settled is an old farmhouse in which Carrie's mother was raised. Carrie and her brothers and sisters return to the village of her mother's youth. At first, it appears that Carrie has chosen an older form of domesticity, but she is an avid reader of *Godey's Lady's Book.* The needlework patterns in the magazine show her how to use the skills she learned in leisure to make money, and indeed, Carrie supports her siblings by selling fancywork. Her work receives such an enthusiastic reception that she opens a school to teach knitting, netting, and crocheting to the women in her village. Carrie is a natural business woman. When she exhausts the market for fancywork in her village, she exports it to the city, where there is a boundless market for her creations. Her success convinces all the ladies in the village to become subscribers to *Godey's.* The story ends, not with Carrie's success as an independent business woman, but with her inheritance of an unexpected legacy. The legacy is not large enough to make her rich, but it returns her to her former, comfortable status, and she is able to enjoy the fruits of the magazine for pleasure instead of profit. This story advertised the usefulness of the magazine and the importance of economic opportunities for women that was a centerpiece of Hale's conservative domesticity and market philosophy. Carrie's economic success, it seems, does not diminish her desire for traditional domestic arrangements.

Godey's put itself forward as a source book for the activities of both pleasure and profit. The *Lady's Book* embraced fancywork and sewing as a regular feature of the magazine, but unlike *Peterson's* and *Frank Leslie's Magazine*, *Godey's* did not employ a fancywork editor. Jane Weaver was the regular fancywork editor for *Peterson's*, which also had a separate sewing editor, Emily H. May, who provided the patterns for the fashions displayed in each issue of the magazine.[51] Frank Leslie seized the opportunity to hire Matilda Pullan when she came to New York in the late 1850s. A well-known and respected contributor to the work pages of both British and American magazines, Pullan began her career in London in the 1840s by contributing fancywork patterns to the *London Review,* the *London and Paris Gazette of Fashion,* and the *Illustrated London Magazine.* She also compiled several books of fancywork instruction. *Treasures in Needlework* (1855), which she wrote with Eliza Warren, was a collection of fancywork patterns that had previously been published in the British periodical, *Family Friend.* The book was dedicated to "lady needleworkers throughout the world." Pullan hoped that they would use her book to produce "those ornamental and useful articles that add elegance to the boudoir and yield a profit to the fancy fair."[52] The prospect of profit was of particular interest to Pullan and Warren. They assured their readers that "no expense [had] been spared" in the preparation of their book to it "worthy of universal acceptance." Only "a very large sale, not only in 'merrie England,' but wherever fair fingers ply the needle," could recompense the authors for their hard work, and they entreated "those who may derive pleasure or profit from the book to extend to it the kindness of a generous recommendation."[53] Recommendations created networks of profit, but the authors balanced their own pleas for profit by acknowledging the use of their book for personal and charitable profit. Yet Pullan and Warren cautioned their readers that it was difficult to earn an income by producing fancywork. Although they received many inquiries about where to sell fancywork, there was no easy answer to this question. It was possible to find places to sell fancywork, usually on commission, but the sale of these creations was "not so remunerative, perhaps, as to constitute a livelihood, but such as will afford an agreeable addition to a limited income."[54] It was easier, the authors conceded, to talk of profit than to earn it. The lesson their readers might learn from this sobering coda was that to write about fancywork was a surer source of profit than to produce it.

Matilda Pullan continued her discussion of the tension between pleasure and profit that characterized the fancywork market in her first American publication. She had come to the United States, she informed her readers, to visit "the dearest and best of all [her] dear and good friends." She wanted to soften the appearance of professional ego that her new career in American might represent, but she also wanted to make it clear to those who were unfamiliar with her work that she had a substantial reputation at home in England. She claimed that her arrival in America had rejuvenated her spirit and inspired her to compile a complete lexicon of fancywork instructions.[55] *The Lady's Manual of Fancywork: A Complete Instructor in Every Variety of Ornamental Needlework* was not dictated by current fashion as her previous manuals had been. This new volume contained instructions for both historical and contemporary fancywork. It was a scholarly treatise that provided detailed instructions on techniques of fancywork, not the patterns themselves. Pullan included historical techniques in anticipation of future revivals and predicted that her dictionary would have continuing value for both student and author.[56] She hoped that her readers would use the manual as a reference book so that rather than devoting space in her column to repetitive instructions, she could include more patterns. Pullan and other fancywork writers had to assume that their readers had no other source of knowledge about technique. Fancywork editors, in fact, imagined themselves as a replacement for the oral culture of women's work.[57] By linking the book market to the magazine market, Pullan made both the book and the magazine more valuable to her readers, who had access to more detailed instructions and a greater number of patterns, and created the possibility of greater profits for her and her publishers. Pullan ended her introduction with a discussion of plagiarism. Her work, she claimed, had been copied or altered slightly by magazines without acknowledgment, and many American magazines had published her work without acknowledgment. Although fancywork editors were certainly familiar with her name, she noted, her name had been "not very justly withheld from American ladies."[58]

The manuals and the work pages in the magazines were testimony to the popularity of fancywork, but they also signaled a shift in its role in women's lives. Because the instruction for fancywork techniques came from books rather than from maternal instruction, fancywork became a form of market knowledge instead of the aristocratic heritage the manuals celebrated. Pullan struggled to maintain a balance between the importance of fancywork as evidence of the taste of natural gentility, tied to a chivalric history of needlework, and the pragmatic need of contemporary authors to claim fancywork patterns and instructions as their own intellectual property.

Pullan underscored the value of the book to her reader. The practice of fancywork was not just a leisure activity, she insisted, because fancywork promoted domestic economy. Women who had been content to purchase fancy items were able to make them more tastefully themselves once the secrets of their production had been revealed. Industry, taste, and skill coincided with good economy. For women who lived outside of large cities and were not able to visit fancy stores, the lexicon offered simultaneous suggestions for both the production and consumption of fancywork, "a mere list of the sorts of work in existence [had] a value of itself."[59] Fancywork was another form of tutorial in the education about genteel living to which the popular book market catered.

Pullan was a commercial as well as an intellectual advocate for fancywork. She waxed poetic about the transformative power of the sewing machine in women's lives. She endorsed Wheeler and Wilson sewing machines and assured her readers that she had researched the matter carefully and could attest to the superiority of this machine. She compared the sewing machine to the Atlantic Telegraph, insisting that it generated an even greater social improvement than the strengthening of the bond between Britain and the United States. "Well may we hail with joy that greater Liberator of our sex, the Family Sewing-Machine," she proclaimed.[60] The sewing machine saved women from drudgery and created more time for fancywork. Pullan also devoted considerable attention to the materials for fancywork, stating that American women were often forced to use inferior materials because merchants did not distinguish between superior and inferior goods. She expected her customers to educate storekeepers by exhibiting their own knowledge of materials. She cited her reputation and the longevity of her career as collateral for the honesty of her opinions, in effect marketing her reputation.

Pullan included in her manual a postscript in which her activities as a fancywork business woman were made abundantly clear. She announced the publication of two related volumes, *Plain Needle-Work* and *The Manual of the Wardrobe,* and reported that, as the result of her research among merchants and manufacturers for the second volume, she was now able to offer her services as consultant to any lady who needed assistance in selecting her wardrobe. She also offered these services, for both wardrobe and fancywork materials, to women who were unable to avail themselves of the advantages of shopping in New York. Ladies were invited to send their requests in writing, and Pullan would make the purchases requested without additional cost to her correspondents. She promised to execute each commission personally. Merchants, grateful for the business, absorbed the cost of Pullan's services. In addition, she agreed to travel as a consultant as long as her expenses were paid, and she pledged to answer all inquiries either personally or under the initials of the correspondent in the pages of *Frank Leslie's Magazine.* Pullan made a special point of offering her services in executing the orders of hair jewelry, assuring her readers that she carried out orders with the "utmost exactitude" and guaranteeing that the hair sent would be the hair used, "a point of much importance to the wearer, though often very cruelly overlooked by the worker."[61] *Godey's Lady's Book* also offered the same service in addition to a shopping service called the Philadelphia Agency.[62] This was superintended by Louis Godey, not Sarah Hale, who made it clear that she was *not* the fashion editor.[63] The initials of the correspondent were published in the magazine to alert her that the order had been filled: "Miss F.G.—sent slippers 29th."[64] *Godey's* also listed items it would supply for readers, which included *Mrs. Hale's 4545 Recipes for the Million* and Godey's Bijou Needle case.[65]

Writing about fancywork and teaching fancywork techniques continued to be the most lucrative fancywork enterprise, especially after the Civil War when the number of women who tried to support themselves by producing fancywork increased. The glut of embroidery and other fancy items in the market meant that prices dropped. Some women who could not afford the materials to make fancy needlework requested that magazines like *Godey's* publish designs for fancywork that could be made from inexpensive or free materials.[66] This request signaled changes in fancywork production that reflected the genteel poverty that many middle-class families experienced after the war. Fancywork that could be made without purchasing materials made leisure activities possible for women without extra money to spend and was something to produce for profit that required no capital.

In the 1870s, Henry T. Williams, editor of the *Ladies Floral Cabinet,* and his coauthor, Mrs. C. S. Jones, introduced a new kind of fancywork that he called "household elegancies."[67] Although it was not their intent, the transformation of elegance into "elegancies" suggested the manufacture of an approximation of elegance, even a form of camouflage for shabby gentility. This fancywork used skills similar to the needlework made popular by the earlier manuals, but the materials were leaves, grasses, pine cones, moss, and other "found" objects. The most popular "household elegancy" was rustic work, which used materials "found 'in the woods and on the shore.'" Although some detractors of rustic work complained that these materials were "common and unclean," the authors argued that these critics had not had the benefit of examining "fine specimens" of this kind of work and had made judgments based on "the clumsy attempts of some novice, devoid of taste or judgment."[68] It was not just the class of work that the criticism of rustic work addressed but the class of those who produced it. The use of natural materials suggested the rural, and therefore unsophisticated, origins of such work or betrayed the possibility of financial instability. Rustic work also seemed to transform fancywork from a leisure activity that stood for (or stood in for) gentility into a craft. Amateur embroidery still looked like embroidery, but "clumsy" rustic work was unrecognizable.

Despite these criticisms, the assertion that well-executed rustic work could be beautiful was consistent with the idea that innate refinement could transform even the most ordinary object into a thing of loveliness. A natural aesthetic was a way to merge economy and taste with novelty. Natural materials allowed a woman "to utilize trifles which would otherwise be valueless . . . enabling the housewife to render her home attractive."[69] The notion of making something out of nothing was popular, and almost any household item

Figure 6. Seed-and-nut wreath, courtesy of the Smithsonian Institution.

could be converted into a household elegancy. Even the lowliest of materials—fish scales, for example—could be sewn on silk or satin in the form of "flowers, leaves, ornamental borders and also birds." These beautiful patterns would "enrich many of those small articles of taste, which always conduce to throw an air of refinement over a home, and give the visitor a favorable opinion of the occupants." Although a significant amount of work was required to clean and prepare the fish scales, Williams and Jones were certain their readers would be "surprised and gratified" by the effect made possible with "a material generally so little regarded as the scales of fishes."[70] They urged their readers to apply their own sense of good taste before they dismissed the medium entirely. For women who yearned for the "air of refinement" but did not possess the financial means to achieve it, the labor may have been well worth it. The transformative ability of taste is made clear when even something as ordinary as fish scales can aspire to an appearance of taste and gentility.

Another form of fancywork that made good use out of everyday materials was the skeletonizing of leaves. In 1863, Edmund Parrish, a member of the Academy of Natural Sciences of Philadelphia and the Philadelphia College of Pharmacy compiled *The Phantom Bouquet. A Popular Treatise on the Art of Skeletonizing Leaves and Seed-vessels, and Adapting Them to Embellish the Home of Taste.*[71] The leaves were used to make centerpieces for the table and pictures for the parlor wall. This technique brought the beauty of natural wonders into the urban parlor.[72] Window gardening had also become very popular. In the 1860s, *Godey's Lady's Book* ran a regular gardening column edited by H. A. Dreer, a Philadelphia florist.[73]

For those whose interest in rustic work was not driven by lack of funds but by interest in the natural aesthetics championed by John Ruskin and his followers, fancy stores offered manufactured naturalness. Artificial ivy, holly, and autumnal vines, described as "perfect facsimiles of Nature's handicraft," were advertised in the back of *Household Elegancies* as more durable than their natural counterparts and strong enough to use instead of wire to hang the rustic picture frames that were also in fashion.[74] Moss and other natural materials were often simulated in wool, an indication that the fashion for rustic work was about the transformation of nature into culture instead of culture into nature. Twig picture frames draped in artificial ivy shared the aesthetic of the carpenter Gothic "cottages" that became popular in at midcentury. Gothic revival architecture emphasized its relationship—however stylized— to the organic forms of nature and presented a romantic vision of domesticity. It was championed first by Alexander Jackson Davis in *Rural Residences* (1837) and later by Andrew Jackson Downing's pattern books for houses, *Cottage Residences* (1842) and *The Architecture of Country Houses* (1850). Both architects presented Gothic revival as a rural style. Although interest in it began to decline after the Civil War, in the 1870s, it was briefly popular again, particularly in urban settings.[75]

The Gothic revival also generated interest in scroll work and fret work. Henry T. Williams, who published fret sawing manuals and sold the saws themselves (used to cut delicate pieces of wood into intricate patterns), played up its potential as a profit-making enterprise. *Fret Sawing for Pleasure and Profit* was written by an "old experienced amateur, who was the *first person* to introduce the art from Germany."[76] The instructions for fret sawing were technical, but the advertisements for the book appeared in the back pages of fancywork manuals, and it was recommended as a pastime for women and children. Items made with a fret saw would "sell quickly and at a good profit," advertisements assured readers: "With this bracket saw, the designs and directions, very desirable articles can be made for Fairs, etc., which will. With it you can *make beautiful articles for presentation gifts.* With it you can *help beautify your homes.* With it you can *make money.*"[77]

Parents were encouraged to give their children a fret saw as a gift. Children would enjoy using it, and it would help "cultivate a mechanical taste.[78] Advertisements always stressed the pleasure of fret sawing, but it was the potential for profit that was its real attraction: "Hundreds are earning large sums of pocket-money by cutting these beautiful household ornaments, and selling among friends or acquaintances, or at the art stores."[79] Matilda Pullan's decorous references to the sale of fancywork for personal gain had been replaced with promises of *large* sums of pocket money. Indeed, the advertisements in the back pages of Williams's manuals addressed the growing number of readers who were interested in ways to make money. By the end of the 1870s, the number of women and men who tried to capitalize on the fashion for fancywork had changed the nature of fancywork. New techniques were invented to allow its producers to make more money; every need was considered and anticipated. Patterns, instructions, and materials could be purchased for any kind of project. Rustic work was, in part, an attempt to resist the artificialities of the market and return to a simple and inexpensive leisure pastime. But in the end the fake ivy was better than the real ivy; it lasted forever, was strong enough to hang a picture with, and was readily available to urban consumers.

Seven

∞

CHARITABLE CALCULATIONS
Fancywork, Charity, and the Sentimental Market

𝓘 n a market filled with all the luxury goods money could buy, the charity fair offered commodities that money should buy. Although fairs resembled markets in practical and symbolic ways, the goods sold at fairs were donated and the profits were used for benevolent purposes. The charity fair was organized along the lines of a gift economy and defined by domestic metaphors of cooperation and reciprocity rather than the market metaphors of individualism.[1] The obligations of reciprocity created a web of exchange that attached moral consequences to the acts of production and consumption associated with the charity fairs.[2] Organizers defined the sentimental economy of the charity fair as an alternative market that operated according to its own system of calculations. The sentimental education about the market, which charity fairs provided, gave consumers a conceptual framework of value and exchange that had a significant impact on the development of market culture as a whole.

Fair organizers made appeals to sentimental benevolence to advertize fairs. Because consumption at a charity fair was virtuous, items ordinarily defined as luxuries became necessities. Good motives justified both the production and consumption of these items. In her essay on "Ladies' Fairs" in *Traits of American Life* (1835), Sarah Hale traced the influence of needlework on the development of civilization: "My readers will easily, without any prompting, refer the improvements of manners to different eras in the art of sewing, from that of necessity to the needle-work of convenience, of elegance, of luxury; and then comes the crowning grace, when the work of fair fingers is made subservient to the luxury of doing good."[3] By connecting the luxurious phase of needlework production directly to the moment it became an essential part of benevolence, Hale argued that both production and consumption could be seen as "the luxury of doing good." Making fancywork to sell at charity fairs was a form of benevolent production, and buying fancywork for the right reasons was virtuous consumption. Fancywork produced and consumed for benevolent reasons could not be criticized as evidence of idleness or self-indulgence. The transactions of the fair provided concrete evidence that the good motives of Christian moralism could restrain and redirect the aggressive self-interest of capitalism.

A charity fair was an efficient way to raise funds in an economic forum that was largely controlled by women. Fair organizers commissioned fancywork and encouraged mothers to set production goals for their daughters. Talent, taste, and benevolence were bound together in this system and prompted a little competition in what was otherwise a cooperative enterprise. Middle-class women often devoted a considerable amount of economic energy to the "business of benevolence." The fairs were designed to raise money for the needy, but they also created a market in which women's production had economic value. Women's production was framed in terms of the need for women to be "useful." Like the idea of women's duty, usefulness linked the virtue and citizenship women to a moral market. Without the ability to claim "usefulness," all women's activities in the market were suspect and threatened the stability of domestic and national harmony. Although the charity fair was an important arena of economic autonomy for women, it was not a market devoid of men. In fact, men played an essential role as consumers of the goods sold at the fairs, but it was a market in which the traditional roles of male producer and female consumer were reversed.

The charity fair was more than just a market for goods, and fancywork was not the only thing on the display. The presence of young women at the tables selling their work tempted male consumers with the prospect of sanctioned flirtation, which accompanied this kind of sentimental exchange.[4] It was the exchange of sentiments that defined the transactions of the fair. Voluntary labor had invested the fancywork with benevolent sentiments, and the flirtation between producer and consumer was another exchange of sentiments that was considered an essential marketing technique. This calculated marketing helped make benevolence, which was an exchange of abstract sentiments, a commonplace part of market exchange. Good habits of production and consumption for both men and women were important for a "good match." Idle women and unsympathetic men did not make good wives and husbands. The charity fair was an arena in which women could display their abilities in sentimental production and men could demonstrate through appropriate consumption their propensity for sentimental behavior.

Charity fairs were usually sponsored by benevolent organizations that provided aid for the poor. Other charitable organizations were founded specifically to aid gentlewomen in reduced circumstances. One of the first organizations of this kind was the Philadelphia Ladies' Depository, founded in 1832. Elizabeth Stott, a wealthy Philadelphia matron who visited the successful Edinburgh Depository on a trip to Scotland in 1831, established the depository, along with six other women, when she returned to Philadelphia. It provided a place to sell the fancywork and fine sewing of women who unexpectedly found themselves in the position of being responsible for their own support.[5] The depository reserved its support for destitute gentlewomen, arguing that they were a group who had been passed over by other, more traditional forms of benevolence. This altruism was based in part on sympathy and in part on the notion that the financial security of all women was, at best, tenuous. The depository preserved the anonymity of the women who sold needlework in an attempt to obviate the humiliation of more public forms of women's work. The Philadelphia Depository, and the other depositories founded on its model, were their own form of successful enterprise. The women who ran them mobilized the strategies of both charity and business to create a hybrid business that functioned successfully but was animated by charitable intentions.

The success of these enterprises depended on their limited vision of eligible women. By restricting Philadelphia Depository to elite women in reduced circumstances, and locating the depository in the heart of the wealthiest part of Philadelphia, the founders could emphasize the potential reciprocity of the enterprise. Women had a responsibility to create a market for women's production, not just out of an interest in Christian charity, but as a safety net for all women. The vicissitudes of fortune meant that regardless of their current economic status, all women must subscribe to the same kind of market philosophy. The depository was an ambitious enterprise. Its founders used the language of a gift economy to lend legitimacy to the production of the unfortunate women who depended on its market and to justify their own business activities. They recognized that charity was a business, but they also strove to define an alternate culture of business that balanced sentiment and profit.[6] This made it possible for women to participate in business activities that did not appear to transgress even the most conservative images of women's social roles.

Although the wealthy women who founded the Philadelphia Depository were able to reinvest any profits of the society in the enterprise itself, the "voluntary" work of benevolence was, for many women, a paid occupation. Benevolent societies hired women to perform the charitable duties essential to benevolent organizations.[7] These women solicited contributions, distributed leaflets, wrote reports, and helped organize new auxiliaries.[8] Women continued to describe their activities in voluntary terms, and as the natural extension of their domestic roles, even if they received a salary for their efforts. That their work appear voluntary was an essential ingredient to the success of their cause. To admit that they worked for pay would have tainted the spontaneity of benevolence that was the centerpiece of sentimental charity: the business aspects of benevolence could not be visible. The success of these sentimental tactics was particularly apparent in the charity fairs where the fancywork was sold. Like the voluntary labor of the charity agents and the invisible labor of housework, the production of fancywork as a leisure activity was a necessary fiction.[9] Fancywork was an ideal product to sell because its production was so easily represented as leisure.

Fairs were communal gatherings, recruitment drives, and necessary fundraisers.[10] Newspaper reports on fairs provide a wealth of information about fair activities and the objects for sale there. On May 17, 1833, for example, the *Salem Gazette* reprinted an article from the *Boston Evening Transcript* about a charity fair to benefit the School for the Blind.[11] The items for sale on each table were described in detail: Miss Catherine Putnam's table offered manuscript volumes; Mrs. Henry Smith's table had so many fascinating items that only a few were mentioned in the article: "To catalogue them all would be to inflict punishment on the reader, so diverse in kind and so numerous in quantity were the useful and ornamental wares exhibited here." The punishment must have been the pain of merely reading about beautiful objects instead of being able to purchase them. At Miss Thayer's table, "all the articles were of *domestic* manufacture, with the exception of one palmetto basket, being made by the ladies who sold them or their friends, from materials purchased or presented to them." Thrift, as well as usefulness and ornament, was praised because it meant greater profit for the charity.[12]

The most intriguing items for sale at the fair were "secret packages." These little packages, their contents a mystery, were sold on speculation and kept in a large box under lock and key until the end of the fair, when the secret was revealed to those who had purchased them. This practice kept interest in the fair alive. The women who organized the fair for the School for the Blind congratulated themselves on having kept the secret: "It should be mentioned to the honor of the much abused sex, that six women kept the secret six weeks not withstanding every art and cunning device used to extort it from them." Two hundred boxes were sold, generating a profit of $450 from these little packages, which "contained nothing more or less than a pair of *dusters* to wipe away the dust which had been thrown in the eyes of the good people for the last six weeks."[13] Gentlemen were reported to "detest" these secret packages. Another table also had secret packages, for only one dollar, that contained a *Blue Stocking* as the prize for an obliging man's generosity. Gentlemen, especially bachelors, were encouraged to patronize the fair. The Blue Stocking poked a little fun at the real reason bachelors came to fancy fairs. The links between the marriage market and the charity fair were not coincidental, both markets tried to reconcile sentimental impulses and economic necessities.

Sarah Hale addressed the objection to public flirtation at fancy fairs in her essay on "Ladies' Fairs."[14] Detractors of the fairs spoke against the impropriety of such a public display of affection, cautioning that "it encourage[d] vanity in young ladies, and [made] the motive of being seen and admired, the predominating one in their hearts."[15] Hale dismissed this criticism by listing other public events considered acceptable for young women in which the danger of display was equal. In addition to the danger of encouraging vanity, critics worried that "the purchase of a ticket will give to any fellow the freedom of the apartment, and the privilege of gazing on the fair managers."[16] Hale agreed that such insolence would wound the feeling of a delicate lady, but she reminded her readers that this vicious and disagreeable sort of man could also buy a ticket to the opera, and no sensible woman would refuse to go to the opera on those grounds.[17] It was the responsibility of the organizers, Hale insisted, to ensure that the fair was managed discreetly and that young ladies were not put in danger. In her arguments in favor women's participation in fancy fairs, she omitted any discussion of the real difference between the role of spectator and the role of saleswoman. Presiding over a table at a fair invited a different kind of public interaction. As participants in a market transaction, these young women were in public in a very different way. Hale collapsed this distinction because it was the sentimental spectacle of the pretty young woman that promised the greatest return on the charitable speculations of the fair. The exchange of sentiments between the fair manager of a fancy table and the male consumer was essential to the financial success of the fair. Gentlemen, Hale argued, would be more likely to purchase items "presented by a fair hand," and would be moved to "unusual generosity" in their purchase of items that had no intrinsic value for them. Their interest in the cause would be increased by the pleasant circumstances of the exchange and might even "encourage other benevolent plans."[18] What Hale described was an act of sentimental consumption. The value of the object was in the experience of the exchange, in the associations with which it was invested. In a gift economy, exchange is defined by courtesy and kindness; it is an economy of emotional transactions.[19] Flirtation was another manifestation of the reciprocity that the charity fair endorsed. It was sanctioned because it fostered benevolent actions. Charity fairs offered a venue in which women could teach men the practices of moral market behavior. The importance of the act of exchange was accentuated by the sentimental potential of the exchange between the seller and the buyer. Because the fancy fair was part of the marriage market, the investment in charity was also a speculation in love.

Social transactions were as important to the success of the fair as the money they raised. In *Little Women* (1868), Louisa May Alcott poked fun at the social "crises" that could occur at fairs. In a moment of social one-upmanship, Jo's sister Amy is unfairly removed from the art table, which is the hub of the fair, to the flower table, a decidedly unpopular one. She is rescued from social obscurity by the good will of Jo, who sends Laurie and his friends to buy all of Amy's flowers and to make her table the center of attention. Once her own ruffled feathers have been smoothed, Amy sends her admirers over to the art table to buy her rival's wares:

> To May's great delight, Mr. Laurence not only bought both the vases but pervaded the hall with one under each arm. The other gentlemen speculated with equal rashness in all sorts of frail trifles, and wandered helplessly about afterward, burdened with wax flowers, painted fans, filagree portfolios, and other useful and appropriate purchases.[20]

Alcott's arch characterization of the gentlemen's purchases suggests that the male impetus for buying fancywork had not changed much in thirty years.

If it was clear who should purchase items at the charity fair, the question of who should produce the fancywork was a more ticklish one. Critics of charity fairs argued that selling fancywork produced by women who donated their time and effort deprived poor women of employment. This was a dilemma for many benevolent societies that did not like to give alms directly to the poor, preferring instead to raise money to provide services or sponsor employment.[21] Fair organizers rarely included poor women's work in the market of the fair. Hale defended this practice by arguing that this did not rob poor women of their livelihood but increased the overall market for fancy-work by making it fashionable. By encouraging men to buy fancy items, the fairs created a demand for fancy goods that the fairs could not satisfy:

> Whatever is fashionable is soon necessary; and the circumstance, that such arti-
> cles as have been sold at the Ladies' Fairs are now kept at many fancy shops, is
> proof that the ingenious and industrious poor are reaping the benefits of this
> trade in trifles.[22]

Despite Hale's optimistic insistence on the ability of the fancywork market to regulate itself, Hannah Lee, writing a few years after Hale published her essays, included some pointed criticism of the sale of fancywork at fairs in her novel, *Three Experiments in Living* (1837). The wide availability of fancywork at fairs, she argued, reduced demand that previously had been met by women in reduced circumstances, whom the fairs did not support, and, despite their benevolent intentions, wealthy women did not always treat poor women fairly in the wage market.[23] Caroline Dall, Virginia Penny, and Dinah Mulock, all writing at midcentury, also contradicted Hale's prediction. Each of these women argued that when wealthy women worked without pay, it devalued the labor of all women.[24]

The poor to whom Hale referred were the unfortunate counterparts of the women at the tables in the fair. Yet Hale argued that these women should not be allowed to sell their work directly at the fairs because the production of fancywork promoted industry in women of leisure that was essential to their health. In addition, it revived the study of needlework, which had become, Hale feared, a neglected part of women's education. The industry of fancy-work saved leisured women from a dangerous "excess of mental culture" as well as indolence and selfishness.[25] Hale's exclusion of poor women from the economy of the fair revealed the complexity of the problem of defining class through taste, as she often did, because taste alone, without economic means, could not sustain social status.

Although Hale was explicit about the value of the production of fancywork for women, she acknowledged that it had no value to the gentlemen who purchased it. These purchases, however, did have value for society. The experience of buying an item from a beautiful and wealthy woman made a second experience of buying such an item from an impoverished woman more imaginable: "The man who purchases articles at a Ladies' Fair is more likely to bestow charity on the next applicant than he who condemns all such means of obtaining money for charitable purposes is to give at any time."[26] Virtuous consumption was an outward sign of inner virtue. The sentimental education that the charity fair provided men helped channel their benevolent tendencies through appropriate channels. Men who shunned that education revealed themselves to their peers as morally deficient in their habits of consumption, thus raising more general questions about their moral fiber. The charitable efforts of the woman involved in the fair recommended her as a wife, and the benevolent impulses of the man recommended him as a husband.

Confining the transactions of the charity fair itself to exchanges between members of the same class was a central component to Hale's definition of the fair as an alternate economy organized as a gift economy. The purchase of a gift created the possibility for giving the gift of charity at the moment of transaction and in future potential transactions, thus keeping the gift in circulation.[27] Both production and consumption were gifts because neither producer nor consumer engaged in the transaction based on personal need. A charity fair could be organized as a gift economy because the goods exchanged were secondary to the sentiments that governed their exchange: they never became commodities. Although charity was the motivating factor in the organization of the fairs, it was a secondary consideration in the transactions. The gift economy was organized by the relationship between buyer and seller as well as by the gift of charity itself. Within the transactions of the fair, there was the possibility for reciprocity that was not possible in the charitable act. Hale explicitly stated that in order for charity to work, it must "bless those who give and those who take" and the "value of the benefits conferred" had to be balanced.[28] Because no reciprocal gift could be expected, the giver of the charity had to ensure that the reciprocity of the act was built into the initial exchange. The moral value of the charitable sentiments had to offset the pragmatic value of the alms given. Therefore, although Hale did not explicitly say it, poor women could not be allowed to sell their work directly at the fairs because class barriers prevented them from participating in the gift economy of the fair, which in its links to the marriage market depended on the possibilities for reciprocity. The act of charity was one way of defining the boundaries between the participants in that economy.[29]

Although Hale found ways to rationalize what she so aptly called the "trade in trifles," other women questioned the intellectual leap from the "valueless" commodities of the fancy fair to the valuable work of charity. Although Juliana Tappan conceded that some items sold at fancy fairs were useful, she worried about the practice of selling *"useless* articles" to raise money. "There is so much time consumed," she fretted, "and so much consulting of fashion, and conformity to the world that I doubt much whether fairs, *as they are now conducted,* are pleasing to God. How little of *Christ* there is in our actions."[30] Tappan's religious concerns highlight the absence this kind of discussion by Hale, whose primary focus was defining the terms of market exchange at the fair rather than exploring the charitable impulse. Whereas Hale argued that ends justified the means, Tappan worried not just whether that was so but also whether the means changed very nature of the justification itself. Could good motives really make trivial objects of fashion necessary? Or did this justification expose the connections between godliness and worldliness rather than maintain the distance between them?[31]

The criticism of fancy fairs diminished as their success in fund raising became a mainstay of charitable enterprises. The antislavery movement made good use of the charity fair as a fund-raiser on the local level.[32] With the advent of the Civil War, charity fairs became a material outlet for a sentimental patriotism nurtured by the nationalist language of fancywork manuals.[33] Women searched for ways to help alleviate the suffering of soldiers, and for Northern women, the Sanitary Commission, a not-for-profit organization founded to help alleviate the suffering of Union soldiers, helped channel the good intentions of men and women on the home front. Women played a large role in all aspects of its work, especially fund-raising. Despite the horrifying conditions of field hospitals and the lack of supplies, the War Department initially regarded the work of Sanitary Commission, "with some want of sympathy," as inconsequential to the war effort. The commission was viewed as "a sentimental body of persons, really only to be countenanced because, somehow or other, they had managed to get the affections of the people," Reverend Henry Whitney Bellows, president of the Sanitary Commission, noted in a speech in 1863.[34] Despite the lack of support from the War Department, the women and men of the Sanitary Commission knew that without the supplies they sent, and the records they organized, the death toll would have been even more devastating. Although the male administrators often used the lofty sentiments of patriotism to define the commission's mission—calling attention to the "unity of plan, earnestness, patriotism, [and] great humanity of purpose" as well as "a broad and positive *nationality of sentiment and influence*"— they often took an extreme antisentimental stance toward its practical work.[35] Because they insisted on common sense over sympathy as the basis for operations, they were criticized for callous behavior. Male administrators rejected a sentimental approach as an obstacle to, rather than impetus of, efficient benevolence.[36] The female administrators, however, took a more balanced view toward the relationship between efficiency and sympathy, channeling "sentimental" energy into the business of fund raising.

The regional organization of the Sanitary Commission created a national network of benevolence that incorporated existing networks of benevolence. One of the first and most successful efforts of the commission was to coordinate the efforts of women's sewing circles, which produced clothing and bandages for wounded soldiers. Sewing made women's patriotism tangible. "As long as the men fight, the women must knit and sew," Reverend Bellows declared, "and the friends at home must furnish the means to alleviate the sorrows and wants of the camps and hospitals."[37] The Sanitary Commission set up regional offices to collect and distribute the production of local aid societies. Mary Livermore, who played a major role in the Northwestern Sanitary Commission office in Chicago, wrote in her autobiography about the notes that accompanied the shirts, drawers, towels, socks, handkerchiefs, and "comfort bags" sent to the commission for distribution.[38] Almost every item, Livermore remarked, had a note pinned to it. She quoted from the most poignant ones:

> MY DEAR FRIEND,—You are not *my* husband nor son; but you are the husband or son of some woman who undoubtably loves you as I love mine. I have made these garments for you with a heart that aches for your sufferings, and with a longing to come to you to assist in taking care of you.[39]

Many of the letters were from young girls; some were romantic overtures and requested that if the recipient of the socks were married that he exchange with a soldier who was not. These letters echoed the flirtatious practices of fairs before the war, but they also demonstrated the pragmatic ways in which sentimental production linked women on the home front to the war.

Women commented on the importance of sewing to the war effort from a variety of perspectives. In January 1863, Sarah Hale included a "Letter from a Lady of New England" in the Editor's Table of *Godey's Lady's Book* that applauded the productive labor of women's needlework not only for its important role in supplying needy soldiers with clothing and wool socks but also for rejuvenating a generation of young women "whose fingers have been too dainty all their lives to do a useful thing."[40] These young women, the author proudly noted, had not joined the war effort in a casual way. They devoted all their leisure time to productive activity, turning their attention to the "highest contemplations of the human mind" rather than the "petty interests of daily life" that formerly had been the focus of their concern. The profound transformation in the character of these young women made possible by this productive behavior suggested, the author professed, a positive effect of all the suffering caused by the war. "The regeneration of so many young hearts almost pays the price of blood and suffering," she opined.[41] It was not enough, this author argued, for women to support their loved ones; it was their responsibility to provide a moral example that went beyond their roles as loving mothers, sisters, and wives and reclaimed their roles as productive members of society. The rest of the letter predicted that the war would make many widows who would need to find work. The work women performed to support the war would be essential in helping to shape the virtue of the postwar era of domestic life. If "work of all sorts will be necessary and *fashionable*," the return of fashionable women to important productive labor would improve their own characters and the national character as well.

Although the author of this letter rejected fancywork as an important part of this productive labor, the organizers of charity fairs saw matters in a different light. Communities both large and small held fairs to raise money for the soldiers. The enthusiasm for these fairs was substantial, but they were still not able to keep pace with the fund-raising needs of the Sanitary Commission. Mary Livermore and Jane Hoge proposed a regional fair of unprecedented proportions that would, they hoped, unite the entire northwest and raise enough money to revitalize the war effort of the Northwestern Sanitary Commission.[42] A centrally organized fair, as Livermore and Hoge saw it, would make the best use of combined resources and generate more public interest. The Sanitary Fair opened October 27, 1863, to great fanfare: "banks closed, courts adjourned, schools were dismissed."[43] Initially, the idea of a fair had met with some skepticism on the part of the male members of the Sanitary Commission. Livermore recounted the reactions of male members of the commission "who languidly approved our plan, but laughed incredulously at our proposition to raise twenty-five thousand dollars for its treasury."[44] At the end of the fair, Livermore calculated the profit at $80,000, which increased to $100,000 when the remaining goods had been sold.[45] The triumph of the fair, she insisted, was due to the organizational ability of women. It was "pre-eminently an enterprise of women, receiving no assistance from men in its early beginnings. The city of Chicago regarded it with indifference, and the gentlemen members of the Commission barely tolerated it."[46] The networks of benevolence that developed out of these fairs changed the opinions of these skeptics, transforming charitable fund-raising and influencing other forms of business as well.

Although many of the goods donated to the fair were agricultural or products of industry, fancywork was an important part of women's contributions. A few of these pieces of fancywork were memorialized by Livermore. She recalled that the sister of one soldier who had lost his life in the war found a small sum of money in his pockets. She "regarded the money as too sacred to be applied to daily uses" and used it to purchase some wool from which she made an afghan, "memories of him who died dimming her eyes and saddening her heart as she crocheted." She donated the afghan to the fair and told visitors the history of its origin. "It was an article of exquisite beauty," Livermore noted, "and was sold at an early day, for one hundred dollars."[47] Women fair organizers recognized the importance of using sentimental narratives of production to create value for sentimental consumption. Another donation Livermore considered the epitome of sentimental patriotism came from a freed slave. She donated a sheet that she had made, and the story of its manufacture increased its value: "Her touching story, pathetically told, caused a speedy sale of her offering, which brought much more than its actual value."[48]

The total amount of money raised through Sanitary Commission fairs during the course of the war was close to $3 million.[49] Even children participated in the fund-raising fever. Livermore recounted that "during the July and August vacation of 1863, the little folks of Chicago were seized with a veritable sanitary-fair mania" and held their own fairs on the lawns and in the parlors of their homes. At one fair to which Livermore been invited, boys and girls cooperated in the planning and execution:

> A boy of eleven stood at the gate as custodian, gravely exacting and receiving the five cents admission fee. Another chap, of ten, perambulated the sidewalks for a block or two, carrying a banner inscribed, "SANITARY FAIR FOR THE SOLDIERS!" and drumming up customers for his sisters under the trees. "Here's your Sanitary Fair for sick and wounded soldiers!" he shouted, imitating the candy vendor who was licensed to sell his wares from a stand just around the corner. "All kinds of fancy goods, in the newest style, and cheap as dirt, and all for the soldiers! Walk up and buy, ladies and gentlemen, walk up!"[50]

In addition to its recommendation of fancywork patterns for ladies to make for fairs, *Godey's Lady's Book* published fancywork patterns for children to make for fancy fairs.[51] Livermore noted that in two weeks during the summer of 1863, the children's fairs in Chicago had raised almost $300 for the Sanitary Commission, a significant sum by any calculation. These fairs were testimony to children's patriotism, and to the lessons they had already learned about the workings of market culture.

The success of the Northwestern Sanitary Fair galvanized other regional branches of the Sanitary Commission to organize their own fairs. These fairs were also very successful fund raisers, but the success of the Chicago fair contributed to substantial changes in the organizing committees of these other fairs and in the spectacle of the fairs themselves. Women's roles in the New York and Philadelphia fairs, for example, decreased dramatically. Women were appointed to head committees for the Metropolitan Fair, as the New York fair was called, but they were not allowed to participate in any of the business matters of the fair, which were to be conducted by men only. Nor were they allowed to be present on the platform at the inaugural proceedings, an omission that caused much unhappiness. Despite their self-professed expertise in matters of business, the male organizers had little experience in the practical matters of organizing and running a charity fair. They refused to take the advice of their more experienced female counterparts, and this created significant obstacles to the success of the fair. The nature of the fair also changed. The New York fair was not be a fancy fair writ large but a new kind of theatrical spectacle that catered to the city's elite and explicitly represented their world view. Admission prices were high, as much as two dollars to see all the exhibits, and the price of admission alone was raised to one dollar. This limited the number of people who were able to attend the fair, although not enough to alleviate the serious overcrowding. The admission fees raised protests about the elitist intentions of the fair's organizers.[52] Although the fair had been reinvented as a new kind of spectacle, the organizers wanted to maintain as much of the closed economy of the earlier charity fairs as they could.

The Philadelphia fair followed the same model of the Metropolitan Fair, which had been an enormous financial success, despite many insinuations about rampant graft. But when men took over the business of the fair, many prominent women refused to participate. The Philadelphia fair was also organized as an event for elites, but the contributions of poor needlewomen were highlighted as a symbolic example of the fair's universal appeal. "At the Great Central Fair held in Philadelphia in 1864, for example, the bookmarkers, Berlin work and bead work on sale had been made and contributed not only by the wealthy, but also by "poor needle-women, who have found spare moments to throw in their mite to the success of our Soldier Brothers," the fair catalog proclaimed.[53] Although the male organizers did not feel they needed the help of their female peers to run the fair, they understood that women's virtuous production lent legitimacy to the profits of the fair.

In spite of the struggles over fair administration, the involvement of women in the Sanitary Commission and other charitable organizations changed many male opinions about women's business aptitude.[54] The language of benevolence itself took on a more businesslike cadence, emphasizing the parity between business and benevolence that reformers had carefully masked before the Civil War. The war created a national network of charitable organizations and sewing circles. This encouraged a coordinated effort so that small sewing circles would not duplicate the efforts of others, creating, for example, a surplus of socks when shirts or scarves were needed.[55] The charity fairs held during the war brought about a dual revolution in fancywork production. They legitimized women's sentimental business activities, but by the end of the war, the enthusiasm for them had worn thin. Disenchantment with the fairs, however, was balanced by an increase in the number of women who hoped to augment their incomes with fancywork production. In an attempt to generate a fashion for novelty, women embraced fads, such as rustic work, which caused a reaction against fancywork rather than a new fashion for it.

The Decorative Arts movement of the Gilded Age scorned the production of fancywork. Women's exchanges refused to accept objects made out of hair, feathers, wax, cardboard, rice, and other plebeian materials.[56] This kind of production was no longer considered worthy of a woman's time; more important, there was no longer a market for it.[57] Despite their dismissal of these unfashionable forms of women's work, the organizers of the women's exchanges and craft cooperatives owed a debt to the charity fairs of their youth.[58] Just as the Sanitary Commission had pulled the disparate charity organizations together into a network of benevolence, sloughing off the language of sentiment in favor of the efficiency of business, the Gilded Age organizations insisted on a new aesthetics of production.

Embroidery was advanced as a form of work that was authentic and beautiful as well as resistant to the commercialism to which other kinds of fancywork had succumbed. Male Pre-Raphaelite artists such as William Morris, Walter Crane, and Edward Burne-Jones designed patterns for embroidery based on natural forms that emphasized their beauty rather than their transformation into whimsy. The participation of male designers in the field changed the definitions of value; what distinguished this new kind of production was its overt market value, the fact that it was "real work," not fancy work.[59] Candace Wheeler, and the other women who organized and supported women's exchanges, expressed a dual purpose in promoting the minor arts and creating a market for the production of gentlewomen in reduced circumstances. Wheeler, who attributed her interest in needlework to the exhibits at the 1876 Centennial Exhibition, remarked that she was particularly struck by the potential for profit that the embroidery suggested: "In those early days I found myself constantly devising ways of help in individual dilemmas, the disposing of small pictures, embroidery, and handwork of various sorts for the benefit of friends or friends of friends who were cramped by untoward circumstances."[60] Wheeler envisioned a way to create a reliable market for women's needlework by adopting a language of art, craft, and history that made the work of fancywork visible again and replaced the language of fancy, whimsy, and trifles that had masked its production before the war.

These two images of needlework, the elegant lady in her boudoir and the destitute gentlewoman huddled over her work, appeared in discussions of fancywork throughout the nineteenth century. What these two poles hid was the prosaic reality of the fancywork business that was visible in Virginia Penny's interviews with fancy workers and Mary Livermore's pragmatic discussions of the production of fancywork for charity fairs. Wheeler and her contemporaries appropriated the discussion of fancywork and reshaped it in aesthetic terms, but the women's market of the charity fair was easily transformed into the women's exchange, and the sentimental enterprise of the charity fair became the nonprofit enterprises of the exchanges.[61] The networks of production and consumption initiated by the charity fair and refined by the Sanitary Commission continued to foster the business of women's needlework. The difficulties, however, remained the same. The aesthetic alliance with the Pre-Raphaelites did not change the fact that the only capital most women had was cultural.

By the 1890s, in Lucy Salmon's opinion, the networks of a women's economy had become a hindrance rather than an asset. Salmon, a historian at Vassar College in the late nineteenth century, objected to the continuing rhetoric of charity that characterized the women's exchange, insisting that it diminished rather than augmented its ability to help needy women because it ignored the rational imperative of competition necessary for successful business. By advocating a network of women producers and consumers and a cooperative work aesthetic, the women's exchanges, Salmon complained, did more to arrest the success of women's enterprise than to aid it because it defined women's work according to different market standards.[62] The networks of women's businesses that had made the charity fairs so successful had changed the market. Women in the late nineteenth century no longer needed the sentimental market strategies of their mothers and grandmothers. Charity fairs, like the benevolent associations they helped support, had changed the social fabric of the economy.

Eight

Roses Are Read

The Symbolic Economy of Valentine's Day

I rejoice that Cards, which used to be reckoned the Bane of Mankind, are now become a thing of real Utility, as the Vehicles of Compliment, Message, and Direction; printed Cards, with proper Blanks, adapted to most Occurrences, Enquiries, and Answers in polite Circles; Condolences in Sickness, Congratulations on Health, Arrival in Town, Marriages and Divorces, Dining, Tea-drinking, Dancing or Rout Invitations; Hopes, Fears, Wishes and even Challenges, with suitable Answers, may be had *ready cut and dried,* by the Dozen; an Invention which saves much Labour in Composition and much Time in Scribbling; obviates bad Spelling; offers legible characters to the Eye, and Intelligible Phrases to the Understanding. . . . By this easy Method, a Courtship, which now blots whole Rheams of Paper, and is spun out through two or three long tedious Years, might be reduced (by the Omission of all Super fluities, and coming to the Point,) to about a Dozen Cards on each Side, and concluded in a Dozen Hours.

—Edward Long, *Sentimental Exhibition; or, Portraits and Sketches of the Times,* 1774

*T*he sarcastic optimism of this eighteenth-century pundit anticipated, by 200 years, the stranglehold on emotional expression that the modern greeting-card industry has on the important business of love. Today a card congratulating a friend on her recent divorce sits in a slot next to a tender plea to confront a drug problem and enter a rehabilitation facility. There are greeting cards for every emotional permutation; no one need be at a loss for words. In some circles, it is even considered an insult to send a handmade card, as if it were evidence that the sender did not care enough to spend money. But for the diehard sentimentalist, the industry has recently introduced kits and computer programs for making cards that satisfy "old-fashioned" impulses to produce a labor of love, with the reassurance that the final product will *look* like a greeting card. Greeting-card companies also reissue historical cards, designed to conjure up the golden age of the nineteenth century. Popular wisdom attributes the origin of greeting-card holidays to the marketing departments of greeting-card companies, and in many cases this is true. Valentine's Day, however, was not invented by the greeting-card industry; on the contrary, the transformation of the valentine from a ritual exchange of self to a written form of affection contributed to the development of the greeting-card industry.[1]

The symbolic economy of Valentine's Day offers a way to examine the struggles over the relationship between property and propriety that preoccupied the emerging middle class at midcentury. The shift from learning to love someone from within the marriage relation to love as a precondition for marriage crystallized not only anxieties about patriarchal authority but also the new relationship between property and propriety that marriage entailed. The debates about married women's property rights suggest that in addition to the reevaluation of the emotional relationships of marriage, the economic relationships were changing as well.[2] The individualism of feeling and choice that the conventions of romantic love proposed challenged paternal control over courtship. The role of individualism in romantic love and its reshaping of courtship bore important similarities to the role of individualism in the market.[3] In both arenas, middle-class parents and children were anxious about the promises and pitfalls of individualism. The celebration of Valentine's Day provided an arena for the investigation of the role of individualism in the marriage market—and, by symbolic extension, in the market as a whole. This gave Valentine's Day its symbolic charge. As an economy of symbols, valentines functioned as symbols of love and the complex relationship between gift and commodity in the exchanges of the marriage market. The celebration of Valentine's Day was symbolic of the interactions of the market as a whole, and the transactions of the marriage market were symbolic of the transactions of the larger market culture.

Marriage was necessarily bound up with class interests. Love, like capitalism, had the ability to blur lines of social distinction.[4] Middle-class ideas about how to behave in the market had inevitable reflections in the marriage market, and the language of romantic love mirrored the individualism of market behavior. The freedom of love to circulate was directly tied to the freedom of capital to circulate.[5] And therein lay some of its attraction and danger. Freedom to choose a mate based on individual love was not unlike freedom of commerce, with the attendant potential treacheries of business partnerships. The danger of doing business with someone unreliable was not unlike the danger of marrying someone unreliable, especially in terms of the loss of capital. Both middle-class and upper-class marriages were intended to combine and conserve capital, but middle-class parents tried to soften this stark economic reality by insisting that money alone was not the basis for a happy union. In order to create a happy home, bride and groom must also be morally and spiritually compatible, their love based on emotional rather than physical passion. Despite these stereotypical niceties, the middle class faced the tricky problem of the financial underpinnings of their domestic ideals. The most vexing question was how to make romantic love consistent with its imperatives of financial stability and domestic happiness. In other words, how to tame the dangerous possibilities of both passion and capitalism. The new manufactured valentine was a symbol of both; its role in the economy of the marriage market was necessarily complicated, holding out both possibility and threat by exposing the links between economic value and sentimental value.

The history of Valentine's Day stretches back to medieval times and beyond, but at the end of the eighteenth century there was an important shift in the celebration of the holiday. In earlier times, the celebration of Valentine's

Day hinged on the choosing of a valentine, often by lot or chance. Although tokens of love were commonly exchanged, the title "valentine" belonged to the person rather than the gift. By the end of the eighteenth century, the valentine had become a written token of affection, transforming not just its semantic definition but also the nature of its exchange, introducing the possibility of the anonymous valentine. By the nineteenth century, Valentine's Day was celebrated primarily in Britain and the United States. In France, legal struggles over the celebration of Valentine's Day led to reduced observation of the holiday. In the French tradition of celebration, once the valentines had been chosen, the woman prepared a meal for the man, and together they attended a public dance. If the man was not pleased with his valentine, he would abandon her and she would then remain in seclusion for eight days. At the end of this time all the women who had been spurned gathered in the town square and burned their valentines in effigy. This ritual frequently escalated into riots, and in 1776, the French Parliament outlawed this practice, beginning the crusade to repress the celebration of Valentine's Day. By 1806, in Metz, anyone who persisted in celebrating the holiday was issued a warning, and by 1816, the police in Metz had successfully curbed observance of the holiday.[6]

Happier versions of the history of Valentine's Day fascinated nineteenth-century celebrants. In the 1850s, valentine stories often contained a nutshell history of Valentine's Day; these were frequently augmented by more detailed histories that appeared in women's magazines every few years.[7] It was not the connection to the Roman feast of Lupercalia, or the martyrdom of Saint Valentine, however, that caught the imagination of a nineteenth-century aficionado. The folk customs of the middle ages, and the genteel celebrations of the seventeenth and eighteenth centuries, seemed to offer an authentic noncommercial celebration.[8] In England, *Godey's* reported in 1854, children went *valentining* from house to house, singing rhymes and collecting favors, not unlike the celebration of Halloween. Another article revived several elaborate rituals to be performed on the night before Valentine's Day to produce dreams of a sweetheart as an augur of impending nuptials.[9] *Godey's* and *Peterson's* published directions for valentine parlor games that drew their inspiration from these older traditions.[10]

The discussion of Valentine's Day in Samuel Pepys's diary was the centerpiece of these valentine histories.[11] In 1851, *Peterson's* culled excerpts from Pepys's discussion of Valentine's Day that were included, verbatim, in subsequent histories of the holiday in both *Peterson's* and *Godey's* for the next twenty-five years. The diary contains a running commentary on the Valentine's Day activities of Pepys and his wife throughout the 1660s. In Pepys's time, the activities of Valentine's Day were not confined to single people. Married people often had valentines who were not their husbands or wives. Nineteenth-century merchants tried to encourage the expansion of the holiday along these lines, providing valentines for every possible relationship and even attempting to extend Valentine's Day into a shopping season rather than a single day.[12] In Pepys's time, the choice of a valentine was based on affection rather than the obligations of betrothal. The traditional gifts were gloves, garters, and sometimes jewelry. Pepys devoted most of his discussion of Valentine's Day to the gifts he was obliged to purchase for his valentines and those that were sent to his wife. He spent considerable energy grumbling about the cost.[13]

Nineteenth-century histories of the holiday emphasized the mutual obligations of the valentine relationship. Although Pepys's discussions of his celebration of the holiday seem lighthearted, nineteenth-century celebrants liked the contractual nature of these old-fashioned customs because the obligations between valentines seemed clearly understood. They offered an appealing contrast to the promiscuous circulation of valentines in contemporary practice. As the conventions of romantic love became more widely observed in the nineteenth century, these histories tied these new celebrations to the past through images of lovers in eighteenth-century costume and nostalgia for the elegance of aristocratic traditions and the simplicity of folk customs, collapsing all the celebrations of "simpler" times into a single nostalgic anachronism. This imaginary history was a foil for contemporary social criticism. It appropriated an imagined aristocratic tradition for an aspiring genteel audience but tempered it with folk simplicity to appeal to a republican sense of virtue. Although this nostalgia implied a narrative of emulation, the invented history and the theme of decline that ran through most of these histories allowed this new audience to reinvent a particular kind of past that distinguished the crassness of modern manners from natural gentility:

> Valentine's Day in the nineteenth century—the sober, intellectual, satirical, nineteenth century—is a very different affair. "These are the days of advance." In our onward march of civilization we have trampled the Maypole under our feet, dethroned its pretty queen, and turned Cupid out of doors.[14]

Mary Moore, the author of this conservative lament, continued by chastising "strong-minded young ladies" for sneering at valentines and considering them "senseless things." At this rate, she predicted, "youth itself will soon be as much out of fashion as the rest." Despite every attempt to simple pleasures of the holiday, Moore noted with satisfaction,

> Valentine's day, although the mere ghost of its former self, still continues to have its old "match-making" propensities; truth still lurks in those annual rhymes, and many a proposal those love lines have contained has ended in smiles and blushes, wedding favors and bride-cake at Whitsuntide.[15]

In the final analysis, modern manners were not capable of stemming the tide of anything as powerful as love. Although the nostalgia generated by these histories inspired many unfavorable comparisons between the sincerity of older modes of celebration and the new commercial ones, these critics did not advocate a return to the old forms of celebration, but employed this nostalgic view of the past in the service of contemporary concerns. The sentimental histories of Valentine's Day in ladies' magazines used nostalgia to draw the line between the valentine as gift and as commodity as much as they lamented the loss of the "genuine" customs of the past that had been abandoned in the enthusiasm for the elaborate manufactured valentines that became the fashion in the 1840s.[16] These histories also served as a gentle but pointed rebuke of celebrants who gave into the excesses of consumption that the manufactured valentines made possible, insisting instead on restraint. With valentines, as with other genres of sentimental consumption, the celebrant tried to identify a certain kind of sentimental consumption that was simple and elegant and possessed a moral market sensibility. As the market for valentines widened, the editors of *Godey's* and *Peterson's* presented themselves as cultural arbiters, asserting an interpretation of the holiday that distinguished appropriate celebration from the appearance of pure commercialism by marking some forms of celebration beyond the dictates of propriety. In courtship, the silent markers of class status were very important.

These accounts of the history of love seem to counter the conventional twentieth-century nostalgia that the nineteenth century was the era of romantic love and pure untainted sentiments. Romantic love thrives on an antimodern sensibility that locates authenticity in the past. Romanticism is fundamentally nostalgic, fueled by continual daydreams about past experience, real or imagined, and the possibility of future repetition.[17] By creating a narrative of redemption, nostalgia becomes one of the most powerful forces for encouraging consumption. A nostalgic view suggests that "appropriate" participation is not governed by the market but by a "higher" sense of taste and moral judgment. The valentine seemed to be a vehicle through which authenticity could be captured, making the act of consumption of a particular kind of card an indicator of taste and authenticity.

The nostalgia for sentiment was not limited to the discussion of Valentine's Day. In an essay titled "Hints for an Essay on Presents" (1845), an anonymous author condemned the corruption of gift giving that had turned a present into something defined by its monetary value:

> In such an age—an age at once ostentatious, haughty and keenly analytical, *presents,* as we were saying, have almost lost their sweet meaning, and become a meaner sort of merchandize—a vile variety of the bribe kind—the most cutting form of dismissal—the most humiliating trick of unresentable insult—in short any thing but what in truth and nature they should be—the spontaneous offering of heart to heart, owing all value to sentiment.[18]

The author complained about the expectation of reciprocity, which in gift giving was a long-term relationship. The insistence on immediate acknowledgment of the gift disrupted the appearance of spontaneity that hid the obligation.[19]

By making his argument historical, and claiming a trajectory of decline, the author gave an authority to his ideas that hid the contemporary tone of his debate. The narrative of decline that he traced was imaginary, a fable of market culture. The real crux of the matter was not the problems with fashionable gift but the overall disappearance of sentiment. "The essence of presents consists, as we have said, in the sentiment of the thing," he complained, "and as all sentiment is out of date, it is not wonderful that presents have become obsolete."[20] His essay was not about the disappearance of presents but the problem of distinguishing presents from commodities.[21] The rhythms of nonmarket life had been transformed by the calculations of market exchange. Conservatives, alarmed by this change, hoped to use sentiment to draw the line between the market and the home.[22] When "properly used," sentiment could remove a commodity from the market and make it into a gift. Without sentiment, all exchange was calculating. The investment of sentiment in goods that the eighteenth-century vogue produced, had become, by 1845, the basis of middle-class market knowledge. But as the number of prosperous men and women grew, it became increasingly difficult to insist on this distinction as consumers embraced commercially produced sentiments in a growing number of forms.

Cupid's Manufactory

Before the late 1840s, British imports dominated the valentine market in the United States. The selection of valentines grew as American manufacturers began to compete with imported valentines, but British imports remained popular and often served as models for American valentine manufacturers.[23] New printing and paper-making technology and the introduction of the penny post made valentines inexpensive to buy and send.[24] In 1848, Thomas W. Strong's Great Depot of Valentines beckoned customers with an advertisement that showed a crowd admiring the window of the store:

> Oh, Ho! St. Valentine's Day! VALENTINES! VALENTINES!—All varieties of Valentines, imported and domestic, sentimental humorous, witty, comic, serious, local and national, got up in the most superb style on lace paper and gold without regard to expense . . . varying from six cents to ten dollars.[25]

Nineteenth-century valentine enthusiasts were torn between the sentimental appeal of a handmade valentine with an original poem and the luscious detail of a manufactured valentine, covered in paper lace and gilt trimmings. These manufactured valentines were loosely based on the handmade valentines. By the end of the eighteenth-century, valentines were often puzzles in the form of love knots, rebuses, acrostics, and riddles. Some were easy; an acrostic, for example, could be easily interpreted by reading the first letter of every line vertically. This usually revealed the name of the recipient of the valentine and was testimony to the cleverness of the sender. Endless love knots were also easy to decode. The best ones featured a text with no discernable beginning or end, emphasizing the perpetuity of true love. Manufactured valentines replaced the intricacies of cutwork valentines with lace paper, silk hearts, mirrors, and printed images of flowers, cupids, and other valentine iconography. Some of these had little messages or daguerreotypes hidden in envelopes or elaborately cut spiral paper, cobweb valentines, which when lifted by a string in the middle revealed another image or message beneath the original one.[26] The pleasures of decoding that these valentines offered contributed to the lighthearted nature of the holiday's celebration.

The transformation to the written valentine at the end of the eighteenth century also produced valentine writers: leaflets or small books that contained poems—"Humorous, Satirical, Tender, Sentimental, Pathetic, Elegant, Fashionable and Amusing"—that could be copied onto valentines.[27] The majority of the valentine writers were directed at trades, with specific poems for different trades that made jokes or puns about the relationship between love and work. Valentine writers were also intended as books of humor to be read: "This Collection which is entirely New, is humbly offered to the Public; and if it serves to pass away an innocent Hour, is all that is aimed at."[28] Often two answers, a positive and a negative, were offered. The poems ranged from lighthearted to cruel, from sentimental to sexual. Many of the poems in the early valentine writers were bawdy:

To a Lady with a Nutmeg Grater (1784)
Perhaps you'll think this present queer

Yet it a meaning has my dear
*   For as you deal in things so nice*
This little thing may grate your spice;
*   And quickly, if you but command,*
My nutmegs shall be in your hand;
*   If nature's grater you'll employ*
'Twill give a taste that cannot cloy
*   Then to my wishes now incline*
Upon the day of Valentine.[29]

Mid-nineteenth-century valentine writers included fewer of these bawdy poems. Jokes about the relationship between love and money superseded those about love and sex.

Eighteenth-century valentine writers offered no instructions for their use. By the mid-nineteenth century, however, valentine writers often began with a preface or introduction that instructed the reader how to conform to the conventions of the sincere valentine. *A Collection of New and Original Valentines—Serious & Satirical, Sublime and & Ridiculous* (1857), for example, contained an "Introductory Treatise on the Composition of a Valentine by a Master of Hearts."[30] The book lamented the tired and stale nature of valentine poems available in other collections. Anyone who wanted to send a valentine, had to "fall back on the above mentioned perennials, or else make use of those senseless lace-paper gew-gaws, which are a degree worse still," the author complained.[31] Individuality had become important in the expression of love, but composing a poem was difficult. The writer created a niche for his book in a competitive market by offering originality for sale. "Whether you would soften the hard heart, or give a hard hit at the soft skull, it must be obvious that nothing can be so telling or so pungent as an immediate emanation from your own heart, or a direct inspiration of your own brain," he admitted, but he conceded that he would happily see his reader cast the book aside, as long as it had been "duly bought and paid for," if his pleas for originality had induced that lover "to rely upon [his] own resources rather than those of the fancy-paper maker, or the coarse caricaturist."[32] These instructions demon-

strate the attempts at reform that characterized the nineteenth-century celebration of the holiday but also suggest the ways in which the business of love
was not all seriousness: humor remained an essential part of the celebration.
But whether a valentine was composed in rapture or with a rapier wit, in order
to conform to the nineteenth-century ideal, it had to be produced by the
sender rather than consumed by him.

In 1850, Benjamin Hager of Bainsville, Ohio, sent a valentine to Harriet
Mackall that was a true emanation from his heart. Although the valentine was
manufactured one, a delicate sheet of embossed paper with a few ornamental scraps, Hager did not rely a printed sentiment to convey his feelings. Nor
did Hager did not trust the penny postman with this valuable missive; the
front of the valentine is inscribed "Presented to Harriet by B. J. H." Inside there
are two poems, "Woman's Love" and "The Love that Lasts," in Hager's handwriting. The last verse of "The Love that Lasts" reads:

> *Dear Harriet such is my love for you,*
> *   It is the kind that never dies,*
> *Which fades not as the morning dew*
> *   But* lives *and* blooms *in paradise.*[33]

Hager did not allow the valentine manufacturer to chose his sentiment for
him or hide behind the coy conventions of the anonymous valentine. The
poems, which extol the purity of love, also champion the domestic ideal.[34] The
ideal valentine of the midcentury middle class both conformed to certain sentimental visual and literary tropes and demonstrated the ways in which the
middle class had invented a form of romantic love that supported the domestic ideal of marriage based on a foundation of religious sentiments. The spiritual language of love also distanced the valentine from the bawdy imagery of
the eighteenth century. The language of emanation and inspiration tied the
expression of love to other forms of evangelical religious fervor. The spontaneity of romantic love was reminiscent of the spontaneity of religious
rebirth. Sentimental love poetry relied heavily on religious images and sentiments consistent with the evangelical Protestant revivalism that swept the

Figure 7. Valentine presented to Harriet Mackall by Benjamin Hager, Norcross Historical Greeting Card Collection, courtesy of the Smithsonian Institution, 1850.

nation. Just as ministers such as Charles Grandison Finney struggled to articulate a powerful religious vision that was consonant with the simultaneous market revolution, disciples of romantic love searched for a basis for familial harmony that also reconciled individual desires, physical and moral, with domestic well-being. The assertion of a vision of romantic love that balanced these imperatives was, among other things, and act of class distinction that, in the case of valentines, tied sincere celebration to moral sentiments.

Like so many of the sentimental rules espoused by the middle class, however, the convention of the sincere valentine was easy to circumvent. The marginalia in one valentine writer suggests one such story.[35] Two of the poems in the volume are marked with the names of two women, Caroline Crawford, in pencil, and Miss Angelia Miller, in pen, both in the same hand. The first poem reads:

> *Lady! these are flowers for thee*
> > *Friendship's hand shall wreathe them*
> *Lady! these are songs for thee*
> > *Memory shall breathe them.*

This poem, which offers friendship rather than love, might be construed as platonic and could be sent to two different women without overstepping the convention of a sincere valentine. The second poem, however, is more explicit in its declaration of love:

> *Doubt not—believe each word you see,*
> > *And treasure up each sacred line,—*
> *Deep from my heart they come to thee,*
> > *Then oh! be thou my Valentine.*

This poem employs a common device of valentine-writer poetry, which was to include a phrase or implication that the poem came straight from the lover's heart in order to mask its generic nature. In addition, the language of emanation served the sender well, implying a spontaneity of feeling. The writer of the marginalia, however, chose to send this poem to two separate women. Even if he did so on two separate occasions, the language of the poem implies that the depth of the love described is irreplaceable. The act of using the same poem to make a declaration to two separate women embodies the greatest (sentimental) fear about the valentine: that it was "manufactured" and the recipient's heart was being trifled with by the sender. The marginalia seems to support the fear that the valentine was a trifle, reusable and interchangeable, not the unique language of communication from one heart to another.

Valentine makers responded to fears about individuality and authenticity by supplying alternate verses that could "personalize" a manufactured valentine. Some manufacturers employed calligraphers to hand write the sentiments so that they would conform to the aesthetics of individual production. The aesthetics of hand production made valentines, especially in the early years of the "Valentine Epidemic," well suited to small-scale production. Stationers who imported valentines, often produced at least some of their own. The imported valentines in her father's store inspired Esther Howland, the daughter of a Worcester, Massachusetts, stationer, to try her hand at making them.[36] By 1850, Esther was well established; her first advertisement, in the *Worcester Daily Spy*, February 5, announced, "Valentines. Persons wishing to select from the best assortment in the City are invited to call on S. A. Howland, 143 Main Street."[37] At the height of her business success, Howland shipped valentines as far as California, and the value of the valentines sold was estimated between $50,000 and $75,000 a year, gross.[38] She superintended all aspects of her business including traveling to New York and Boston on business.[39] Howland's sentimental enterprise, the New England Valentine Company, remained part of the family business. She did not become sole proprietor until 1876.[40] Her father fell ill around the same time, perhaps the reason for the transfer of ownership. Increasingly, Esther devoted her time to caring for him, and she mortgaged the business heavily to help pay for his care.

In a 1901 interview in the *Boston Globe*, Howland discussed her enterprise.[41] She presented her role as more maternal than managerial, casting the business as the logical extension of her household duties and community responsibilities. She hired girls from families she knew, and several of them,

Figure 8. Valentine from the New England Valentine Company, Norcross
Historical Greeting Card Collection, courtesy of the Smithsonian Institution.

impoverished by their fathers' bankruptcies, lived with the Howlands until they married.[42] The structure of her business resembled the ordinary daily activities of women, as if it were the logical extension of women gathered to do fancywork, which helped deflect attention away from the profit motive and the labor. Because the women she hired were "friends" of the family, she provided a comfortable and pleasant work environment, well lighted and not overly taxing. To hire workers from families whom she knew also helped erase the difference between Howland and the women who labored for her. Howland's negotiations within the confines of her family business bear some important similarities to the negotiations of courtship, another kind of family business. Her enterprise mirrored the tensions in the marriage market between property and propriety in ways that suggest the centrality of these conflicts to middle-class market culture and the usefulness of examining the production and consumption of valentines as a symbolic economy.

As the profitability of the valentine business grew, competition from other valentine manufacturers eroded Howland's business, and her sentimental model could not compete with increased mechanization of production. Her interview in the *Boston Globe* is of particular interest because it is a response to a more general discussion in the press at the turn of the twentieth century about the commercial tendencies and possibilities of holidays.[43] The interview was prompted by more than just an interest in her as a local personality. Her history provided an authentic history for Valentine's Day, playing on the same kind of nostalgia that the magazine histories of the holiday had fifty years earlier.

In 1879, Howland sold her heavily mortgaged business to George Whitney, her biggest competitor. Whitney also started his valentine business with help from his family. When he returned to Worcester after fighting in the Civil War, he went to work for his brother Edward, who was already established in the stationery business. Edward had also been involved in manufacturing valentines with their older brother Sumner, who had died in 1861. His widow, Lura Clark Whitney, had continued the valentine business from her home after her husband's death.[44] In 1869, Edward ended his partnership with George and established his own wholesale paper business, located next door to George's fancy goods and valentine business. They maintained a close business relationship throughout the rest of their lives. As George Whitney's valentine business grew, he bought out other valentine manufacturers, even large New York firms such as Berlin and Jones. By the time he bought out Esther Howland in June 1879, he was well established as a leader in the valentine industry.[45] Whitney built the largest valentine factory in the world, and by 1883, he had additional offices in both New York and Chicago. Unlike Howland, he was able to successfully make the transformation from family enterprise to manufacturing concern.

In Britain, where valentine manufacture had became a large-scale business concern much earlier, the "Great Valentine Economy" inspired humorous articles about valentine production in *All the Year Round,* a magazine edited by Charles Dickens. In "Cupid's Manufactory" (1864), the narrator, curious about the origin of the "pictorial rash" that breaks out in stationers and book sellers to woo an "affectionate public" each year, pays a visit to the premises of Cupid and Company, located at Thirty-five Love Lane, a mysterious address that is not available through the post office directory. The essay humorously highlighted the disjunction between the romantic expectations of the author and the drab reality of the business world.[46] The narrator expects to find the building decorated as if it were a valentine; instead, he finds the most ordinary of manufacturing concerns: "Neither the red rose, nor the blue violet, nor the sweet carnation, embowers the windows; these being wholly unadorned, rather dingy, and provided each with a wire blind, on which are painted, in the severest prose, the words 'Cupid and Co., Manufacturers.'"[47] After waiting in Cupid's counting house, the narrator is at length introduced to Cupid himself. He is struck by Cupid's appearance:

> It had never occurred to me to picture the God of Love, even in his manufacturing capacity, otherwise than in a full set suit of wings and with a bow and arrow. . . . I had thought of Cupid as he appears on high days and holidays. But here he was "in business." No doubt the wings were carefully doubled down under the broadcloth, and the bow and arrow were probably hung up in the best bedroom with the pink fleshings, ready for Sunday.[48]

Humorous descriptions of Cupid's manufacturing capacity were the natural counterpart to the laments over the decline of authenticity.

The remainder of the article describes the valentine manufacturing process in detail. The heavy work of die stamping is done by men, whereas "twenty neat-handed nymphs" are hard at work coloring the lithographs. Once the valentines have been assembled, they are sent before six "nymphs" who are the "committee of taste." The narrator comments favorably on the working conditions. The workers seem cheerful, healthy, and strikingly pretty; the rooms are light and well ventilated. In short, Cupid's manufactory offered appealing contrast to the "the languor and weariness which are painfully apparent in the work rooms of the milliner and dressmaker." In his endorsement of the favorable working conditions, the author commented that "if the Song of the Valentine were written, it would form a happy contrast to the Song of the Shirt."[49] Valentines produced in sweatshop conditions would have upset the fragile truce reached in middle-class market culture between the aesthetics production and the aesthetics of consumption; the conventions used to describe the workers create a sentimental work atmosphere, much as Esther Howland's description of her enterprise mobilized the sentimental conventions to mask labor, and as Godey and Hale's sentimental business language had set the terms for *Godey's Lady's Book.*

A similar tone is evident in a second description of valentine workers in an article written in 1874. This article also described the workers in as "crowds of happy-looking girls working at their delicate trade." They seemed to be interested and amused by their work, "contented and well-to-do young women, nicely dressed and nicely mannered." Echoing the earlier article, the author of this article reaffirmed the appropriate relationship between the production of valentines and their consumption: "We fancy they could scarcely be otherwise than contented and well-to-do under the kind and genial management of that famous house."[50] This almost makes it sound as if they are receiving the valentines instead of making them, as if their work were a leisure activity rather than a means of livelihood.

Even the poet laureate of love, in Cupid's employ, was a creature of the market, but his appearance fulfills the narrator's romantic expectations: "He had raven ringlets, wore a cloak with a velvet collar, and had a fine phrensy in his eye." After quoting from some of the poet's verses, the narrator remarks, "If it be alleged that the poet-laureate of Love is somewhat halt, it must be remembered that Love himself is blind." The poetry, he reminds us, is worth two pence a line, "but the great difficulty in dealing with the valentine poet is to make him comprehend that brevity is not only the soul of wit, but also the essence of economy."[51] The poet never hesitates to spin his poems out to twelve lines to make an even shilling. The poet is not the only one pocketing a tidy sum; despite the "hard practical nature" of the nineteenth century, Cupid's business increased yearly.[52] The narrator ends on a philosophical note: "The iron of our age has not entered the national soul so deeply, after all."[53] The humor of this pieces hinged on the unmasking of the relationship between the sentiment and profit. Pointed reference is made to the methods of maximizing profit, from Cupid's businesslike demeanor to the financial calculations of the poet. Although these sly remarks point out the seeming contradictions of sentiment and profit, they retain the fiction of workers as pretty, well-to-do nymphs. No one purchasing a valentine wanted to see the shadowy image of a consumptive factory operative peering out from behind Cupid's shoulder.

Love in a Bank Note World

In 1845, *Niles' National Register* remarked on the popularity of Valentine's Day and its effect on postal delivery. "Between twenty and twenty-five thousand of these missiles of the wicked little blind deity, were deposited in the New York post office on the 14th," it reported. With the addition of more than "two hundred extra penny posts for the day, some fifteen thousand of them were delivered."[54] The enthusiastic celebration of the holiday far surpassed the ability of the infrastructure to support it. Mary Moore, writing in 1861, poked gentle fun at the excess encouraged by the introduction of the penny post in the 1840s:

> Postmen were known to have fainted beneath the weight of Cupids, doves, Hymen's temples, and gold rings their bursting bags contained. One misanthropic man of letters committed suicide on Valentine's eve by throwing himself, bag and all into the river . . . leaving a note on the bank stating his reasons for the act:

hatred to marriage, and a desire to save his fellow creatures from that misery, as *the wooer on the fourteenth of February was generally a fool by the first of April.*[55]

This "perfect inundation of sentiment" had, according to *Godey's*, spoiled the celebration of the holiday, allowing rampant commercialism to taint the pure exchange of sentiments that had once been the hallmark of Valentine's Day celebrations. In 1849, *Godey's Lady's Book* published an editorial recommending "A New Fashion for Valentines," proposing an alternative to the expensive, manufactured valentines that *Godey's* pronounced insincere.[56] The opulence of the manufactured valentines raised uncomfortable questions about whether they were an appropriate representation of sentiments that were intended to be outside the crass exchange of the market. These questions were addressed in "A New Fashion for Valentines," which begins with a short vignette of Valentine morning. Miss Eveleth has just received a lavish valentine that her friend, Miss Selina Simpkins, pronounces absolutely lovely.[57] Eveleth, however, objects to the *printed* nature of the sentiment and proclaims the card a "miserable compliment." Simpkins, whose valentine aesthetics are not so refined, retorts that the card "is very beautiful and must have cost at least fifty dollars." Eveleth bases her evaluation of the valentine on different criteria: "No gentleman of talents would send a Valentine that he did not write, and none but a vain fool would send such an expensive toy, that is not of the least worth either for use or ornament. Probably the dunce who sent it has not paid his tailor's bill for the year."[58]

Her objections to the valentine are numerous: reliance on printed poetry bespeaks a lack of education and originality, the expense of the valentine gratifies the ego of the sender as much as it flatters the recipient, the card has no use value, and finally, it is evidence of profligate tendencies. Miss Eveleth and Benjamin Hager share the same valentine aesthetics: "little poems, generally devoted to tender passion, *written by the person who sent the valentine.*"[59] Women wanted valentines to be a form of male fancywork that demonstrated the same sentimental codes of production that defined women's production and corresponding consumption. This editorial vignette reminded readers that a man's spending habits were an important indicator of his character and taste. Conspicuous consumption raised questions about a man's character

Figure 9. Valentine, Norcross Historical Greeting Card Collection, courtesy of the Smithsonian Institution.

rather than confirming his eligibility. To trust an object of the market, like a fancy valentine, with private feelings suggested that he might be too much of the market himself, which raised questions about his social status.

Printed valentines, even those that conformed to sentimental aesthetics, could not escape their resemblance to other market missives: "Now the title is bestowed on *printed* doggerel, bought in market and distributed through the penny-post, with no more of sentiment to consecrate the offering than though these Valentines were patented recipes for colds, or notices of a new milliner's shop."[60] Valentines often spoofed their relationship to advertisements. One British valentine from circa 1850 poked fun at the extravagances of courtship by spelling out the material advantages of marriage. At the bottom is inscribed "SOMETHING LIKE A VALENTINE."[61] These jokes mocked the economic aspects of courtship by putting a price on love. The humor of these valentines softened the economic realities they mocked, but it also framed the illusive value of romantic love in familiar terms, exposing the fundamental uneasiness about definitions of value that preoccupied the middle class. The market transaction ascribed value to the valentine, but complicated its role in the priceless gift economy of romantic love.[62]

Although the editorial in *Godey's* soundly criticized the contemporary celebration of Valentine's Day, it was not in an attempt to curtail its celebration, but to promote an advertising scheme to capitalize on the market for valentines. The editorial proposed the magazine as the ideal valentine. It was a good value in comparison to fancy valentines, for it cost only three dollars and lasted for the whole year. It was, moreover, designed expressly for ladies, unlike *Graham's Magazine*, *Union Magazine*, and the *Columbian*, which the editorial also recommended.[63] The editorial made a distinction between printed sentiments of the valentine and the printed sentiments of *Godey's Lady's Book*. Although printed valentines had many shortcomings, they had become "quite the rage" because many lovers did not have the leisure, or, one might surmise, the talent, to compose original valentine verses. If this was the case, it was still preferable to a book of poetry and mark a poem that expressed the appropriate sentiments. Books suggested included *Female Poets of America, Mrs. Sigourney's Poems, Women of the Bible, Women of the Scriptures, The Female Poets of England*, and *Women of the American Revolution*.[64] Works by female authors were highly recommended, although a list of male poets was also offered: Bryant, Longfellow, Halleck, Willis, Percival, Hoffman, Simms, Morris, Sargent, Street, and Holmes. These books were "rich ornaments for the parlor and boudoir" and demonstrated the good taste of the sender. The distinction was made on the basis of taste and content rather than form, emphasizing the importance of discriminating taste to delimit an appropriate celebration of the holiday. The editorial suggested that if a man would win a woman's heart, he must learn to buy what she would have chosen for herself or to buy a book that would encourage an intellectual relationship between a future husband and wife.

This editorial, although unsigned, was most likely written by Sarah Hale. Despite its disparagement of the affinities between valentines and advertisements, Louis Godey often used this comparison when it was useful:

> GODEY'S VALENTINE. We shall be anxiously looking out, on the proper day, for those valentines that our friends have, from time to time, so kindly promised us. It does not matter to us particularly whether we receive them on the very day or not. It may be before, or after, or now. We allude to those sundry "promises to pay." In all cases, we will return our autograph.[65]

Godey used Valentine's Day as a humorous advertisement for his magazine, capitalizing on the prevailing humor that linked love and money. The following year he made the link between subscription and remittal and valentines even more explicit:

> We publish in this number a Valentine story, and the supposed origin of St. Valentine's day. These two articles are for our subscribers. In return, we should be pleased to receive a Valentine from them, inclosing $3, $6, $10, or $20. It can be addressed as follows:—Registered. L. A. Godey, 113 Chestnut St., Phila. We shall promptly answer the receipt of every such Valentine.[66]

Godey joked that delinquent subscriptions could take the form of a valentine, just as the magazine could, and he went even further, suggesting that the gift of a subscription was more than just an ordinary valentine. It was a de facto proposal of marriage:

> If the following will not make the ladies subscribe, nothing we can say will have

any effect. The editor of the "Flushing Journal" says: "Godey's Lady's Book" for February is as usual a book for the ladies. The sending of a copy of "Godey" to a lady is now the way of popping the question. All the young lady readers of "Godey" contrive to get married before their subscriptions expire. There is an incommunicable something in the "Lady's Book" that swells the matrimonial statistics of the United States. A postmaster on the Island, through whose office pass some fifty copies of "Godey," says that he never sees the name of a new female subscriber, but that he is sure that a certain interesting event will shortly occur.[67]

Like most discussion of the market in *Godey's Lady's Book*, these humorous subscription reminders blended discussions of property relations with prescriptions for propriety.

These discussions of valentines were not the first time *Godey's* had linked love with advertisements. In 1837, the magazine had published "Wives by Advertisement," a scathing condemnation of fortune hunters that sparked several essays in response. Its author, R. Shelton MacKenzie, characterized a man who would stoop to advertising for a wife as beneath the most vicious pauper. The need and the desire to advertise for a wife provided evidence that his character was such that he could not obtain a wife by any other means, regardless of the flattering light in which he portrayed himself in the advertisement. Men who advertised for wives, MacKenzie claimed, desecrated the institution of marriage by using it as a ruse for financial gain. It was the fortune that the advertiser sought that turned courtship into a market transaction: "He puts himself up to the public bidding, for the unworthy to purchase. He lays aside the dignity of his sex, and avows himself desirous of a life-union with age, deformity, vice—so that they be thickly gilded. He proclaims that he is in the market, like any other commodity."[68] The act of advertising made him into a commodity. The commodity life of a bachelor, for MacKenzie conceded that men were more frequent advertisers than women, stripped the sentimental veil from marriage and revealed it as a sequence of bargaining and speculation. The nature of the proposal solicited by the advertisement demanded a commodity to be exchanged rather than a heart to be given. The marriage license became a contract in a business deal. By advertising himself,

Figure 10. Cupid, Auctioneer, from *Godey's Lady's Book*, 1864.

a man put himself in the same category as the other commodities praised in the adjacent advertisements:

> It *is* a fact, that the advertisements which invite women to matrimonial alliances, just as they are invited to bargains at auction or shops, are not jests, to see if females would notice them; they are what they avow; and it is an ascertained circumstance that many *mesalliances* have been formed through this very *delicate* medium.[69]

For a woman to answer such an advertisement was not only to reduce herself to the level of the advertiser but also to call her own motives into question. "Bankrupt, indeed, in charms and character must she be who would proffer herself as the spouse of a wife-advertiser for the fulfillment of such a speculation," MacKenzie declared.[70] To participate in the speculation for love required by the advertisements for marriage was to enter the market. A marriage bought and paid for could not escape the original transactions: "Strive they for happiness? That, also, is not a marketable article. . . . They buy each other, as we buy cattle. Their qualifications must be discounted in the bargain. They *cannot* love: theirs is a contract from which delicacy shrinks, and at which pride revolts."[71]

A marriage of the market promised to be a confidence game, either a rake who intended to spend the fortune or a woman who was deep in debt and needed a scapegoat husband to cool his heels in debtors prison for her. To purchase love was to forego the possibility of honesty or constancy. The sexual nature of such a liaison also raised problems, as to marry under such terms was legal prostitution of the mind and body, testimony to a woman's prurience. Marriage relations became market relations, a spiritual union became the consumption of a commodity.[72] For a man to allow himself to be bought, to reduce himself voluntarily to a commodity, was to become a slave. The distinction between economic and private status was eliminated.[73]

The responses to this essay took a more lenient view of the subject. The following May, *Godey's Lady's Book* opened with a letter on the topic signed by "Coelebs," a reference to Hannah More's novel, *Coelebs in Search of a Wife* (1809). It offered a different perspective on the subject of the marriage market.[74] "Coelebs" outlined extenuating circumstances in which, he felt, it would be acceptable for a lady or gentleman to advertise for a spouse. He cited the difficulty of procuring an introduction to a lady beyond his immediate circle, stating that social rigidity precluded both men and women from making happy marriages by circumscribing their circles of acquaintance. He gave an example of a "private advertisement" that took place at a wedding in South Carolina, where each guest wrote the name of another guest whom she or he would be willing to have as a life partner. The results were tabulated by an disinterested party, and those who had chosen each other were informed. Nine marriages resulted out of a total of fourteen couples. Several gentlemen confessed afterward that they would not have had the courage to propose under other circumstances.[75] The terms of this "private advertisement" were different, however, because they facilitated marriages a particular social circle rather than between two strangers. A closed market, "Coelebs" implied, did not have the same stigma as the open market.

Coelebs turned this story about private advertisement into a form of genteel public advertisement, using himself as an example. His analysis of the problem of "matrimonial connexions," which had been masquerading as an essay, was an advertisement. He described himself in the most flattering terms: a substantial fortune, an ardent admirer of the female sex, well educated, an abhorrence of cant and "ultra religion," and possessing a strong desire to be married. He defined his prospective bride in stringent terms:

> The lady I would wish to be between twenty and thirty years of age, rather hand-some than decidedly ugly; and above rather than greatly below middling height; and possessed of a respectable fortune. Now these three conditions I consider as bagatelles, compared with the following, which are, a first rate and accomplished education, pure piety, and of a respectable family.[76]

By listing the expected criteria first, and undermining their importance with the second set, he spoofed the usual form of advertisement as well as the sentimental conventions of womanhood and dared his reader to catch him in the joke. He was not alone in his unfulfilled search for a wife, he revealed; he had two friends who also found themselves in a similar situation. This confession was a further advertisement of his own charms. The sincerity of his interest in matrimony, and the misfortune that circumstance had brought upon him should, he argued, allow the extraordinary measure of advertisement in a public paper. He ends his "letter" with a request for advice on the matter. Coelebs managed to advertise himself by stating his intention to do so. His spoof of the form became an advertisement.[77]

Two answers to this "dissertation on the difficulties of forming matrimonial connexions" appeared in the August issue. The first was from a matron who signed herself "Iola" and suggested that Coelebs had greatly exaggerated the difficulty of gaining introductions. Gentlemen, she noted, have ways of becoming acquainted with each other. A bachelor, by polite attention to the wives of his acquaintances, could be introduced to their unmarried friends. It was the behavior of the lady in the activities of life, rather than her qualifications on paper that indicated whether she would be a good wife.[78] She also condemned the idea of advertisement on the grounds that it excluded the parents from participating in the marriage decision, a complaint also leveled against valentines. In order to maintain class status, parents, particularly fathers, had to be able to subject prospective lovers to a certain amount of financial and personal scrutiny. Marriage by advertisement precluded this.

The second letter was not a rebuke but an answer to the advertisement: "Here is a second epistle from a young and amiable lady, we opine: if 'Coelebs' is still in that state of waiting and watching for opportunities, which he so pathetically describes, he has now an opportunity of speaking out."[79] This letter is dated May 7, 1838, an indication of the promptness with which its author, Anna, replied to Coelebs's advertisement. Anna offered a feminine perspective on the difficulties of the marriage market. Women who would make the best domestic partners were overlooked in favor of "gay and trifling votaries of fashion and frivolity." She agreed with Coelebs that social constraints were to blame and advocated the acceptance of greater social intercourse between men and women. The bulk of her letter read like a treatise on women's education, but she ended with her own advertisement. Although she listed many positive qualities, she admitted that she was neither beautiful nor rich, thus revealing her need for advertisement.

The final installment of this series, from a southern lady who signed herself "Cahokia," appeared in October 1838. Unlike Anna, Cahokia saw through Coelebs and accused him of "seeking amusement in the shape of adventure." She questioned the possibility that "a man who is as intellectual and imaginative, as his writing bespeak [*sic*] him, could reach the age of thirty untouched by the tender passion—such an impossibility is only for the stoic."[80] Coelebs's problem, as Cahokia defined it, was ambition: a market sentiment unseemly in courtship. She condemned his references to fortune and suggested that in the South no woman could be won with anything short of chivalric gallantry, of which there was no evidence in Coelebs's letter. She declined to describe herself, but chided Coelebs for not describing himself with the necessary detail for an informed decision. Although she did not want to be equated with the women described in MacKenzie's article, she could not resist the advertising possibilities of the letter. Certain that her anonymity was impenetrable, the author invited Coelebs to continue the correspondence: "If it should be the wish of Coelebs, I have not the least objection to continuing the correspondence; provided, Mrs. Hale will allow an unoccupied corner of her interesting periodical to be devoted to such little matters."[81] Cahokia proposed a public literary flirtation. Her letter was an advertisement for both her literary "skills" and her desire for a connection with Coelebs.[82]

Hale was unwilling to relinquish such a corner, and this letter was the last of the series, but a similar sequence appeared in 1844. The February issue contained a poem entitled "Advertisement" signed C. W. D. It outlined the required attributes of a wife: education, grace, virtue, freedom from sin, and last but not least "a good share of 'TIN.'" The April issue contained two responses to the poem. The remainder of the responses, Hale noted, would be sent to C. W. D. at his request. The poems spoof the requirement of "tin," and the whole exchange was humorous rather than polemical. R. Shelton MacKenzie's vitriol had been given way to a playful humor that despite its barbs conveyed a certain legitimacy to advertising for love.

In 1850, Sarah Hale inaugurated her own little matrimonial advertisement on the behalf of the male editors of *Godey's Lady's Book*. She conceded that ladies had a history of preferring military men, but, she noted approvingly, "that time appears to be rapidly passing away." Ladies were showing a decided preference for "the modest and retired members of the corps editorial and for the bloodless glories of the quill and the scissors." Despite this good fortune, Hale informed her lady readers, "quite a number of our friends appear not to be conscious of the great price that has been set upon their worth and intelligence, and the astonishing rise which these commodities have taken in the matrimonial market."[83] She suggested that any lady who was interested should send her portrait, which would be tastefully arranged in the "editorial gallery where the editors might study them and select a suitable consort." These humorous defenses of matrimonial advertisement suggest that, as in all things, good motives were paramount—and the imagined community of the magazine assured that these connections would be kept within the boundaries of class the magazine defined.

Although middle-class celebrants of Valentine's Day were expected, at least according to Miss Eveleth, to confine themselves to sincere, tasteful, and restrained forms of celebration, the valentines themselves betray a spirit of merriment. Nowhere was this more evident than in valentines that mimicked the familiar documents of middle-class life: marriage licenses, checks, and bank notes that reveled in the puns and double entendres that the affinities between the languages of love and money offered. Marriage licenses were sweet: "Marriage solemnized at St. Bride's Church, Matrimonial Lane, in the County of Cupidshire by Rev. Peter Tiethemtight, M.A., Joseph Wedlock, Clerk."[84] Promissory notes were serious: "I Promise to pay Miss —— on Demand a Loving Heart, a Good Temper, Industrious Habits, and strict attention to Early Hours, in consideration of her becoming my partner for life."[85] The bank notes, however, were the most whimsical. They came in different denominations, 50 and 100, although they did not specify what the units were. Instead, they conveyed a hyperbole of sentiment: "Secured by the Whole Stock of Truth, Honour and Affection." Although this mimicked the form of an actual banknote, it also poked fun at the precarious security of real banknotes by securing the love represented with something beyond monetary value. One particular run was issued from the State of Matrimony on the Bank of True Love, but testimony to a different kind of attachment, that of the publisher to his profit. The banknote also bears the name of its manufacturer, his address and date of publication because it is a copyrighted design. For all the implications of timelessness, the valentine is grounded firmly in Pennsylvania in 1852. The sender of the valentine, acting as cashier, could make the promissory note out to his beloved: "I promise to pay to —— on demand the homage and never-failing devotion of sincere affection. —— Cash'r. Cupid, Pres't." Cupid appears in his business capacity, this time as a bank president rather than a manufacturer, but humor of Cupid in business dress seems to have been irresistible. The humor of the juxtaposition was the exposure of the oxymoron of the marriage market: love prompts marriage but money sustains it. This kind of comic valentine demonstrates the blurred boundaries of middle-class celebration. The aesthetics and the jokes that distinguished these document valentines were aimed at a middle-class rather than working-class audience, but their gentle irreverence did not conform to the criteria outlined by Miss Eveleth or practiced by Benjamin Hager. Despite their protestations of sincere love, they would have been an unlikely choice for a serious proposal

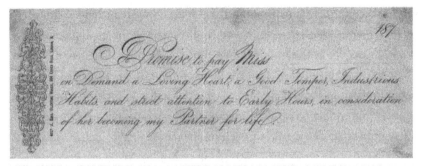

Figure 11. Valentine "promissory note," Norcross Historical Greeting Card Collection, courtesy of the Smithsonian Institution.

Figure 12. Valentine "bank note," courtesy of the Library of Congress.

of marriage, nor would they have been appropriate for a platonic valentine. Rather, they fell in the middle, suggesting that some participants in the traditions of the holiday had a sense of humor about its serious side without either succumbing to the rancor of cheap comic valentines or relinquishing the sentimental aesthetics of the fancy valentines.

Courtship was a process in which the intersections of the public and private spheres were particularly visible and particularly troubling. The language of romantic love shifted the focus away from the productive aspects of economic partnership, which had underpinned marriage in the past, to emphasize a moral and spiritual bonding that, at least in definition, transcended financial constraints. This could not, however romantics might try, erase the very real economic elements of marriage. A man was financially responsible for his wife and children. A suitor was required to prove his eligibility not only through sincere protestations of love, but also through evidence of a solid financial situation and sensible habits of consumption. He was obliged to represent himself in such a light to the father of his love in order to gain possession not only of her heart, but also of her body and possibly her fortune. Even the lighthearted treatment of these subjects represented by comic valentines introduced a sober, economic note into the symphony of tangling eye-strings.

Be Mine

The metaphor of possession was commonly used in the language of romantic love. One valentine contained a series of jokes: "Why is a little dog with a tail in his mouth like a prudent husband? *Because he makes both ends meet;* Why are ladies like arrows? *They can't go off without a beau and are all in a quiver till they get one;* Why am I to call you *my* ever dearest? *You are to become my proper tie (property);* If Cupid were to take a situation for what would he be best fitted? *A buss conductor;* What is the first thing a lady looks for in church? *The hims;* Why are deep sighs like long stockings? *They are both high ho's (high hose)."*[86] All the jokes are puns on different aspects of courtship, but the property joke is the most interesting, especially as its pun is decoded on the valentine. The language used to discuss marriage centered around the idea of possession, or the words of another valentine: "Tis happiness we have in view and mine is in possessing you."[87] The language of possession reflected the split between the possession of the heart that the rhetoric of romantic love espoused, and the possession of the body, both sexual and economic, that conjugal property rights of marriage still entailed. To marry was to be possessed, emotionally, bodily, and economically. The juxtaposition of happiness and possession was common: "Dearest name the happy time that I in truth shall call you mine." For even the most romantic woman, the common refrain of "Be Mine" must have had a double ring.[88]

Valentine stories in women's magazines also explored the relationship between property and propriety that fueled the humor of comic sentimental valentines. Before 1849, there was almost no mention of Valentine's Day in

Godey's, but between 1850 and 1880, the February issues always contained a story or poem about Valentine's Day and often an engraving as well. The duplicity of the valentine as a romantic go-between in these valentine stories is striking. Even when a valentine facilitates the union of two lovers, there is always a high price to pay for its services. The valentine serves as test of love, but at great emotional cost. The stories often focused on the negative aspects of valentine exchange: mysterious, cruel, and misunderstood valentines. The promises of emotional freedom that romantic love seemed to offer were, in many senses, hollow. The rituals of courtship remained tied to patriarchal prerogatives; women were still given by their fathers to their husbands. Even seemingly private transactions such as the exchange of valentines were subject to paternal scrutiny. The valentine fiction addresses the power relations between men and women through the symbol of the anonymous valentine, which offered two forms of power: the power of a heart to read the emanation of true love in any form and the power to manipulate the exchange by obscuring its true origin, prompting a false reading.

The anonymous valentine lent a Gothic cast to a sentimental ritual. Instead of operating as an extension of the convention of the transparent emotion of sentimental love, the valentine encoded it. The Gothic accents of the stories in *Godey's Lady's Book* suggest that, like Gothic novels from the early Republic that examined and critiqued the hierarchies of traditional society and the excesses of individualism, the authors of these valentine stories struggled to express and resolve moments of transgressive behavior, specifically the transformation in the rituals of courtship that the acceptance of romantic love abetted.[89] The exchange of valentines was examined through other forms of exchange, such as gambling and mysterious contracts. The juxtaposition of the happy ending and the mysterious, even sinister, role of the valentine appealed to the reader on two levels; it fulfilled her desire for a tale of requited love, and addressed her concerns about the changing nature of courtship and the role of trifles in the serious business of love.

"Kate's Valentine" (1850), by Harry Sunderland, a Gothic tale despite its happy ending, relates a story of a valentine wager.[90] Its narrator, Kate's uncle and guardian, begins by describing his niece in indulgent and patronizing tones.

Figure 13. "Kate's Valentine," from *Godey's Lady's Book*, 1850.

Kate has independent opinions and good sense for her twenty-one years, her uncle admits, but "her knowledge of human nature is not very deep; nor is she as wise in all her conclusions as she is led to imagine."[91] The story hinges on her uncle's attempt to "educate" her about Valentine's Day. For the last several years, Kate had been expressing her distaste for the holiday: "The Valentine epidemic, which raged so violently, she considered a social disease emphatically. It was no healthy manifestation of right feelings in her estimation."[92] Her characterization of the disease as a social one points directly to the importance of such a ritual in forms of social definition. Kate shies away from the irrationality and frivolity of a valentine. She knows the seriousness of a declaration of love, and prefers, at least so she claims, to have a lover appeal to her common sense rather than her sense of romantic indulgence. For Kate, love is a very serious business, and she desires a certain amount of control.[93]

Her uncle characterizes her demand for a lover to appeal to her common sense as silly. He challenges her to a wager, claiming that if she receives a valentine from the right young man, she will not reject him. Kate, echoing the sentiments of Miss Eveleth, retorts that she will spurn any man who insults her with a valentine for "no man of good sense would stoop to such trifling." Her uncle, however, does not leave the wager to fate but assures himself of winning, by sending an anonymous valentine to Kate himself. He hopes she will think it is from Loring, the suitor to whom, her uncle has observed, she is most partial. Kate's uncle justifies this deception because Loring seems unable to express his feelings to Kate on his own. The valentine he sends contains a bracelet and a poem: "This little love-token, dear Kate, is for thee: / Accept it, and keep it, and wear it for me." True to her uncle's prediction, she is not mortally offended when she receives it. But her uncle does not choose to collect the new hat that was to be his prize. He waits until the valentine has finished its work. The valentine is a double wager: the wager for the hat stands in for the wager for the heart.

Kate seems to change her mind about valentines. She always wears the bracelet whenever Loring comes to call, and she begins to exhibit the classic signs of love, or as her uncle calls it—heart disease: failing appetite, loss of color, and loss of weight. In time Loring asks Kate's uncle for her hand, and once Kate and Loring are engaged, she wears the bracelet constantly. A month before the wedding, her uncle comments on it. He extracts a confession from her that it is a love token and a valentine. Not just any valentine, but a sincere one, not one from a trifler. Kate blushes deeply at each revelation. Her uncle has scored his first point; Kate did not spurn the sender of the valentine. He is not content, however, to drop the issue. He recites the poem from the valentine. Kate, who has told no one about the valentine, starts with surprise. Her uncle reveals his ruse: "'But I'm afraid, Kate,' said I, with a meaning smile, and a voice half-regretful in its tone, 'that you wore it less for the real than for an imaginary giver.'"[94] Kate suddenly realizes that the bracelet was from her uncle, not Loring. Kate's uncle wanted to expose her hypocrisy, and in doing so he proves her both wrong and right. She did accept the valentine, contrary to her statement, but she was also correct about the potential treachery of the valentine.

Her uncle's revelation leaves Kate momentarily stricken: "She covered her face suddenly with her hands and sat motionless for some moments. In a little while, I saw a tear come stealing through her fingers. My feelings were touched, for I feared lest I had done violence to hers by this little confession of the truth."[95] The story is a sequence of confessions. The first confession is Kate's distrust of valentines, which appears to be a false and unfounded confession. She had tried to resist the gamble of the valentine for the "sure money" of common sense, but she could not resist the seduction of the valentine's speculation. The second is the confession of the valentine itself, which Kate reads as a confession of love from Loring. The next confession is her uncle's confession of what he calls the truth. His truth, however, is the confession of deception. He sent the anonymous valentine in the hope that Kate would interpret it as a gift from Loring. This false valentine, it appears, has preempted any genuine confession of love that Loring might have sent to Kate; she ignored her other valentines once she had received what she thought she wanted. Her uncle waited for Loring to confirm his love before he makes his own confession.[96] The success of his manipulation of their courtship remains dependent on Loring's unconscious cooperation. The tentative suitor was a stock character in valentine fiction. The fiction of individual choice must be maintained for her uncle's ruse to succeed.

When Kate recovers from the shock of her uncle's confession, she declares, "Henceforth I will wear it for the real giver." Her uncle, clearly gratified by that decision, ends his story with a final comment about Kate's wedding night: "On her wedding night Kate wore her Valentine bracelet; and I am weak enough to believe—if the sentiment may be called a weakness—that she prized it even more highly than if Loring himself had been the giver."[97] In this final confession, her uncle places himself, through the symbol of the bracelet, on Kate's arm on her wedding night. Kate's uncle, who was originally happy to have his valentine misinterpreted, wants to reclaim it. His "giving" of Kate to Loring is not unconditional. Having masqueraded as Kate's lover, her uncle does not seem willing to relinquish that role. His confession intrudes on the love of Kate and Loring, and his purpose in confessing becomes suspect. It is not simply that he wants Kate to acknowledge that she changed her mind, nor does he claim his wager; in fact, he never mentions the hat. He wants to reassert his power over her, to strip her talisman of its meaning and assign it new meaning. Romantic love—and its messenger the valentine—would appear to invest the lovers with control of their love, but the activities of Kate's uncle make it clear that the power is easily recouped by the displaced patriarchal figure. The valentine was an essential prop in the drama of romantic love, a parlor theatrical still produced and directed by, although no longer starring, the patriarchal figure.

Kate is a sentimental pragmatist. She understands the necessary compromises of domestic happiness and familial prosperity. The story blurs the lines between filial love and conjugal love and reaffirms the dominant bond as that with the father figure. This story, and many of the others published in the magazine, is about the relations between men in the marriage market. Kate's behavior is dictated by propriety and prompted by filial duty and respect, but the strategies of emotional possession used by her uncle suggest an unsettling affinity with property relations. The exchange of the valentine becomes synonymous with the exchange of Kate. For Kate, the valentine is a contract. By accepting it, she is subject to its terms. The anonymity makes it a form of blind trust. She questions the propriety of the valentine, but her uncle controls the terms of both property and propriety.

Although the "happy ending" of this story seems compromised to the modern reader by the capitulation of the heroine to the manipulations of her uncle, even though he has her best interests at heart, the uneasy truce between paternalism and individualism suggests a period of transition rather than a reassertion of paternal authority. The Gothic accents are clues to this instability. Kate's uncle proves his point, but the terms of his success also prove Kate's point. Kate's uncle insists that the valentine is merely a vehicle for a message of love, and has no inherent meaning of its own. If it is the right message, he argues, the fact that it is delivered by a valentine is irrelevant. Kate, however, has a more subtle understanding of sentimental commodities. She knows that the medium is the message, and thus the acceptance (or consumption) of the valentine, cannot be detached from the conditions of its production, which in this case are further complicated by anonymity. If the conditions of production are hidden, the true meaning of the message is illegible. Although he does not acknowledge it, this is exactly why Kate's uncle is able to use the valentine to reassert his paternal authority.

"St. Valentine's Day" (1864), by S. Annie Frost, also addresses the question of paternal authority, by taking the masquerade of the anonymous valentine one step further.[98] The heroine, Maggie, has double cause to celebrate the fourteenth of February, for it is her birthday, and this year, her eighteenth. For four years a secret lover has been sending her a valentine that contains a $500 bank note. This year the envelope contains not only the money but also a letter to Maggie, and one to her father, Dr. Lossing, who knows the seriousness of the situation and takes Maggie into his study for a private conversation: "The deep gravity of his manner, the mysterious letter, filled Maggie with a vague dread, and she trembled violently as she followed him."[99] The letter is from Herbert Arundel, whom Lossing reveals to be Maggie's true father. Lossing and Arundel had been college friends and "wild boys," who lived a life of "fashionable extravagance and dissipation." Love showed them the error of their ways, and they swore to reform in order to be worthy of "the daughter of a leading physician and . . . the orphan niece of a wealthy banker." Lossing was taken on as a student by the father of his beloved and managed to prove himself in five years time. Arundel was not so lucky; Margaret's uncle did not approve of him, and their relationship had to remain a secret. He struggled against his evil desires and went to work for the bank where her uncle was director. In time, both Lossing and Arundel found spiritual guidance and were thoroughly reformed. After three years, an embezzlement scandal rocked Arundel's bank, and he was framed. He was tried, found guilty, and sentenced to a lengthy jail term. Two weeks after the trial, he escaped with Margaret's help; they were married and went to California.

Five years later, Margaret appeared on Lossing's doorstep on a wild evening in February. Herbert had lost everything in a fire. She had come to

Figure 14. "St. Valentine's Day," from *Godey's Lady's Book*, 1864.

beg her uncle for assistance and receive a pardon for her husband. Her uncle had refused. She fainted in Lossing's arms and gave birth to Maggie at two o'clock Valentine morning, dying shortly afterward. Lossing agreed to act as Maggie's father until Herbert could clear his name. Herbert sent a yearly sum to support Maggie, a portion of which he included in a valentine. This year, the letter to Lossing enclosed in the valentine includes a newspaper clipping revealing the identity of the true embezzler, who had been caught for another crime. As chance would have it, Herbert, under his assumed name, had been a juror in the trial, and the accused, in an attempt to clear his conscience, had identified him as the same man he had framed twenty-three years earlier, because he also had been in love with Margaret.

Maggie is shocked by the news. Lossing leaves her alone to think things through while he tells the others. Maggie's first thoughts turn to Albert, her "brother," who has always been her favorite, whose name was her first word, and whose company she has always preferred to any beaux. Now that he is not her brother, she fears she has no claim on his affection. Her thoughts are also of her newly found father and the years of loneliness he must have suffered separated from any family. After a short time, Herbert Arundel is shown into the room, and he meets his child for the first time. They both remain in the doctor's house for a few weeks as Herbert "weans" Maggie from her family. Eventually he takes her away to preside over his own establishment, where he sequesters her for a year. Maggie is lonely and homesick, but she conceals her true feelings from her father. At the end of the year, her father decides to allow Maggie to reenter society and to renew contact with the Lossings. He admits to jealousy of her former ties to them, but when she requests that they be allowed to come visit, he consents.

During the course of the year, Maggie has come to understand her love for Albert in a new way. This year her valentine is from him, and it contains a ring and proposal that Maggie takes to her father. It is clear to Herbert that this is what Maggie desires, but he stipulates that Albert must come and live with them because he cannot part with her: "She clung to him, whispering: 'Nothing shall part us Father!' Long, long he held her closely in his arms and then with a fervent kiss and a whispered blessing her father put Albert's ring upon her finger."[100] This story reads like a classic Gothic tale. At the beginning of the story the reader believes the sender of the mysterious valentine to be the hero and potential lover. When he is revealed to be Maggie's unknown father, his status is changed. But the reader quickly learns that Maggie has always harbored unarticulated incestuous feelings for her "brother" Albert. Now that Albert is not her brother, she allows these feelings to transform themselves into romantic love. Her father, having asserted his paternal rights of possession by sequestering her for a year, is forced to relinquish Maggie to Albert. By giving up the role of lover to reassert his rights as her father, he must give up the control of her body he asserted by sequestering her. The transference occurs when the lover-turned-father fervently embraces Maggie and puts the ring of the brother-turned-lover on her finger, effectively placing himself physically between them. By sending a valentine proposal, Albert tries to circumvent the traditional practice of asking the father for the daughter's hand, but having appropriated Arundel's discarded medium of communication with Maggie—the valentine—he has relinquished the right to place the ring on Maggie's finger himself. Following the dictates of propriety, Maggie allows her father to not only approve the proposal but also dictate the terms of the marriage itself. Albert must go and join Maggie and her father, he will not be allowed to take Maggie for himself. Propriety insists that Maggie acquiesce to her father's wishes, and so she remains the property of her father's heart.

Maggie, like Kate, understands the pragmatic nature of sentimental relations. She, too, must revise her understanding of the nature of the sentiments conveyed by the valentine, and reevaluate her feelings first for the anonymous sender, and then for Albert. Once she knows Albert is not her brother, the strength of her feelings can only be understood in romantic terms, just as her romantic interest in the anonymous sender of the valentine must be reinvented in familial terms. In both stories, the women question the propriety of the valentine and the men assure them that everything is in order. Both Kate's uncle and Lossing know the secret origin of the valentines: they control the terms of both property and propriety.

The valentine fiction in *Godey's Lady's Book* suggests an interconnection between the market and romantic love rather than a confirmation of the separation of love from market concerns. The fiction and the valentines themselves also suggest the continued strength of patriarchal prerogatives at the heart of sentimentalism, yet another indication that the conflation of sentimentalism with feminization obscures the real power relations of middle-class culture. The negotiations of the marriage market bore a striking resemblance to the negotiations of the sentimental market that Esther Howland, Sarah Hale, and Matilda Pullan experienced, and that authors such as T. S. Arthur and Mary Virginia Terhune explored in their magazine fiction. Sentimental enterprise was a series of compromises between familial obligation and personal ambition, a resistance to the market and an acceptance of it on carefully negotiated terms.

The conventions of romantic love incorporated the individualism of the developing market culture and the evangelical Christian belief in an ecstatic experience of God's love; to fall in love was to experience the same sensations as a spiritual rebirth. Romantic love offered a translation of physical attraction, recasting the impulse to couple as a spiritual union of souls. By giving a concrete form to the exchange of hearts, the valentine contributed to the commodification of love. Romantic love insisted that true love knew no boundaries and was not confined by worldly necessities, but romantic love was about the exchange of the ultimate commodity: the heart. The valentine represented the heart. It was a sentimental talisman, a reification of love.

The dissatisfaction with the commodity form of the valentine that the fiction in *Godey's Lady's Book* and other women's magazines expressed was testimony to the failure of sentimental commodities to fully satisfy the desires they provoked. The expectations that sentimentalism engendered in the creation of personal relationships based on emotion, and the promise of material possessions whose purchase would provide another opportunity to experience emotion, contributed to an experience of consumption in which satisfaction was by definition unattainable.[101]

Although the conventions of romantic love proposed a new kind of marriage that was not determined by the merger of family fortunes, its language of possession and exchange betrayed a refashioning of the rituals of market culture within sentimental culture. The relations of romantic love were not unlike the consumption of sentimental luxuries. As people became accustomed to purchasing the sentiments of a valentine or a piece of fancywork, they began to contemplate the consumption of all forms of sentiment.

By 1880, both the valentine market and valentine exchange had changed. Esther Howland went out of business in 1879, not just because her role as daughter superseded her role as entrepreneur but also because Valentine's Day was becoming big business and small entrepreneurs like Howland had more difficulty competing. The acceptance or even embrace of manufactured sentiment was also explored in valentine fiction, which concerned itself less with the problem of paternal authority than with the skills of reading a manufactured valentine correctly. While middle-class ideology struggled to protect the difference between property and propriety, the visibility of the market relations of courtship, the negotiation of family capitalism, the demands of the marriage market, and the embryonic consumer culture that the valentine fiction addressed revealed a breakdown in the strict divisions between property and propriety. The conventions of romantic love paralleled the individualism of a developing market culture. The valentine was an incorporation of the terms of market exchange into the world of courtship itself. As an economy of symbols, Valentine's Day played an important role in the acceptance of manufactured sentiment by middle-class consumers. As a symbolic economy, celebration of the holiday provided a ritual in which the new relationship between property and propriety could be explored. In one sense, this was merely a perpetuation of the role that courtship had always played in the financial alliances of families. But because the language of romantic love denied its market relations, it set in place a new series of mechanisms for discussing and interpreting the relationship between property and propriety.

$\mathcal{N}ine$

A Tempest in a Teacup

Spinoff Products in the Sentimental Marketplace

*T*hroughout the nineteenth century, readers of Susannah Rowson's novel of sentiment, *Charlotte Temple* (1791), made pilgrimages to the grave of a real woman named Charlotte Stanley in Trinity churchyard, New York, which had been mistaken for the grave of the fictional heroine.[1] At some point, the stone was even changed to read Temple instead of Stanley.[2] The search for the grave of a real Charlotte was prompted in part by the subtitle, *A Tale of Truth,* and by the fact that Rowson did not deny the existence of Charlotte's grave. The frontispiece engravings of Charlotte Temple's grave encouraged the search, and pilgrimages to the Stanley grave invented a body for the fictional Charlotte, even if it was only a corpse, collapsing the boundaries of the fictional and the real. The power of the sentiments portrayed in the novel demanded that a "real" body had "felt" them.[3]

The borrowed grave drew pilgrims, numbering in the thousands, according to an article in the *New York Daily Tribune* in 1900.[4] Discussion of these pilgrimages more than 100 years after Rowson's novel was published signaled an attraction to more than just the touching story of Charlotte's lost virtue. This interest celebrated the touching naïveté of readers who brought flowers, locks of hair, and other keepsakes to leave at the grave stone. Like the Esther Howland interview in the *Boston Globe* (1901), which was testimony to a nostalgia for a celebration of Valentine's Day governed by "right feeling" rather than commercial success, the article about the pilgrims to Charlotte's grave described an authentic reading experience that was an explicit contrast to the indiscriminate consumption of texts that seemed to characterize popular reading habits at the turn of the century.

In the age of American Nervousness, these stories of innocent reading seemed to portray a lost market culture that offered an appealing contrast to the jaded commercialism of the moment.[5] The nostalgia for these market experiences was a yearning for a moment before self- knowledge, before cynicism and calculation. In the name of nostalgic innocence, all the complexity of the debates about market culture that had engaged antebellum men and women was erased.[6] Nostalgia always has an ideological component. It constructs relationships between people and things that reinforce a hierarchical understanding of the world defined by taste. Powerful enough to resurrect discarded notions of good taste through a reconstructed narrative of the past, it creates desire where there has been an absence of desire. It collapses historical distinctions in the service of a usable past. What little we know about sentimental spinoff products comes from antiquarian collectors and nostalgic grandchildren waxing poetic about the past. At the end of the nineteenth century, nostalgic narratives helped collapse all forms of sentimentalism into either sweet sentiment or mawkish sentiment.[7] This nostalgia for the commodities of sentimentalism suggests that spinoff products capture the Zeitgeist of sentimental culture.[8] It is no coincidence that spinoff products appear to be the quintessence of late capitalism; their appearance in the mid-eighteenth century at the birth of literary sentimentalism suggests the relationship between sentimental narratives and commodities that lies at the core of market culture.

The reading practices that surrounded the novel from the beginning of its popularity provide a way to see the links among visual, material, and textual reading. The spinoff product is as old as the sentimental novel. Samuel

Richardson's *Pamela* (1740) inspired a wide range of spinoff products, including a fan, a straw bonnet, a teacup, waxworks, engravings, and a series of paintings.[9] These intersecting and interdependent forms of reading helped shape some of the new ways that commodities were understood to contain and convey meaning. The novel was written for readers who habitually read objects and images as well as texts. Although reading novels was, for most people, a new experience in the late eighteenth century, that experience was shaped by older material and visual forms of religious reading, equally nuanced and educational, which the novel helped to reinvent in secular forms. Before the experience of reading a novel was codified and defined as the primary experience of sentimental reading, the other forms in which sentiment could be read existed as congruent reading experiences.[10]

As the sentimental novel gained popularity in America at the end of the eighteenth century, the capacity to blur the boundaries between life and fiction prompted admonitions from ministers and mothers alike, who echoed the fears of their European counterparts about the dangers inherent in the act of reading a novel. Critics, such as Samuel Miller, feared that reading novels, particularly novels of sentiment, would lead to moral turpitude and social anarchy. This reaction was tempered, over time, by a grudging acceptance of the possibility that novels could teach the lessons of moral restraint by exposing the dangers and consequences of sentimental excess. Although the laments of these early critics may seem a bit like a tempest in a teapot to a modern reader, novel reading did play an important role in the transformation of ideas about social hierarchy and cultural literacy, although these changes did not manifest themselves to any great extent until the first decades of the nineteenth century.[11]

Spinoff products were the eye of a similar storm: a tempest in a teacup. Because they were trifles, they were not subject to the scrutiny focused on the novel. Although the vogue for spinoffs seemed trivial by comparison to the more important changes in which novels participated, spinoffs were part of a shift in the understanding of commodities in everyday life. Spinoff products reveal a much more diverse readership of sentimentalism than previous scholarship has suggested. The "irreverence" of some of the spinoffs helps correct the misapprehension of sentimentalism as primarily a feminine middle-class phenomenon and raises questions about the use of the term "feminization" to describe the rise in the cultural power of the novel. The hints of this broad audience help reveal a more complex reading revolution in the early nineteenth century and suggest the importance of a reading revolution of objects and texts as a catalyst for a revolution in market culture.[12]

Spinoff products encouraged an acceptance of a kind of sentimental value in which sentimental associations could be bought.[13] *Sentimental* value implies that the object is priceless because it is defined by sentiment. Sentimental *value* suggests that if sentiment has a value, it also has a price. The early appearance of spinoff products for sentimental texts and performances suggests that a market for sentimental goods developed simultaneously with private definitions of sentimental value. Sentimental value was defined by much more than just the convention of investing goods with sentiment.[14] Although middle-class men and women insisted that investing goods with sentiment removed them from the circulation of the market, they knew from experience that this was not a foolproof endeavor. Sentimental narratives increased the possibilities for consumption rather than curtailing them, As the prosperous urban population grew in the 1840s and 1850s, it was increasingly difficult to enforce the vision of market behavior based on dictates of "good motives" that Sarah Hale had helped to popularize in the 1830s.

Fanny Elssler and Jenny Lind, two of the most famous performers in the antebellum period, benefitted financially from the carefully crafted sentimental personas that defined their public images. The public images of women performers were shaped by the same ideology that dictated women's private behavior.[15] In both public and private worlds, the sentimental images of womanhood were tied to women's role in market culture. This connection is evident in the spinoff products that tried to capitalize on the sentimental value of these sentimental personas. Fanny Elssler was a Viennese ballerina. In the early decades of the nineteenth century, the ballet was seen as a lower-class amusement, and ballerinas were often assumed to be prostitutes. Henry Wikoff, the impresario who brought Elssler to America, was well aware of these stereotypes and went to significant lengths to reinvent Elssler in genteel terms in order to expand her audience. He approached Elssler in Paris with a lucrative business proposition from the Park Theater in New York and served as her escort on her tour of the United States and Cuba. Although Elssler's reputation as a dancer was fantastic, her moral reputation was suspect. Elssler, although more discreet than most dancers, had two illegitimate children and a string of passionate affairs to her name. Wikoff knew that to make her American tour a financial success, he would have to convince the women of American society that the ballet was not just intended for a male audience. His ally in this project was Harriet Grotes, an English woman of wealth and stature, and a friend of Elssler. Grotes tried to introduce Elssler to the expatriate American community in Paris. Elssler met with an initial rebuff from Mrs. Adeline Wells, who spoke for her peers when she said, "Not that I do not believe Fanny Elssler to be a very interesting person, but there must be a line drawn between a woman *sold* and a woman *given.*"[16] Her husband, Samuel Wells, who had taken an interest in Elssler, convinced his wife to meet her, and Mrs. Wells was so favorably impressed with the dancer's demure appearance and genteel behavior that she supplied her with several letters of introduction to prominent members of New York society.

These letters were the key to Elssler's social and financial success in America. Her invitations from New York's wealthiest families helped to dispel criticism about her character. Wikoff's tactic of securing the approbation of the elite class, and the enthusiasm of the working class, allowed a middle-class audience to appreciate the social sanction of Elssler's public gentility and enjoy the performance as well. Her social success and her critical acclaim packed the Park Theater night after night. Wikoff succeeded in increasing the audiences for Elssler's performances, and together they transformed the social demography of the audience. One reviewer called Elssler a "Powerful magician!" He noted how she had "destroyed all demarcation" and "humanized the most savage affectation." Her ability to capitalize on sentimental aesthetics drew an elite audience to regard her performance as a respectable form of culture. So many wealthy patrons clamored to see her that they overflowed into the "part of the theater called 'the hell,'" transforming it "into an Eden, where sparkled the most fastidious and disdainful houris of New York."[17] Elssler's demure persona allowed this new audience to insist that the performance was uplifting as well as entertaining.[18]

By performing the private attitudes of the sentimental woman in the public sphere, Elssler managed to transcend the crude stereotypes often applied to women who made their living on the stage. Her crossover did not dampen the ardor of her male admirers, however, as "moustaches, imperials, whiskers and long locks" crowded the stage door every night, hoping for a glimpse of Elssler in the flesh.[19] Elssler was criticized for depriving children of food by enticing fathers to spend money on tickets to her performances rather than fulfilling their paternal duties. The endless supply of "Elsslerana" also targeted a male audience. Besotted admirers could purchase cigars, boot polish, boot jacks, shaving soap, and champagne. For those who might have had to choose between feeding their children and celebrating Elssler, there was Elssler bread. Women admirers also had many choices to commemorate Elssler: boots, stockings, garters, corsets, shawls, dresses, parasols, and fans, as well as a few boats and horses, bore her name. One contemporary critic described the sensation as "elsslermaniaphobia."[20]

Elssler's acceptance by the elite families of New York was invaluable advertising as her tour progressed. When she performed in Washington, Congress adjourned, unable to meet quorum. She was invited to the White House by President Van Buren, whose son John had dined with her in New York. In Philadelphia, the actress Fanny Kemble attended all her performances. Even in Boston, she was entertained by the leading families. Elssler cemented the good will of Boston matrons, including Sarah Hale, by purchasing many items at the Ladies' Fair held to raise money for the Bunker Hill Monument, and by giving a benefit performance that raised almost $600 for the cause.[21] After this performance, a tartan dress with black velvet collar and cuffs and brass buttons, based on Elssler's costume for her signature dance, the Cracovienné, became the height of fashion, as did statuettes of Elssler in the costume.

Elssler's tour of the United States and Cuba was an unprecedented financial success, but the constant presence and attentions of Wikoff wore thin Elssler's public image of sentimental womanhood. In 1841, toward the end of her tour, Nathaniel Parker Willis launched an anti-Elssler campaign, suggesting that

Elssler was Mrs. Wikoff in fact, if not in name.[22] Willis's campaign was a success, and Elssler brought her tour to a close. In the midst of a depression, without the broad audience that her sentimental image had made possible, her performances became much less profitable. Although Elssler was not able to sustain the sentimental image she and Wikoff had created, her initial commercial success transformed the image of women performers in lasting ways.

Fanny Elssler's tour paved the way for the success of Jenny Lind ten years later. Lind's European success had been even greater than Elssler's substantial triumphs. Lind, whose vocal technique was reported to be unsurpassed by any other living singer, had given a command performance for Queen Victoria. Her sizable donations to charity and modest deportment made her appear to be a paragon of womanly virtue. Unlike Elssler, Lind had lived a life untouched by scandal, although she was the illegitimate daughter of a divorcée who had refused to marry Lind's father. The details of her unhappy childhood, and her triumphs over her mother's terrible temper and resistance to her career, were sentimentalized in her biography, subtitled *A Struggle Against Difficulties,* published by P. T. Barnum to introduce her to the American public.[23] Although Lind's European success had not depended on the advertising gimmicks that had made Barnum famous, he knew his audience. He built a market for her musical talents by aligning her with public sentiment. He wooed both the Swedish Nightingale and her audience with the same techniques. To Lind, he promised profits large enough to sustain her charitable impulses; to her prospective audience, he emphasized Lind's benevolence and natural talent. By offering the public a touching story of Lind's private life, Barnum succeeded in making her appear a worthy recipient of public attention for her triumphs over adversity. Her natural talent assuaged fears about ambition; Barnum represented her as an ordinary person whose spiritual purity made her a natural wonder.[24] By promoting her thus, he offered his audience both the thrill of seeing a sensation and the assurance that despite her public stature, Lind remained a private woman, and her virtue was more than just a public performance.

The "Jenny Lind Enterprise," as Barnum sometimes called his venture, was not as much of a departure from his usual tricks of showmanship as it might seem. Barnum's first successful exhibit, Joice Heth, whom he billed as George Washington's nurse, required a similar kind of sentimental marketing. According to a series of exposés in the *New York Herald,* Barnum had helped to "create" Heth, artificially aging her by extracting her teeth and feeding her on a diet of whiskey and eggs. He also forced her to memorize hymns and details of George Washington's life so he could present her as a source of the piety and virtue of Washington's character. Thus, with a sheaf of forged documents that proved her identity, he created a sentimental persona for Heth.[25] This exhibit appealed to the patriotism of his audience, but the humbug exploited the struggle over the legacy of the founding fathers.[26] Barnum banked on the fact that his audience, even those who were abolitionists, would be attracted to Heth because of her connection to Washington rather than her identity as an aged victim of the cruelties of slavery. With such an exhibit, Barnum attempted to straddle the class lines of his potential audience. Heth's freakish nature appealed to a rowdier audience seeking amusement. Her sentimental associations lured a more respectable audience who could not resist the possibility that through this person they might be able to be connected to Washington, himself. This was appealing, even through the uncomfortable avenue of slavery.

Barnum used his fictional persona, Barnaby Diddleum, author of *The Adventures of an Adventurer,* which was serialized in the *New York Atlas,* to explore the contradictions Heth represented.[27] Diddleum relates the tale of how he acquired Heth, thus becoming a Yankee slaveholder. This oxymoronic identity delights Diddleum, who takes special pleasure in duping abolitionists with his new exhibit. Barnum not only mercilessly exploited the competing impulses of sentimental abolitionism and patriotism but also spoofed the idea of sentimental value. If investing a "thing" with sentiment removed it from the market, Heth was a pointed reminder of the folly of that practice. Sentimental value was much more likely to be bound up with the calculations and exchange of the market than to succeed in erasing the history of exchange from the life of a commodity. Heth's sentimental value, defined by her "sentimental education" under the tutelage of Barnum, and by the nostalgic consumption of her person by those who paid admission to see her, was entirely fictitious, framed by imaginary sentiments.

Barnum, as Diddleum, also exposed what he saw as another abolitionist conceit. He insisted that Heth greatly enjoyed the hoax and was a willing participant, preferring to earn glasses of whisky for herself rather than demand wages to then save and use to free her family members.[28] Slaves and slavery were not exclusively defined by the sentimental images of abolitionism, Barnum insisted. Heth exposed what he saw as the hypocrisy of radical abolitionists, who, by denying any bond between slave and master, denied the complex role of slavery in the social fabric of American society. As New Englanders, P. T. Barnum and Sarah Hale, although they appeared to be two ends of a spectrum, shared a pragmatic acceptance of slavery as an integral part of the national economy. They were unmoved by the tactics of moral suasion. Hale saw abolitionism as an exhibition of excessive and untutored sentiment, and an obstacle to the necessary culture of restraint that must govern all market relations. Barnum saw it as its own humbug, rife with contradictions, just begging to be exploited. Barnum's ability to imagine and articulate these contradictions, as well as contribute to their popularization through direct advertising and fictitious complaints, suggests a certain dark enjoyment of the contradictions of market culture.

It may have been a coincidence that Barnum began to exhibit Heth in the same year Congress instituted a series of gag rules concerning the discussion of slavery, beginning with the Pinckney gag rule, in May 1836.[29] His choice to use Heth to play on the social discomfort about slavery, however, was no coincidence. The gag rules did not succeed in removing the debate about slavery from public attention, although they did curtail the possibility of civilized public political discussion of the issue. This sense of political constraint seems to have opened up many discussions of slavery in popular culture.[30] Not only southerners thought abolitionists were troublemakers.

Barnum's speculation in Heth also capitalized on another, more self-critical humbug. He began to exhibit Heth in the depths of the depression that followed the Panic of 1837. In addition to his attempts to make abolitionists uncomfortable, Barnum also reminded his audience that false speculation, rather than slave labor, was the most pressing economic issue of the moment. Like any nostalgic construction, Heth presented a fantastic invention of the past that seemed to make sense of the present. Her (imaginary) bond to Washington, and her lifelong identity as his nurse was an arch commentary on the fragmentation of the relationships between workers and employers that depression had made clear. In the reverse publicity campaign Barnum initiated after the interest in Heth died down, he anonymously insisted that she was an automaton rather than a live person, suggesting that machines presented a greater a trick on the working men and women of the North than slavery.

Barnum's own career was testimony to the fickle nature of speculation. After his success with Joice Heth, he experienced an extended financial dry spell. The empty pockets of his audience meant that no speculation, however topical or fantastic, could persuade people to trade their only pennies for a ticket to see humbug. But in the 1840s, after a period of financial hardship, Barnum's fortunes began to improve. Although Barnum himself did not subscribe to Hale's rhetoric of economic restraint, he began to see the possibilities that rhetoric might offer as a marketing strategy, and his promotion of Jenny Lind owed a great deal to his public invention of himself as a member of the middle class and the growth of this new market.[31] Barnum emphasized Lind's charitable image to dispel the criticism about personal profit that Elssler had experienced, but this profit was also his best advertisement. He made regular announcements of the sums Lind donated to charity in each of the cities she visited; this allowed him to advertise the overall success of the tour without stripping away the sentimental veneer. He took a page out of Hale's book by promoting the idea that money made through good motives would support the "luxury of doing good."[32] *Godey's Lady's Book* congratulated Barnum on numerous occasions for bringing Lind to America at the height of her career, tacitly confirming his marketing campaign.[33]

Although Lind turned her profits over to sentimental causes, other speculators capitalized on her image for purely profit-oriented ventures. The enthusiasm for Lindiana demonstrated how difficult it was to control the terms of sentimental value. Whereas *Godey's* offered instructions for tasteful hats, cloaks, and mantillas named for Lind, the more obstreperous members of her audience enjoyed Lind's image on or association with a wide range of much more prosaic commodities. The spinoff market was vast, with cigars, needles, paper dolls, etched whiskey bottles, tea kettles, china, gloves, pianos, opera glasses, chairs, sofas, beds, sleds, and even sausages, puddings, and brandy bearing her name.[34] Numerous engravings of her portrait were produced, and a series of polkas and songs were named for her. As soon as Lind's diminutive slipper had touch the shores of America, "the furor commenced" and shopkeepers, *Godey's* noted wryly, lost "no time in making the most out of the popular taste for novelties." Once she had arrived, there was an explosion of available goods: "At Stewart's, Beck's and Levy's there was no difference; but in the Bowery, Canal Street, or Eighth and Second Streets in Philadelphia, Jenny Lind plaids, combs, silks, car-rings, work baskets, bonnets, and even hair-pins were advertised and recommended."[35] This distinction between shopping destinations indicated that the majority of these spinoff products were targeted at a lower-middle-class and working-class audience. For many of these men and women, spinoffs were all they could afford. Most working-class men and women could afford to listen only outside the theaters in which Lind performed, hoping to hear whatever came through the open windows.[36] Barnum kept ticket prices high to create a "natural" segregation of audiences. Despite the popularity of products bearing Lind's image or name with this "fresh air" audience, *Godey's* was quick to point out that these items bore no real relation to Mademoiselle Lind and were nothing better than a "barefaced shopkeeping ruse." Nevertheless, they were a highly successful ruse, and "half the American public [were] wiping their heated brows with Jenny Lind pocket-handkerchiefs, or dressing their hair with Jenny Lind combs."[37] Lind's popularity, true to Barnum's predictions, transcended class boundaries. The prominence of male consumers of Lind spinoffs also indicates the appeal of sentimental commodities for men, even those who had occasion to mop their heated brows. Nor were these consumers insignificant if *Godey's* estimate of their number was accurate even by half.

There were a few spinoff products that did bear a more genuine relation to Lind and targeted a more elite clientele. The Jenny Lind riding hat, for example, was modeled on one that had been a gift to Lind from John N. Genin, a celebrated Broadway Hatter whose shop was next to Barnum's museum. Genin bid $225 for a ticket to Jenny Lind's first concert. As Barnum

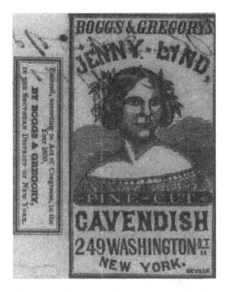

Figure 15. Boggs & Gregory, Jenny Lind
Fine Cut Cavendish Tobacco, ca. 1850,
courtesy of the Library of Congress.

predicted, the publicity Genin received as a result of his bid was well worth
the price of the ticket.[38] *Godey's* described Genin's hat in lavish detail and
included a description of the Jenny Lind bandeaux: a hair piece done by a professional coiffeur to imitate Lind's own hair style. The hat, the bandeaux, the
songs, and the Jenny Lind piano, sold by Boardman and Gray, made logical
sense as spinoff products. Some spinoffs, such as the bed, still popular today,
were associated with Jenny Lind's name but had no visual representation of
her attached to it. Girandoles, a form of candelabra designed for the mantle-
piece, were often cast in the form of literary characters from the novels of Sir
Walter Scott and Washington Irving or from famous historical scenes such
as the *Spirit of '76* and the *Capture of Major Andre*. Both Lind and Elssler, and
later Little Eva, were immortalized in this fashion. These girandoles indicate
an interest in incorporating the image of the celebrity or the novel character
into the parlor in a permanent manner, suggesting that a middle-class audience, which might not have been tempted by Lind sausages, would have been

Figure 16. Jenny Lind girandole, courtesy of the Strong Museum, Rochester, NY.

more inclined to purchase elegant alternatives. The popularity of the sausages and the cigars indicates how flexible the spinoff market was and how easily the desire to possess a talisman of Lind's celebrity could be satisfied. These ephemeral products needed merely a label change to capitalize on the popularity of the celebrity of the moment. The cigar was the most common spinoff product from any sentimental narrative or enterprise.[39] The cigars, like the boot blacking and shaving soap, targeted the male audience for these sentimental performances.

Just as Barnum had tailored his presentation of Heth to capitalize on contemporary anxieties and enthusiasm, his marketing of Lind was based on the same kind of logic. In part, Barnum's sentimental publicity campaign was an implicit reference to Elssler's fall from grace almost ten years earlier, but Barnum engaged the issues of the day as he sought to create the perfect public persona for Lind. In his presentation of Elssler, Wikoff had played on the "surprise" of her virtue to lure women to the theater. With Lind, Barnum did not have a questionable reputation to create a stir. But the issues surrounding the public appearances of women had changed substantially in the decade between 1840 and 1850. By 1850, the question was no longer whether a virtuous woman could appear on stage but how a virtuous woman did appear on stage. Barnum's ability to create the frenzy surrounding Lind's tour was not merely the popularization of her sentimental image; it was his ability to suggest Lind's capacity to personify the reconciliation of two of the most controversial issues in the early 1850s: the controversy over slavery, simmering barely beneath the surface after the fragile Compromise of 1850 and the question of a woman's property rights.

Lind's arrival in America in September 1850 coincided with the rapid fragmentation of any harmony the Compromise might have brought as southern slaveholders lost no time sending slave catchers north to recover lost slaves under the favorable conditions of the newly passed Fugitive Slave Law.[40] Because of her perfect balance of public womanhood and charitable behavior, abolitionists hoped to claim Lind as a supporter of their cause, and after her split with Barnum, she seems to have made a few overtures in that direction, but while under contract with Barnum, Lind's public image was shaped by

Barnum's politics on slavery. Lind modeled a pragmatic kind of charity. She focused her benevolence on feeding and clothing the worthy poor, steering clear of any charitable associations that based their arguments for need on social change.[41] Rumors circulated that Lind had donated $1,000 to the cause of abolitionism, and Barnum, who may have started the rumors, squelched them in a letter to Thomas Ritchie, editor of the *Washington Daily Union*, a proslavery paper.[42] This public denial was nicely timed to coincide with the beginning of Lind's southern tour, assuring southern audiences that the money they paid for their tickets would not support a cause so contrary to their interests. Barnum used this controversy to let his southern audiences know that despite her independence, Lind's understanding of sentimental economics was akin to their own: she did not equate her public self-ownership with a call for self-ownership more broadly understood.[43] In spite of Lind's celebrated benevolence, which modeled the correct mode of public womanhood, she could not help but raise questions about the definitions of sentimental property relations. Barnum had made a reputation for himself in the 1840s by mocking the economic hypocrisy of abolitionism. With Lind, he again raised the specter of inconsistency between the economic relations of sentimental benevolence and the arguments over wage labor and slave labor. Both northerners and southerners claimed their own economic system as the one defined by right sentiments. Because abolitionists turned a blind eye to the injustices of wage labor, Barnum discounted their commitment to the sentimental economics of antislavery, preferring the paternalist arguments of southern slaveholders, although there is no indication that he examined this ideology with the same scrutiny.

Lind was Barnum's answer to the fractious politics of slavery at the beginning of the 1850s. Barnum worked hard to create the impression of Lind's universal appeal across class and regional divides, and he was frequently accused of buying positive reviews. In Barnum's vision, Lind's morally uplifting music, and her personification of a market culture that united the country based on common economic motives rather than conflicting systems of labor and morality, was as much key to her unprecedented economic success as his familiar tricks, such as the appearances of Lind "doubles" and intentional mobs outside the theater.

Lind's association with Barnum was profitable for many people, but she severed her business relationship with Barnum in June 1851 after ten months, before the end of their contract. Although Lind felt that Barnum's marketing campaign was not consistent with her sense of decorum, their split diminished rather than increased her profits. Lind did not understand Barnum's ability to balance controversy and entertainment. Unlike Elssler, who was forced to cut her tour short by scandal, Lind's popularity declined when she publicly embraced respectability through her marriage to Otto Goldschmidt, her accompanist. There was public rejoicing that Lind had finally, at the ripe old age of thirty, fulfilled her womanly destiny, but her marriage also diminished her popularity in two important ways. First, it eliminated the possibility for sensational speculation about her. Once she was a married woman, her veiled sexuality lost its interest and she lost the lower half of her box office.[44] Second, it complicated her sentimental economic persona. As a single woman, she represented a pure kind of female enterprise, but as a married woman, she became the embodiment of all the thorniest issues in the contemporary debates about married women's property rights. Her marriage to Otto Goldschmidt seemed anticlimactic for someone as famous as Lind, and the public nature of her wealth provided fodder for the arguments of those who, like Sarah Hale, were public advocates for married women's property rights. Lind's larger-than-life image of both sentimental womanhood and sentimental enterprise made it hard to strip her of the ideal image of independence that she had modeled just a few months before.

The hoopla that characterized Lind's tour was replaced with the uproar generated by *Uncle Tom's Cabin*, which was serialized in the *National Era* beginning in May 1851 and appeared in novel form in 1852. After she had severed her ties to Barnum, Lind wrote Stowe a letter praising *Uncle Tom's Cabin* for its contribution to "the welfare of our black *brethren*."[45] The rapid sale of the novel was matched by the equally rapid proliferation of spinoffs. Stowe's novel inspired at least fourteen proslavery novels, several of which turned her metaphor of the cabin on its head.[46] In addition to these novels, there were numerous commodities that offered additional ways to both purchase and represent the sentimental politics of the novel. A contemporary enthusiast writing in *Putnam's Monthly* coined the term "Tomitudes" to describe these tributes to the success of the novel.[47] The spinoff products from *Uncle Tom's Cabin* included scarves, dishes, vases, candlesticks, a board game, wall paper, carpets, and fabric. The domestic furnishings suitable for a middle-class parlor refigured the symbolic domesticity of the cabin. These domestic furnishings were not only intended to remind people of the horrors of slavery, however, but also the beauties of right sentiment and the threat of slavery to those moments. Slaves could have right sentiments as long as they were dictated by touching narratives and frozen in beautiful objects. These spinoffs joined a long tradition of objects, starting in the eighteenth century with Josiah Wedgwood's medallions depicting a kneeling slave, which were intended to prompt sympathy for slaves.[48] William Lloyd Garrison depended on a statue of a kneeling slave, which he kept on his mantle, to renew his commitment to the suffering of slaves.[49] The American Anti-Slavery Society distributed handkerchiefs and other objects with the image of the kneeling slave on them to keep the "speechless agony" of the slave in the hearts of those who worked for the cause or to touch the feelings of those still to be persuaded.[50] The wish to own the image of Uncle Tom, or Little Eva or Topsy, however, was not always based on deeply held antislavery sentiments. Purchasing a spinoff appeared to lend credence to abolitionist sensibilities because it gave an economic value to the sentimental commitment, but not all enthusiasts who bought spinoffs from *Uncle Tom's Cabin* shared Garrison's commitment to abolition. For many, the objects they bought renewed their sympathy for the characters in the novel as much as for the real slaves they were intended to represent. If Garrison had to remind himself of his commitment, imagine how easily others might have allowed their attention to be distracted.

The act of purchasing a spinoff had important connections to the economic underpinnings of slavery. Although abolitionist arguments based in moral suasion increased in popularity after William Lloyd Garrison began to publish the *Liberator* in 1831, economic arguments contrasting slave labor and wage labor were also important to the growth of antislavery sentiment in the North. The "rational" arguments about the relative virtues of these two economic models made by gradualist abolitionists were often contrasted with

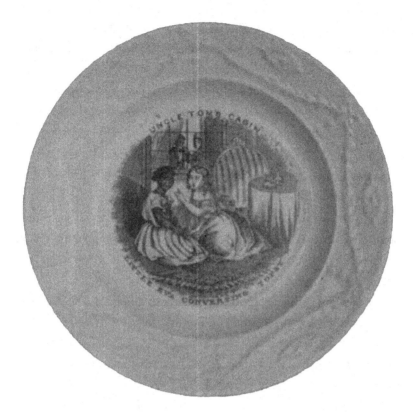

Figure 17. *Uncle Tom's Cabin* plate, courtesy of the Harriet Beecher Stowe Center, Hartford, CT.

the "emotional" appeals of the moral arguments made by immediate abolitionists. The issue over which both groups stumbled, and their ideas inter-
sected, was the fate of emancipated slaves. Neither group could imagine the
possibility for successful domestic coexistence, in the North or the South, for
free people of both races. Colonization seemed to offer the best solution.
Harriet Beecher Stowe was a proponent of this view and demonstrated its
importance to her vision of the successful end of slavery through the relationship of Miss Ophelia and Topsy. Miss Ophelia, an antislavery northerner
who cannot abide slaves, must learn to love one. Topsy must allow herself to
be domesticated by Ophelia. Once the bonds of sympathy have been established between these two (Ophelia initially could not bear to even touch

Topsy), Topsy can be sent off to Liberia to continue the civilizing process there by teaching her own race. Thus Stowe could inculcate domestic ideals in Topsy and insist on the value of sentimental bonds between white and black women while safely fixing a civilized Topsy in her appropriate sphere—Africa.[51]

In Africa, Topsy could be part of another community in which black domesticity as it was imagined in *Uncle Tom's Cabin*, could exist as it could not in the North or the South. The distance, in this case a whole continent away, was essential to the feelings of sympathy. As Adam Smith had reminded his readers, sympathy was not absolute. He who sympathized with another did not forget that he stood apart from the one who gained his sympathy; this distance was essential for sympathy to be possible.[52] The consumption of the spinoff products from the novel was governed by similar logic. Although these objects brought images of slaves into the parlor, they contained them as images of ideal moments of sentiment that seemed to preclude the possibility of social unrest always present in the minds of even the most fervent abolitionists. If Stowe had convinced her readers that Uncle Tom was a man, not just a piece of property, the spinoff products handily turned him back into property. These objects could be invested with sentiments learned from the novel and extended by the consumer's heart, but they were a constant reminder of the contrast between a female consumer's sense of self-ownership and the bondage of the slaves. This distance was essential to the political economy of sentimental abolitionism, and the very opening that Barnum exploited. Also, the insistence of northerners that only they understood the sentimental economics of slavery was testimony to their lack of personal experience with dynamics of the slave market and the complex sentimental bonds between a surprising number of masters and slaves.[53]

Many of the spinoff products for children were intended to teach children how to be good through virtuous play. There was a Topsy-Turvy doll with Little Eva on one side and Topsy on the other. The Topsy-Turvy doll represented the metaphorical transformation of Topsy into Little Eva as she learned to be good. The didactic effect of the doll was easily undermined, however, for Little Eva could just as easily turn into Topsy. An Uncle Tom mechanical bank encouraged young readers to save their pennies, but whether this was to buy Tom his freedom or buy gingerbread for themselves was, of course, ambiguous.[54] One game, "Uncle Tom and Little Eva," focused on the separation and reunion of families. In order to win the game, a player had to be the first to reunite the entire family.[55] This suggested that this was possible. This game and other popular ones, such as the Mansion of Happiness, a game of courtship and marriage, instructed while they entertained, but were easily susceptible to the inversion of their moral lessons.

The plethora of spinoffs inspired by the novel offered an oblique way to create a balance between political sentiments and market sentiments that the reader engaged in the text and had prompted Stowe to write the novel itself. Harriet Beecher Stowe, with characteristic public modesty that belied her private calculations, explained that she had two reasons for writing *Uncle Tom's Cabin:* to do her part, however small, for the cause of abolitionism, and to earn enough money to purchase a silk dress.[56] This assertion, though intended to convey Stowe's womanly modesty and lack of economic calculation, suggests an uncomfortable parallel between the silk dresses bought by southern women with money earned by slave labor and Stowe's dress, bought with money earned by the labor of fictional slaves. In both cases, women owed their ability to participate in market culture to the labor of slaves.

Stowe's argument against slavery was based on her attempt to reformulate the market relations of commodity exchange in sentimental terms. By emphasizing the loss of familial love as the true cost of slavery, Stowe rendered the moral cost of exchange disproportionate to the use value of the slave torn from his family. She argued that slavery did not make economic sense because it did not make sentimental sense.[57] By calling attention to the lack of balance between exchange value and use value, Stowe identified the commodity in question as a sentimental one. A slave/commodity could not be exchanged because his/its sentimental value rendered the cost of ownership too high for any market bid. Stowe hoped that sentiment had the ability to curtail market exchange, even to remove a commodity from the cycle of exchange. But as Barnum had shown, this was not a transparent process. The spinoff products exposed how easily the logic of Stowe's sentimental marketplace could be inverted.

Barnum was quick to seize on the ways that the possibilities of inversion could support his politics of national harmony rather than Stowe's divisive abolitionist politics. In 1853, Barnum brought H. J. Conway's dramatization of *Uncle Tom's Cabin* to the famous Lecture Room in his American Museum. Moses Kimball, owner of the Boston Museum, had commissioned this adaptation, and it had played with great success in Boston. Conway's adaptation differed dramatically from George Aiken's theatrical adaptation of the novel, which was then running to great acclaim at the National Theater in New York. Whereas Aiken's version strove to stay true to Stowe's sentimental abolitionism, Conway turned Stowe's novel on its head and wrote a play that maintained only the skeleton of her story. Although called *Uncle Tom's Cabin*, it told an entirely different story about slavery. Conway championed the bonds among white, male northerners and southerners, made all the slave characters beholden to white benefactors, and used this new story to argue aggressively for the preservation of the Union at any cost.[58] Barnum capitalized on the popularity of the novel to sell tickets to a play that contradicted almost every moral lesson in Stowe's book.

P. T. Barnum and Sarah Hale were once again united in their criticism of *Uncle Tom's Cabin*. Hale, who had published stories by Stowe before she wrote *Uncle Tom's Cabin*, did not review the book, although she favorably reviewed several of the response novels.[59] When she reviewed Stowe's subsequent novels, she used the review as the opportunity to skewer Stowe rather than discuss her book. Hale's review of Stowe's *Dred* demonstrates her dismissal of Stowe as an author: "This is a handsomely printed work, and will doubtless prove otherwise attractive to the author's friends."[60] She reissued her own first novel, *Northwood*, in 1852, with a new introduction that was a pointed critique of Stowe's work, without mentioning her by name. Hale informed a new generation of readers that she had written this novel "when what is now known as 'Abolitionism' first began to disturb the harmony between the South and the North." Her only motive, she asserted, had been to search for the truth of the issue from the "retirement of her mountain home." She had looked to the Constitution, the word of God, and the history of humanity, rather than fractious debates, for her answers, and in twenty-five years, she affirmed, her views had not changed. "The great error of those who would sever the Union rather than see a slave within its borders," she lamented, "is that they forget the *master* is their brother, as well as the *servant*." To counter Stowe's argument about the sentimental economics of abolitionism, Hale asserted that abolitionism did not make sentimental sense because it did not make Christian or economic sense. For a new generation, reading *Northwood* for the first time, as well as for those who had read it in their own youth, her novel would, she hoped, teach the true spirit of Christian philanthropy and promote harmony between the North and South.[61] The following spring, Hale published *Liberia; or Mr. Peyton's Experiments* (1853), which outlined the advantages of colonization, not only as solution for the African, "who among us has no home, no position and no future," but also to the tribes of Africa who would benefit from the civilizing and Christian influence of former slaves.[62] Despite their very public differences on the subject of abolitionism, Hale and Stowe shared a vision of sentimental economics in which colonization of freed slaves was the only answer.

In May 1851, the *National Era*, a prominent antislavery newspaper, advertised the publication of a new story by "Mrs. H. B. Stowe" a few weeks in advance as a way of encouraging their subscribers to get their accounts in order lest they miss an installment of "Uncle Tom's Cabin, or the Man that was a Thing." Stowe's story promised to be "the length of the Tale by Mrs. Southworth, entitled Retribution."[63] Although Stowe was already a popular writer and able to draw readers based on her own reputation, Southworth had a greater following among readers of the *National Era*, as well as a reputation for lengthy stories. Toward the end of the serialization of *Uncle Tom's Cabin*, one subscriber wrote to ask if Stowe's story could be bound in a single volume with Southworth's *Mother-in-Law* and *Retribution*. Although the answer was no— Southworth's books had already been published separately, and Stowe's book was already being stereotyped by the Jewetts of Boston—publication of this request in the pages of the *National Era* suggests that this was a frequent request and readers considered the work of Stowe and Southworth together.

Although Stowe and Southworth shared abolitionist sentiments, Southworth, as a resident of Washington, DC, encountered realities of slavery in a more immediate fashion. In 1854, she published "A Warning to the Public" in the pages of the *National Era* stating that Annie Taylor, a nine-year-old mulatto girl, whom Southworth had recently manumitted, was missing and presumed kidnaped. Southworth warned readers to not to purchase her or, if Taylor had already been sold under false pretenses, "to take immediate steps toward the recovery of the purchase money."[64] This advertisement demonstrates Southworth's personal commitment to abolition, but it also suggests that the readers of the *National Era* might be slave owners themselves, revealing the complex nature of slave culture in the nation's capital.

As a southerner, Southworth played an interesting role in the world of anti-slavery fiction. In a review of *The Wife's Victory*, by Mrs. Southworth, the following year, the editor of the *National Era* was careful to inform readers that another book that had appeared that year, *The Inebriate's Hut*, was not by their own dear Mrs. Emma D. E. N. Southworth, but by a "*Northern Mrs. Southworth*" who sought to capitalize on the name of the more famous Mrs. Southworth. Southworth's writing style incorporated many literary genres: the sentimental, the Gothic, the tall tale, the plantation story, melodrama, moral allegory, and black minstrelsy. Her ability to meld these traditions into a single gripping narrative was the secret to her popularity. Her politics, like her writing, were based on unification rather than division, and although she supported gradual abolition, she was unwilling to put the Union in jeopardy.[65] In 1857, Southworth signed an exclusive contract with Robert Bonner, publisher of the *New York Ledger*. Bonner assiduously avoided any suggestion of sectionalism in his paper. Southworth, who had always appealed to both northern and southern audiences was well suited to this task. Although her stories were avidly consumed by a wide audience, Southworth did not abandon her earlier positions on slavery. Instead, she recast her discussion of slaves and slavery as part of a reexamination of stereotypical oppositions of all kinds. Her skill with melodrama and her use of descriptive names lent themselves well to exposing the false dichotomies of black/white, master/slave, man/woman, girl/boy, villain/hero, and independence/dependence, to name a few.[66] One of her most famous novels, *The Hidden Hand*, serialized in 1859, explores all of these dichotomies through the exploits of one of Southworth's most beloved heroines, Capitola the Madcap.[67]

Southworth's Capitola was celebrated in both the United States and Britain through a fashion craze for Capitola hats, suits, and boots as well as a few boats and a racehorse that bore her name.[68] The sartorial spinoffs must have resonated with readers because Capitola's own disguise in boy's clothing, and her subsequent transformation into a "young lady" through the purchase of an appropriate and extensive wardrobe by "Old Hurricane," her guardian, were an important symbol of Capitola's appeal as a heroine. She retained the resourcefulness and pluck of her initial masquerade as newsboy, even after her transformation into a young lady of property, not to mention her use of additional disguises throughout the novel. Capitola clothing might have offered a way to exhibit appreciation of the novel and participate in a personal kind of masquerade. The dramatizations of the novel must have tickled the audience's funny bone as they contemplated the humor of a costume of a costume of a costume. Although the slaves in *The Hidden Hand* are caricatures, with the exception of Nancy Grewell, the midwife who rescues Capitola, they are caricatures of personality types. Southworth does not caricature slaves as a group. Although she relies on comic form, she teaches her readers important lessons about independence of action and thought. Those who were capable of independent action and thought—men, women, and slaves—deserved self-ownership, Southworth argued.

After the Civil War was over, the issue of slavery was largely written out of popular fiction as the causes of the war were revised to conform to the politics of reconciliation.[69] Southern authors such as Augusta Evans, who had been a fervent Confederate supporter, wrote novels that glorified the lost civilization of the antebellum South. Her novel, *St. Elmo* (1867), was enormously popular and generated a wide variety of spinoff products. In some cases, the spinoff was not an ephemeral piece of material culture, such as shaving soap or boat blacking, but a person or a place. *St. Elmo* inspired the naming of at least thirteen towns in Alabama, Tennessee, Georgia, California, Colorado, Illinois, Kentucky, Louisiana, Mississippi, Missouri, New York, Texas, and Virginia, and many southern towns had a St. Elmo Hotel. In addition, there were a number of girls' schools, steamboats, railway coaches, and blue-ribbon dogs, not to mention a cigar, a blend of punch, and a camellia named for the novel. Southerners named their houses "La

Bocage" after the Murray family estate. Daughters were named after the exemplary Edna Earle, and sons were named after the novel's brooding hero, whose moral reform imbued the name St. Elmo with the associations of virtue and excellence.[70] In 1939, Earnest Elmo Caulkins, an advertising executive, commented in the *Saturday Review of Literature:* "I once attended an advertising meeting at which four of the members were named Elmo or St. Elmo. In some cases the name survives into the second generation."[71] The name St. Elmo came to stand in the abstract for quality and gentility of the "lost" southern way of life and offered at least one way to heal the wounds to southern pride.[72]

Elizabeth Stuart Phelps's novel *The Gates Ajar* (1868) also proposed a spiritual vision that she hoped would heal the wounds of the Civil War. The novel chronicles the recovery from grief of a young woman named Mary, whose brother Royal was killed in the war. Mary's Aunt Winifred is the catalyst for her recovery; Winifred comes to visit, bringing a vision of heaven as a domestic paradise, and converts Mary to her religious views. She also converts a wide circle of townsfolk, and, by the end of the novel, the minister himself.[73] The problem with heaven, the flock of Dr. Bland and Deacon Quirk confide in Aunt Winifred, is that it sounds dull; nobody does anything, they "just [float] around in heaven—you know—all together—something like jujube paste!" or "glorify God and sing Worthy the Lamb!" They are not comforted by Deacon Quirk's assurance that those who enter heaven "shall be clothed in white robes with palms in [their] hands, and bow before the Great White Throne."[74] Aunt Winifred promises that heaven will be like earth, except the material possessions that had been unattainable in life—a piano for one poor girl, and machines to fix for the son of a farmer—will be available in heaven. Heaven is a place where domesticity torn asunder by death can be reconfigured. Phelps caricatures Deacon Quirk's vision of heaven to show Aunt Winifred's material heaven as sensible by comparison. She points out that a piano is no more material than the harps that Quirk admits are in heaven, and that the palm fronds he imagines everyone carrying would have to come from somewhere, so trees and meadows are not far-fetched.

The Gates Ajar continued the trend toward personal spiritual interpretation that sentimental fiction encouraged, and its spinoffs offered spiritual placebos in commodity form. There were wing collars, the style a pun on the title, tippets, the ever-popular cigars, funeral wreaths to speed the dead to Aunt Winifred's heaven, and in Britain, a patent medicine that offered a free copy of the novel in pamphlet form with every bottle. This medicine was Phelps's personal favorite among the spinoffs. She remarked on the spinoffs with some amusement in her autobiography; her only complaint was that she did not receive any percentage of their profits.[75] By including the novel in pamphlet form, free with the medicine, the relationship between novel and spinoff changed. With the medicine, the spinoff appropriated the text itself and presented it as a secondary form, an advertisement specifically for the medicine. The "gift" of the novel with the medicine implied that the purchaser of the medicine could just as easily discover the novel through the purchase of the medicine as she or he could be drawn to purchase the medicine for its association with the novel. In the novel, Phelps portrays medicine as powerless against death, but she presents spiritualism as a powerful cure for grief. The patent medicine equated the spiritual with the "medical" and, by inverting the relationship between spinoff and text, replaced spiritual healing with medical healing. The transformation of the text from the sources of the desire for the spinoff product to advertising in which the meaning is shaped by the product represents an important shift in the role of narrative in its relationship to the consumption of commodities, and it signals the rise of a new era in advertising.

Lydia Pinkham's *Vegetable Compound,* which appeared on the market shortly after *The Gates Ajar,* offered a similar conflation of spiritual and medical solutions to women's problems. Pinkham's medicine promised to cure women's ailments, suggesting the needless suffering of a "woman's condition" was no longer necessary. She attempted to dispel associations with other patent medicines by insisting that the alcohol content was minimal and all the ingredients were natural. The label bore her portrait as her personal testimonial that she held her product to the same standards to which she held herself. She encouraged women to write to her with their problems so that she could prescribe a cure. Women began to write about all kinds of problems, and her correspondence department, which had begun as a "medical" service, became an outlet for confessions of spiritual, emotional, and physical problems.[76]

The novel and its spinoff products stimulated an evolving relationship between sentimental value and economic value. As the luxury market expanded, cultural meaning became the premier value bought and sold. The secular translation of the moral narratives of religion in the novel and the artifacts of faith in spinoffs gave the sentimental associations of these goods a cultural power that their ephemeral nature disguised. Reading sentiment was both a literary and commodity venture. Novels did not merely discuss the market, they were imbedded in a circle of commodity relations. The novel prompted a form of "everyday theatricals," reenactments of manners, gestures, and rituals from the novel recast as part of the reader's life.[77] Spinoff products helped model a new understanding of market behavior and commodities.

$\mathcal{E}pilogue$

∞

THE SMOOTH MISCHIEFS
OF SENTIMENT

In December 1877, when Sarah Hale bid her readers farewell, she had just entered her ninetieth year. Her retirement from the literary editorship of *Godey's Lady's Book* coincided with Louis Godey's decision to sell the magazine. Godey was in poor health and lived less than a year after the magazine was sold.[1] Hale outlived him by only a few months. Their deaths seem to mark the end of an era. By the late 1870s, *Godey's* had lost its position as the grand dame of women's magazines. Hale's obituary in the *New York Times* referred to it as "a Philadelphia magazine of the old school."[2] Hale was lionized for the longevity of her life as an author: "Her life all but spanned the history of our nation under the existing polity and she saw that wonderful material growth of her nation that has place it among the great nations of the world."[3] But her literary production, with the exception of *Northwood*, was described in terms of antiquarian interest: "She wrote first and last more than 20 books, mostly of that peculiar type that one associates with the round table, with its red-and-black spread, the high posted bedstead, the wooden mantel, with gilt china ornaments, and the white muslin curtain of the 'spare room' in the low farmhouse where, perchance, one has passed a few careless vacation days."[4] Although *Godey's* did not go out of circulation until 1898, at the time of Hale's death, it was a relic of a bygone era.[5]

In the aftermath of the Civil War, a crisis of confidence, caused by the perception that reason and morality had failed to restrain the destructive passions that had led to war, undermined the sentimental market philosophy of an aging generation. The rhetoric of restraint—both commercial and moral—that had animated conservative visions of the national economy and national culture in *Godey's Lady's Book* rang hollow when it seemed as if all sense of restraint had been thrown to the winds. The growing disinterest, and even disdain, for the moral world described by sentimentalism was interpreted as the failure of sentimental ideas to reform the market. The very nature of the national economy had changed. The shift from household production to a market economy in the antebellum period contributed to a significant increase in the consumption of manufactured goods.[6] The breakdown of household economy opened the door to the metaphor of family business as the parlor became a site of economic production that supported the cultural identity of the middle class, but the moral authority of this economic vision was challenged by the devastation of the Civil War. The links between domestic and political economy that had been the mainstay of economic lessons taught by Sarah Hale and her contemporaries were obscured by the development of industrial capitalism. The tensions between capital and labor that caused such anxiety in the late nineteenth century were contrasted with a nostalgic version of antebellum commerce in which the links between domestic economy and political economy that permeated the sentimental rhetoric about economics were remembered as the moral economy of the agrarian past rather than the logic of an urban middle class. Nevertheless, the sentimental education about economic life had a lasting effect on the economic consciousness of middle-class Americans. Even if they had forgotten the source of their market knowledge, the links to a sentimental vision of moral economy were stronger than the perception that these ideas were outdated. After the war, northerners promoted their vision of the economy as the national vision of the economy. As the market expanded, public debates about the progress of national economic development continued to be influenced by the desire to curb the tendency toward the excesses of luxury, but the roles of consumption and production in the process and the relationship between culture and economics took on new meaning.

Charlotte Perkins Gilman, a grandniece of Catharine Beecher and Harriet Beecher Stowe, published her first major work, *Women and Economics: The Economic Factor Between Men and Women as a Factor in Social Evolution,* in 1898. Gilman, following in the footsteps of both her great aunts, particularly Catharine, was interested in the relationship between the organization of home life and science and economics. Unlike her aunts, Gilman rejected the moral language of Christianity in favor of the more scientific language of ethics. She framed her argument around the ideas of evolution and a reexamination of the category of "natural" rather than interpreting the world through a Christian lens. Although she agreed with Beecher and Stowe that the home should be subjected to intellectual scrutiny, Gilman disputed their claim that the home was the center of society. She remained unconvinced by the description of husbands and wives as partners in the business of life and questioned the logic of marriage as a model of complementary relations, or "copartnership," to use Mary Virginia Terhune's term. A wife "is in no sense a business partner," Gilman asserted, "unless she contributes capital or experience or labor, as a man would in a like relation."[7] In her opinion, rather than describing the true nature of domestic economic relations between men and women, importing the language of business relations into the domestic sphere perpetuated inequality. Terhune, Hale, and others had argued for economic interdependence. For Gilman, the coded language of duty that earlier generations had used to claim the dignity of domestic economy meant the denial of women's fair wages, and nothing short of economic independence for women was acceptable.[8] By challenging the definition of marriage as the natural state of society, Gilman challenged the logic of sentimental economics. For polemical reasons, she took at face value women's rhetorical insistence that their work was not labor. In doing so, she helped erase the memory that the parlor had always been home to work as well as leisure.

Women of Gilman's generation, born in the 1860s, questioned the separation of politics and economy that had been so important to earlier generations. Gilman had experienced her own mother's struggle to support her children after her divorce, and she struggled financially in the years after her own divorce. Like many progressive reformers, she saw politics as an effective way to rationalize social practice. She was adamant that economic opportunities for women could not be ad hoc. As she argued in *Women and Economics*, women's lives were not naturally defined by motherhood and household responsibilities, nor did these roles preclude a woman's ability to work for pay. Society must recognize that women's roles were constructed and should change to accommodate their need to work for money. For Gilman, it was not enough to use the metaphors of business to describe home life; the home must be made into a business and women's domestic responsibilities professionalized. Catharine Beecher had argued almost sixty years earlier that domestic economy must be taught by professionals, and Gilman took that suggestion one step further, arguing that it must also be performed by professionals. Children must be raised, food must be prepared, houses must be kept by women who had been trained to do these tasks so that all women could benefit. Women who did domestic work would be paid for their work; other women would be free to pursue professional careers without the dual anxieties of career and home. Hale and her contemporaries had argued that women were free to pursue careers as long as they did not neglect their domestic duties. Gilman argued that women who pursued careers had the right to neglect their domestic duties.

Gilman presented her case by using the powerful metaphors of economic individualism and competition. An economy based on the bonds and obligations of friendship and familial relations would marginalize women, she feared. She wanted to move away from domestic dependency and argued for an ethical economy in which everyone was a civilized and competitive stranger. Despite her overt rejection of the sentimental logic that had governed the economy of charity fairs and other female enterprises, Gilman's ideas were an extension of this way of thinking about the market. Although she preferred the stance of a dispassionate scientist to that of a domestic moralist, her arguments had a familiar ring. Like earlier writers on domestic economy, Gilman argued for the necessary integration of the spheres of home and market, and like the ethical economists, who were her contemporaries, she saw no chance for social harmony without this integration.[9] Although *Women and Economics* is usually studied as a rejection of the shackles of Victorian domesticity and as a pivotal work in the transition to the feminist thought of the New Woman, the grounding of her ideas in the earlier literature about women and economics suggests important continuities in the economic sensibilities of the nineteenth and twentieth centuries.[10] By rejecting the economic compromises of antebellum women outright, Gilman lost as much as she gained. The compromises of sentimental economics remained persuasive to a majority of women into the twentieth century. Women continued to find the language of sentimental pragmatism convincing, using new version of it with considerable success, as the careers of Brownie Wise in the 1950s and Martha Stewart in the 1980s attest.[11] The disdain of Gilman and her contemporaries for these compromises contributed to the marginalization of the market strategies of many women as much as it claimed legitimate ground for women's economic activity. Once sentimental strategies became detached from production, their associations with consumption came to define women's primary market activity as consumption. The rise of consumer culture, therefore, could be described as a process of feminization.

Thorstein Veblen also contributed to this characterization. His *Theory of the Leisure Class* (1899) was published a year after *Women and Economics*. Although Veblen's discussion of the roles women played in economic life is complex and ironic, his insights are often reduced to a shorthand characterization of women as conspicuous consumers. Perhaps this is because he made no secret about his disdain for the strident economic language of the New Woman, but more likely it is because he categorically dismissed the idea that the work middle-class women did in the parlor was real production.[12] For Veblen, middle-class women's claims to usefulness were merely ceremonial.[13] Like Gilman, he discounted the pragmatic underpinnings of the sentimental rhetoric these women used. Once people lost the ability to see the balance inherent in this rhetoric, it is no wonder it seemed hollow.

So much of the history of consumer culture has centered on a rhetoric of disenchantment about the homogeneity of mass culture and fear that acts of consumption lack the authenticity of production.[14] By focusing on how people engaged a new market culture and grappled with the complexities of these new experiences rather than focusing on an abstract imaginary world of desire, this book tells a different tale about the rhetorical understanding of the relationship between production and consumption. Recovering antebellum debates about this relationship helps link the rise of new forms of advertising in the late nineteenth century to a well-established discussion of the practical uses of sentimental language. Although advertising encouraged fantasy, it was firmly rooted in the compromises of everyday life. Advertisers joined a discussion about the meaning of production and consumption, indulgence and restraint, and moral economy and moral turpitude that had engaged their grandmothers and grandfathers.

The growth of advertising in 1880s was an indication that people were more willing to embrace the desire for goods rather than counsel restraint. Where good motives had indicated that a person should choose between opportunities for consumption and limit the acquisition of goods and experiences, advertising suggested that there was a way to inculcate the idea of good motives into all commodities and consumption experiences. Where there had been a growing sense that sometimes luxuries could be necessities, advertising began to persuade consumers that luxury was necessity. Advertisers encouraged readers to believe that they were able to discern the difference between good and bad advertising. As a result, all consumption encouraged or sanctioned by good advertisement could be seen as moral. When a consumer's motives were directed by good advertising, they were, by association, good motives. By making this connection, advertisers asserted that these distinctions alleviated the burden on the individual consumer to make these choices.[15] This shift from personal morality to collective morality demonstrated how malleable sentimental rhetoric was. The daydreams inspired by the narratives of advertising are as much about restraint, whether self-imposed or unavoidable, as about indulgence.[16] In addition to offering an opportunity to enjoy the fantasy world of consumption, they provide a way to puzzle out the pragmatic decisions about what is possible and what is practical. Even people given to self-indulgence have to choose sometimes. People for whom the rhetoric of restraint and the ideal of moral market culture are appealing use their daydreams toward rational ends. Restraint is pleasure as well as denial. Whereas Hale had mobilized sentiment in the name of restraint, postwar advertisers were equally willing to mobilize sentiment in the name of indulgence. Although the emphasis on good motives remained, the definition of those motives changed. Advertising suggested that consumption was based in a rational assessment of personal and social needs. By educating the consumer, advertisers facilitated the fulfillment of those needs. Women and men read advertisements for information and assessed the sentiments they expressed before they made purchases. For middle-class consumers, advertising helped to rationalize the market.[17]

The problem of how to reconcile prosperity and morality—property and propriety—remains the central organizing principle of middle-class market culture.[18] As each new middle class invents itself, the terms of this balance are renegotiated. This moral cycle is a prerequisite for a renewal of the "middleness." The legitimacy of a new middle class depends on a partial repudiation of the previous moral structure of market relations in favor of a new moral logic that answers the rise of new conditions. The moral cycle holds important clues to the history of consumer culture and the influence of sentimentalism. We are continually persuaded by a moral language of the market that balances sentimental desire with pragmatic need. As Alexis de Tocqueville noted, Americans "maintain that virtue is useful and prove it every day."[19] Each generation determines the balance that defines their vision of a moral economy. The smooth mischiefs of sentiment drive our economic imagination, for not only is their fraud a successful one, but each generation is convinced that its moral vision is not susceptible to mischief, only to succumb to the latest wiles.

Acknowledgments

Herman Melville's invocation "Oh, Time, Strength, Cash and Patience!" expresses with eloquence the exquisite agony of writing a book. I have been very lucky to have my own prayers of this nature answered by many friends, family members, and colleagues. I would like to thank the archivists and librarians at Yale University's Sterling and Beinecke Libraries; Harvard University's Baker, Houghton, and Schlesinger Libraries; the New York Public Library; the Library of Congress, especially Cynthia Earman; the National Museum of American History; Lied Library at the University of Nevada, Las Vegas; the Strong Museum; and the Harriet Beecher Stowe Center. I am also grateful for financial support for this project from the National Museum of American History and for a New Investigator Award from UNLV.

I would like to thank Barbara Miller Lane, my mentor at Bryn Mawr College, whose example both intellectual and professional I have always tried to emulate. Her confidence in me gave me the courage to try to live up to her expectations. I owe Jean-Christophe Agnew, my dissertation adviser, a great intellectual debt. He listened with only a slightly raised eyebrow to my enthusiastic torrent about my choice to write about valentines for his seminar on consumer culture, and he began a long sequence of well-placed suggestions about sources and methodology that helped turn enthusiasm into analysis. My copy of his book, *World's Apart*, is perhaps the greatest testimony to this intellectual debt. It is a palimpsest, the margins filled with my moments of eureka as I read and re-read those pages, rediscovering their meaning as my own thinking evolved. In the last phase of revising this book, I came across a piece of marginalia written in some early reading of the last chapter that announced: THIS IS IT! Where the arguments in this book approach lucidity, my debt to him is clear. Where they remain fuzzy, they might have benefited from yet another reading of *World's Apart* and the scribbling of another layer of marginalia. I especially want to thank Ann Fabian, who has been both mentor and friend throughout this project. She has always been a model of collegiality, intellectual curiosity, and achievement. She showed me how to imagine historical problems in new ways. Her advice, queries, intellectual example, and kind support has sustained me in ways I cannot express.

Nancy Cott was an invaluable member of my dissertation committee. She always asked hard questions and pushed me to clarify my thinking. I thank Laura Wexler for her very helpful comments. I thank Charlie McGovern for the valuable insights into this project that he offered every time we discussed it. I thank him also for his warm friendship and his ability to make the fellows program at NMAH one of the most intellectually rewarding experiences I have had.

I thank Adam Green for a lunch conversation that prompted me to write a seminar paper on Valentine's Day and Elizabeth Abrams, Ed Balleisen, Brooke Barr, Dan Belgrad, Nancy Bercaw, Scott Casper, John Cheng, Cassandra Cleghorn, Karin Gedge, Carolyn Goldstein, Jeanne Lawrence, Margaret McFadden, Stephen Rachman, Shawn Rosenheim, Douglas Rossinow, Laura Saltz, Peggy Shaffer, Carol Sheriff, Karen Suchenski, Charlotte Sussman, and Glenn Wallach for years of interesting conversations about this project.

I am grateful for conversations with Richard Brodhead, Helena Curtis, Michael Denning, Shelley Foote, Richard Fox, William Gienapp, Rodris Roth,

Alan Trachtenberg, Lynn Wardley, and Bryan Wolf that have helped strengthen and clarify my ideas about nineteenth-century America. I thank George Schulman for his intellectual example and for many stimulating conversations in the earliest phase of this project, which have continued to shape my ideas throughout the writing of this book.

I thank the members of the UNLV History Department faculty seminar series for their interest in the chapters I presented and their good advice. I especially thank Gregory Brown, Chris Rasmussen, David Tanenhaus, Michelle Tusan, and Mary Wammack for their suggestions and help with this manuscript, and Andy Fry and Eugene Moehring for their support. I thank Chris Wiatrowski for her invaluable help finding sources and learning to use new and old technology in the library and for her friendship. For my students, both graduate and undergraduate, who made me explain many times what cultural history was and above all why history mattered at all. I especially thank Bill Bush, Caryll Dziedziak, Gerry Evans, Matt Lay, Melise Leech, Heather Lusty, Carole Terry, and the members of my graduate colloquium on market culture for their intellectual companionship.

At Smithsonian Books I thank Mark Hirsch for his enthusiasm about his project and his support at a most important time in my career; Joanne Reams, Brian Barth, and Emily Sollie; and my editor, Jeff Hardwick, whose help in the last stages of writing was indispensable and some of the best I have ever been given. I also thank the anonymous readers of the manuscript and Karin Kaufman for her skillful copyediting and kind patience during the process.

Because this book is about the marketplace and the home, I want to thank all who helped me balance those responsibilities in my own life. I thank all the people who have taken such good care of my children through the years I worked on this project: Jenifer Stenfors, Melanie Paris, Rebecca Horacek, Alexandra Clinton, Arianne Pichon, Amy Robinson, and the staff of the University United Methodist Child Development Center, especially Diana Alvarez, Margaret Bourgon, Geri Devereaux, Nancy Easton, La Nora Gallo, Nicholas Grainger, Carissa Haeck, Talisha Henderson, Lindsay Hendricks, Christina Hernandez, Hilary Hinchman, Valerie Phillips, Deena Rooke, Carole Simpson, Tabitha Sorvillo, and Zanni Van Antwerp. I thank the friends who have sustained me through this process. Jill Caskey participated in more conversations about Valentine's Day than anyone should have to. She has been an intellectual anchor and a kindred spirit from our first days in college. I am grateful to Regina Cosnowsky and Bruce Carvalho, whose visits to Las Vegas have been true bright spots in the long process of finishing this book, and Karminder Brown, Vicki Hom, Jackie Maloy, Andrew Oshiro, Kelli Quinn, and Jayne Wynes, whose interest in my progress helped me finish.

I cannot characterize my entrance into the world of print as evidence of my commitment to familial duty, as did so many of the nineteenth-century women who appear in the pages of this book. A dissertation and the book that follows from it are, by definition, a product of ego, but they are also a form of autobiography and so I find my family written everywhere in the pages of this text. I thank all of them for many years of patience and tolerance of crazy work schedules, deferred vacations, and the other disruptions to family life that accompany writing. This book has been its own form of sentimental enterprise and by extension a kind of family business. I thank my grandmothers, Marguerite Beale Johnson and Virginia Armistead White, and my great-aunt Margaret Beale who did not live to see this project finished but provided tangible and spiritual links to nineteenth-century sentimental culture through artifacts and stories. Marguerite Beale Johnson left a legacy of twentieth-century Victorianism that fed my imagination. Margaret Beale told me stories about my great-grandmother, Cynthia Moore Beale. Virginia Armistead White read and discussed parts of this book; her insights were astute and helped me to see the complementary nature of seeming contradictions. I thank Chick and Judy Nelson, for many years of intellectual interest and practical support. I thank John, Emily, Isobelle, and Victoria White and Hilary, Bob, Alex, and Clara Jacobs. I thank Ben White for offering helpful criticism while at the same time sparing my feelings. I thank Lynn Cooper for her personal support and professional example. I thank my father, Harrison White, for his intellectual example, his unstinting criticism, and his belief in and support of me. My discovery of links between his work and my own was a great surprise and a great gift. I thank my mother, Cynthia White, for her indispensable help with all intellectual and family matters, our many interesting conversations on the subject of this book, her careful editing and delicious suppers, and her assuming the responsibilities of our household, which could pass for a three-ring circus.

I thank my children, Phoebe, Cyrus, and Jasper, who have lived this book from the very beginning of their lives. This book is for Phoebe, who made her own books, much more beautiful and illuminating, on the backs of my drafts, and in the summer I was finishing this book began her first titled work, *Cyrus Tales*. She wanted to know when her name would appear in my book, and now she can read it for herself. It is for Cyrus, who frequently asked with cheerful optimism if I was done with my book yet. And it is for Jasper, whose sense of humor made the final stage of this project so much happier. Most of all, I thank my husband, Ethan Nelson, who gave me the valentine that inspired this project and the title for the book. He is always able to help me see both the forest and the trees, and without him, none of this would have been possible.

Notes

Introduction

1. Massachusetts, vol. 2, 683, R. G. Dun & Co. Collection, Baker Library, Harvard University Business School. 2. "Made First Valentine in United States: Miss Esther Howland of Quincy Tells How She Built Up a Big Business. Oldest Valentine Known," *Boston Globe*, February 14, 1901, p. 6. 3. Franklyn Howland, *A Brief Genealogical and Biographical History of Arthur, Henry and John Howland and the Descendants of the United States and Canada* (New Bedford, MA: Published by the Author, 1885), 351–52. 4. Ruth Webb Lee, *A History of Valentines* (Wellesley, MA: Lee Publications, 1952), 61. 5. See Stuart Blumin, *The Emergence of the Middle Class: Social Experience in the American City, 1760–1900* (New York: Cambridge University Press, 1989); Philip Scranton, *Proprietary Capitalism: The Textile Manufacture at Philadelphia, 1800–1885* (New York: Cambridge University Press, 1983). 6. See Susan Coultrap-McQuin, *Doing Literary Business: American Women Writers in the Nineteenth Century* (Chapel Hill: University of North Carolina Press, 1990); Wendy Gamber, *The Female Economy: The Millinery and Dressmaking Trades, 1860–1930* (Urbana: University of Illinois Press, 1997). 7. See Amy Dru Stanley, "Home Life and the Morality of the Market," in *The Market Revolution in America: Social, Political, and Religious Expressions, 1800–1880*, ed. Melvyn Stokes and Stephen Conway (Charlottesville: University Press of Virginia, 1996), 75; Winifred Barr Rothenberg, *From Market-places to a Market Economy: The Transformation of Rural Massachusetts, 1750–1850* (Chicago: University of Chicago Press, 1992), 4, 7. 8. Tony A. Freyer, *Producers versus Capitalists: Constitutional Conflict in Antebellum America* (Charlottesville: University Press of Virginia, 1994), 4; Douglass C. North, *The Economic Growth of the United States, 1790–1860* (New York: W. W. Norton, 1966), 48. 9. See Sean Wilentz, *Chants Democratic:*

New York City and the Rise of the American Working Class, 1788–1850 (New York: Oxford University Press, 1984); Christine Stansell, *City of Women: Sex and Class in New York, 1789–1860* (New York: Knopf, 1986) for histories of an urban working class. 10. See Sam Bass Warner Jr., *Streetcar Suburbs: The Process of Growth in Boston, 1870–1900* (Cambridge: Harvard University Press, 1962). 11. Those in the middle class were not exclusively urban dwellers, although there was a population concentration of the professional classes in cities and towns. In New England, where rural men and women participated in the market economy in significant ways, there was a provincial middle class tied to the urban middle class by culture if not kinship. See Catherine E. Kelly, *In the New England Fashion: Reshaping Women's Lives in the Nineteenth Century* (Ithaca, NY: Cornell University Press, 1999), 8–17; Adam Sweeting, *Reading Houses and Building Books: Andrew Jackson Downing and the Architecture of Popular Antebellum Literature, 1835–1855* (Hanover, NH: University Press of New England, 1996); and David Schuyler, *Apostle of Taste: Andrew Jackson Downing, 1815–1852* (Baltimore: Johns Hopkins University Press, 1996). 12. See Betsy Blackmar, "Re-walking the 'Walking City': Housing and Property Relations in New York City, 1780–1840," *Radical History Review* 21 (fall 1979): 131–48. 13. See Daniel Horowitz, *The Morality of Spending: Attitudes Toward the Consumer Society in America, 1875–1940* (Baltimore: Johns Hopkins University Press, 1985). 14. See Ann Douglas, *The Feminization of American Culture* (New York: Knopf, 1977); Thorstein Veblen, *The Theory of the Leisure Class* (New York: Penguin, 1979); and Lori Merish, *Sentimental Materialism: Gender, Commodity Culture, and Nineteenth-Century American Literature* (Durham, NC: Duke University Press, 2002). The engravings of store interiors that served as advertisements for commercial establishments frequently figured men as consumers, often in a family group with women and children. These engravings, which were intended to draw people into the store by representing imagined customers, suggest that ideal consumer behavior included the whole family. See Blumin, *Emergence of the Middle Class.* 15. See Edward Balleisen, *Navigating Failure: Bankruptcy and Commercial Society in Antebellum America* (Chapel Hill: University of North Carolina Press, 2001), 71–73, for a related discussion of what he calls commercial moralists. 16. New cultural/economic histories of religion: R. Laurence Moore, *Selling God: American Religion in the Marketplace of Culture* (New York: Oxford University Press, 1994); Leigh Eric Schmidt, *Consumer Rites: The Buying and Selling of American Holidays* (Princeton, NJ: Princeton University Press, 1995); George M. Thomas, *Revivalism and Cultural Change: Christianity, Nation Building and the Market in Nineteenth-Century United States* (Chicago: University of Chicago Press, 1989); Colleen McDannell, *The Christian Home in Victorian America, 1840–1900* (Bloomington: Indiana University Press, 1986). 17. James Livingston, *Pragmatism and the Political Economy of Cultural Revolution, 1850–1940* (Chapel Hill: University of North Carolina Press, 1994); William James, *Pragmatism and Other Writings*, ed. Giles Gunn (New York: Penguin Books, 2000), xxi–xxiii. 18. I am grateful to Harrison C. White for conversations on this subject. 19. Drew McCoy, *The Elusive Republic: Political Economy in Jeffersonian America* (Chapel Hill: University of North Carolina Press, 1980), 33. 20. See also Margaret R. Hunt, *The Middling Sort: Commerce, Gender, and the Family in England, 1680–1780* (Berkeley and Los Angeles: University of California Press, 1996), 4–5. 21. On the idea of self-fashioning, see Scott E. Casper, *Constructing American Lives: Biography and Culture in Nineteenth-Century America* (Chapel Hill: University of North Carolina Press, 1999). 22. See Walter Johnson, *Soul by Soul: Life Inside the Antebellum Slave Market* (Cambridge: Harvard University Press, 1999) for a similar argument. 23. For other arguments about moral economy, see Michael Merrill, "Cash Is Good to Eat: Self-Sufficiency and Exchange in the Rural Economy of the United States,"

Radical History Review 3 (4): 42–71; James Henretta, "Families and Farms: Mentalité in Pre-Industrial America," *William and Mary Quarterly,* 3rd ser., 35, no. 1 (January 1978): 3–32; Christine Heyrman, *Commerce and Culture: The Maritime Communities of Colonial Massachusetts, 1690–1750* (New York: W. W. Norton, 1984); Steven Hahn and Jonathan Prude, eds., *The Countryside in the Age of Capitalist Transformation: Essays in the Social History of Rural America* (Chapel Hill: University of North Carolina Press, 1985); and Christopher Clark, *The Roots of Rural Capitalism: Western Massachusetts, 1780–1860* (Ithaca, NY: Cornell University Press, 1990). 24. See Douglas, *Feminization of American Culture;* Colin Campbell, *The Romantic Ethic and the Spirit of Modern Consumerism* (Oxford: Basil Blackwell, 1987); and G. J. Barker-Benfield, *The Culture of Sensibility: Sex and Society in Eighteenth-Century Britain* (Chicago: University of Chicago Press, 1992). 25. Jean-Christophe Agnew, *World's Apart: The Market and the Theater in Anglo-American Thought, 1550–1750* (New York: Cambridge University Press, 1986), 7. 26. For other discussion of nineteenth-century consumer culture, see Richard Wightman Fox and T. J. Jackson Lears, eds., *The Culture of Consumption: Critical Essays in American History, 1880–1980* (New York: Pantheon Books, 1983); Richard Wightman Fox and T. J. Jackson Lears, eds., *The Power of Culture: Critical Essays in American History* (Chicago: University of Chicago Press, 1993); T. J. Jackson Lears, *Fables of Abundance: A Cultural History of Advertising* (New York: Basic Books, 1994); Elaine S. Abelson, *When Ladies Go A-thieving: Middle-class Shoplifters in the Victorian Department Store* (New York: Oxford University Press, 1992); Kathy Peiss, *Cheap Amusements: Working Women and Leisure in New York City, 1880 to 1920* (Philadelphia: Temple University Press, 1986); Miriam Formanek-Brunell, *Made to Play House: Dolls and the Commercialization of American Girlhood, 1830–1930* (New Haven, CT: Yale University Press, 1993); Wendy Woloson, *Refined Tastes: Sugar, Confectionary, and Consumers in Nineteenth-Century America* (Baltimore: Johns Hopkins University Press, 2002); Susan Porter Benson, *Counter Cultures: Saleswomen, Managers, and Customers in American Department Stores, 1890–1940* (Urbana: University of Illinois Press, 1988); William Leach, *Land of Desire: Merchants, Power, and the Rise of a New American Culture* (New York: Pantheon Books, 1993); Schmidt, *Consumer Rites;* Ellen Gruber Garvey, *The Adman in the Parlor: Magazines and the Gendering of Consumer Culture, 1880s to 1910s* (New York: Oxford University Press, 1996). 27. See Christopher Clark, "The Consequences of the Market Revolution in the American North," in *The Market Revolution in America: Social, Political, and Religious Expressions, 1800–1880,* ed. Melyvn Stokes and Stephen Conway (Charlottesville: University Press of Virginia, 1996), 30, and Livingston, *Pragmatism,* 21–23, for related discussions of nineteenth-century market transformation. 28. Wendy Motooka, *The Age of Reasons: Quixotism, Sentimentalism and Political Economy,* in *Keywords: A Vocabulary of Culture and Society,* by Raymond Williams, rev. ed. (New York: Oxford University Press, 1983), 280–83; *Eighteenth-Century Britain* (New York: Routledge, 1998),94. 29. Motooka, *Age of Reasons,* 103. 30. Raymond Williams, *Keywords: A Vocabulary of Culture and Society,* rev. ed. (New York: Oxford University Press, 1983), 280–83. 31. Douglas, *Feminization of American Culture,* 4–13. 32. Nina Baym, *Women's Fiction: A Guide to Novels by and about Women in America, 1820–1870* (Ithaca, NY: Cornell University Press, 1978) was of the first revisionist studies of nineteenth-century popular fiction. Baym emphasized the realism of women's fiction in her analysis of the sentimental novel as a female Bildungsroman. Jane Tompkins, *Sensational Designs: The Cultural Work of American Fiction, 1790–1860* (New York: Oxford University Press, 1985), argued that sentimental fiction performed important cultural work by making controversial ideas understandable and acceptable and transforming public opinion about moral issues such as slavery. The explicit cultural agenda of sentimental fiction renders it alien to a modernist imagination that prefers to think of fiction in terms of form rather than content. The success of the realism of sentimental fiction was its ability to make controversial ideas, such as the vision of a slave as a man, common sense or realistic. Once this goal had been accomplished, however, the stridency with which the fiction had preached its lesson seemed stale and overwrought. See also Philip Fisher, *Hard Facts: Setting and Form in the American Novel* (New York: Oxford University Press, 1987). Other scholars have contributed to the reclamation of sentimentalism realism by focusing on women's literary careers. In *Private Woman, Public Stage: Literary Domesticity in Nineteenth-Century America* (New York: Oxford University Press, 1984), Mary Kelley argued for the realism of sentimentalism by pointing out the striking similarities between the lives of women writers and the fictional characters they created. Susan Coultrap-McQuin, in *Doing Literary Business,* explored the relationships between women writers and their publishers. She demonstrated that the literary market in the mid-nineteenth century was a congenial atmosphere for women writers rather than the perilous terrain that Kelley had mapped. Male publishers adopted a style of business that emphasized the sentimental values that women writers espoused. This created a literary culture in which the patriarchal relationship between publisher and author extended to both male and female authors. Coultrap-McQuin emphasized the serious, professional manner in which women conducted their careers, helping to revise the image the Kelley had portrayed of the accidental author. Both of these books have helped to situate literary sentimentalism in its cultural context. Susan K. Harris, *Nineteenth-Century American Women's Novels: Interpretive Strategies* (New York: Cambridge University Press, 1990) asserted that these novels were open to a range of interpretations helps complicate the more ideologically inflected arguments of previous works on sentimental fiction. 33. See my essay, Elizabeth Alice White, "Sentimental Heresies: Rethinking *The Feminization of American Culture,*" *Intellectual History Newsletter* 15 (fall 1993): 23–31. 34. Lori Merish has the most sustained discussion of this relationship in *Sentimental Materialism.* See also my dissertation: Elizabeth Alice White, "Sentimental Enterprise: Sentiment and Profit in American Market Culture, 1830–1880" (Yale, 1995). 35. See Margaret Cohen, *The Sentimental Education of the Novel* (Princeton, NJ: Princeton University Press, 1999) for a discussion of French sentimentalism and its emphasis on emotional abandon. 36. See John Mullan, *Sentiment and Sociability: The Language of Feeling in the Eighteenth Century* (Oxford: Clarendon Press, 1990). 37. David W. Robson, *Educating Republicans: The College in the Era of the American Revolution* (Westport, CT: Greenwood Press, 1985). 38. See Albert O. Hirschman, *The Passions and the Interests: Political Arguments for Capitalism Before its Triumph* (Princeton, NJ: Princeton University Press, 1977), 4–5. 39. Agnew, *Worlds Apart,* 175. See also John Reader, ed., *On Moral Sentiments: Contemporary Responses to Adam Smith* (Bristol, UK: Thoemmes Press, 1997); Patricia H. Werhane, *Adam Smith and His Legacy for Modern Capitalism* (New York: Oxford University Press, 1991); Motooka, *Age of Reasons;* Jeffrey T. Young, *Economics as a Moral Science: The Political Economy of Adam Smith* (Cheltenham, UK: Edward Elgar, 1997) for additional discussions of the importance of *The Theory of Moral Sentiments.* 40. Clifford Geertz, *The Interpretation of Cultures: Selected Essays* (New York: Basic Books, 1973); Arjun Appadurai, ed., *The Social Life of Things: Commodities in Cultural Perspective* (New York: Cambridge University Press, 1986); Mary Douglas and Baron Isherwood, *The World of Goods* (New York: Basic Books, 1979); Chandra Mukerji, *From Graven Images: Patterns of Modern Materialism* (New York: Columbia University Press, 1983). 41. Young, *Economics,* 58, 65, 69. 42. See C. A. Gregory, *Gifts and Commodities* (London: Academic Press, 1982); Georg Simmel, *The Philosophy of Money,* trans. Tom Bottomore and David Frisby, ed. David Frisby, from a first draft by Kaethe Mengelberg (New York: Routledge, 1990). 43. Max Weber, *The Protestant Ethic and the Spirit of Capitalism,* trans. Talcott Parsons (London: Allen & Unwin, 1958); Campbell, *Romantic Ethic.* 44. Gillian Brown, *Domestic Individualism: Imagining Self in Nineteenth-Century America* (Berkeley and Los Angeles: University of California Press, 1990); Shirley Samuels, ed., *The Culture of Sentiment: Race, Gender and Sentimentality in Nineteenth-Century America* (New York: Oxford University Press, 1992); Merish, *Sentimental Materialism;* Bruce Burgett, *Sentimental Bodies: Sex, Gender, and Citizenship in the Early Republic* (Princeton, NJ: Princeton University Press, 1998); Mary Louise Kete, *Sentimental Collaborations: Mourning and Middle-Class Identity in Nineteenth-Century America* (Durham, NC: Duke University Press, 2000); Mary Chapman and Glenn Hendler, eds., *Sentimental Men: Masculinity and the Politics of Affect in American Culture* (Berkeley and Los Angeles: University of California Press, 1999); Isabelle Lehuu, *Carnival on the Page: Popular Print Media in Antebellum America* (Chapel Hill: University of North Carolina Press, 2000). 45. These didactic formulas, as Jane Tompkins has argued, reveal the important cultural work done by popular fiction and demonstrate the value of these sources for any work of cultural history. Tompkins, *Sensational Designs.* 46. See Andrew Burstein, *Sentimental Democracy: The Evolution of America's Romantic Self-Image* (New York: Hill and Wang, 1999). 47. See Richard L. Bushman, *The Refinement of America: Persons, Houses, Cities* (New York: Knopf, 1992); C. Dallett Hemphill, *Bowing to Necessities: A History of Manners in America, 1620–1860* (New York: Oxford University Press, 1999). 48. Karen Halttunen, *Confidence Men and Painted Women: A Study of Middle-Class Culture in America, 1830–1870* (New Haven, CT: Yale University Press, 1982). 49. See Hirschman, *Passions,* 71, for a related discussion of the characterization of commerce as a positive social force. 50. Livingston, *Pragmatism,* 41, 44. 51. In his essay, "Coming Up for Air: Consumer Culture in Historical Perspective," Jean-Christophe Agnew briefly characterized the antebellum period as an "urban commercial culture." Throughout this book I argue it does not make sense to skip from the consumer society of the eighteenth century to the consumer culture of the late nineteenth century. A better understanding of market culture in the antebellum period is necessary if we are to understand the development of consumer culture in the late nineteenth century. See Jean-Christophe Agnew, "Coming Up for Air: Consumer Culture in Historical Perspective," in *Consumption and the World of Goods,* ed. John Brewer and Roy Porter (New York: Routledge, 1993), 19–39. 52. David Waldstreicher, *In the Midst of Perpetual Fetes: The Making of American Nationalism, 1776–1820* (Chapel Hill: University of North Carolina Press, 1997), 55. 53. McCoy, *Elusive Republic,* 7. 54. Waldstreicher, *In the Midst,* 68, 71, 76, 78. 55. See Paul Johnson, *A Shopkeeper's Millennium: Society and Revivals in Rochester, New York, 1815–1837* (New York: Hill and Wang, 1987); Mary Ryan, *Cradle of the Middle Class: The Family in Oneida County, New York, 1790–1865* (New York: Cambridge University Press, 1987); Blumin, *Emergence of the Middle Class;* Wilentz, *Chants Democratic;* Stansell, *City of Women;* and Sven Beckert, *The Monied Metropolis: New York City and the Consolidation of the American Bourgeoisie, 1850–1896* (New York: Cambridge University Press, 2001). 56. See Nancy Cott, *The Bonds of Womanhood: Woman's Sphere in New England, 1780–1835* (New Haven, CT: Yale University Press, 1977) for a similar argument about domestic ideology. 57. See Hirschman, *Passions.* 58. See Richard D. Brown, *Knowledge Is Power: The Diffusion of Information in Early America, 1700–1865* (New York: Oxford University Press, 1989). 59. "Godey's Arm Chair," *Godey's Lady's Book* 45 (July 1852): 99. 60. See Linda K. Kerber, "Separate Spheres, Female Worlds, Woman's Place: The Rhetoric of Women's History," *Journal of American History* (June 1988): 9–39; Jeanne Boydston, *Home and Work: Housework, Wages and the Ideology of Labor in the Early*

Republic (New York: Oxford University Press, 1990); Lori D. Ginzberg, *Women and the Work of Benevolence: Morality, Politics and Class in the Nineteenth-Century United States* (New Haven, CT: Yale University Press, 1990); Monika M. Elbert, ed., *Separate Spheres No More: Gender Convergence in American Literature, 1830–1930* (Tuscaloosa: University of Alabama Press, 2000); Laura McCall and Donald Yacovne, eds., *A Shared Experience: Men, Women and the History of Gender* (New York: New York University Press, 1998); and Cathy N. Davidson, ed., "No More Separate Spheres!" special issue, *American Literary History* 70, no. 3 (1998): 443–668. The focus of women's history has turned toward an investigation of the ideological role of gender in both public and private culture. See Nancy F. Cott, "On Men's History and Women's History" in *Meanings for Manhood: Constructions of Masculinity in Victorian America,* ed. Mark C. Carnes and Clyde Griffen (Chicago: University of Chicago Press, 1990): 205–11; Stanley, "Home Life"; and Jeanne Boydston, "The Woman Who Wasn't There: Women's Market Labor and the Transition to Capitalism in the United States," in *Wages of Independence: Capitalism in the Early American Republic,* ed. Paul A. Gilje (Madison: Madison House, 1997), 39. Mary Poovey, *Uneven Developments: The Ideological Work of Gender in Mid-Victorian America* (Chicago: University of Chicago Press, 1988): 3–4. 61. Stanley, "Home Life," 78, 81; See also Elizabeth Blackmar, *Manhattan for Rent, 1785–1850* (New York: 1989), 112, 126. 62. Blumin, *Emergence of the Middle Class,* 68. 63. See Cott, *Bonds of Womanhood,* and Susan Strasser, *Never Done: A History of American Housework* (New York: Pantheon Books, 1982). 64. Boydston, *Home and Work,* xv. Boydston has argued that in a system in which labor was increasingly defined by its wage, housework could no longer be seen as labor. 65. See Stanley, "Home Life," 74–96.

1. Good Motives

1. Lydia Huntley, *Moral Pieces in Prose and Verse* (Hartford, Conn.: Sheldon & Goodwin, 1815); *Notable American Women: A Biographical Dictionary,* ed. Edward T. James, Janet Wilson James, and Paul S. Boyer (Cambridge: Harvard University Press, 1971), 3:289. 2. Although Child was almost a generation younger than Sigourney, Sedgwick, and Hale, her early success as an author links her to this group of authors rather than to those born after 1810. Her embrace of the abolitionist cause, however, suggests that she was somewhat of an anomaly in this group. 3. Bruce Mills, *Cultural Reformations: Lydia Maria Child and the Literature of Reform* (Athens: University of Georgia Press, 1994), 1. 4. Marshall Foletta, *Coming to Terms with Democracy: Federalist Intellectuals and the Shaping of American Culture* (Charlottesville: University Press of Virginia, 2001), 3–5, 11. 5. Victoria Clements, "'A Powerful and Thrilling Voice': The Significance of Crazy Bet," in *Catharine Maria Sedgwick: Critical Perspectives,* ed. Lucinda L. Damon-Bach and Victoria Clements (Boston: Northeastern University Press, 2003), 41. 6. Edward T. James, Janet Wilson James, and Paul Boyer, eds., *Notable American Women, 1607–1950: A Biographical Dictionary,* vol. 3 (Cambridge: Belknap Press, 1971), 289; Edward T. James, Janet Wilson James, and Paul Boyer, eds., *Notable American Women, 1607–1950: A Biographical Dictionary,* vol. 2 (Cambridge: Belknap Press, 1971), 112. 7. Carolyn L. Karcher, *The First Woman in the Republic: A Cultural Biography of Lydia Maria Child* (Durham, NC: Duke University Press, 1994), 13–14. 8. Karen Woods Wierman, "'A Slave Story I Began and Abandoned': Sedgwick's Antislavery Manuscript," in *Catharine Maria Sedgwick: Critical Perspectives,* ed. Lucinda L. Damon-Bach and Victoria Clements (Boston: Northeastern University Press, 2003), 122–25. 9. Karcher, *First Woman in the Republic,* 191–92. 10. James, James, and Boyer, *Notable American Women* 3:288. 11. Mary Kelley, ed., *The Power of Her*

Sympathy: The Autobiography and Journal of Catherine Maria Sedgwick (Boston: Massachusetts Historical Society, 1993), 19–22. 12. Karcher, *First Woman in the Republic,* 2–3. 13. Quoted from "Wheeler's History of Newport, New Hampshire" (1868), in *The Lady of Godey's: Sarah Josepha Hale,* by Ruth E. Finley (Philadelphia: J. B. Lippincott, 1931), 29. 14. At William and Mary, where the works of Adam Smith and John Locke were part of the curriculum, they were taught, in part, as a critique of Federalist policy. Robson, *Educating Republicans,* 161–62, 165, 170–71. 15. Dugald Stewart and William Paley remained on lists of recommended reading into the late nineteenth century. In *What to Read, and How to Read* (1871), Charles Moore included works by Stewart and Paley as well as Adam Smith, Harriet Martineau, and Sarah Hale. See Charles H. Moore, *What to Read, and How to Read, Being Classified Lists of Choice Reading, with Appropriate Hints and Remarks, Adapted to the General Reader, To Subscribers to Libraries, and to Persons Intending to Form Collections of Books* (New York: D. Appleton, 1871). 16. Review of *Elements of the Philosophy of the Human Mind, Godey's Lady's Book* 50, no. 6 (June 1855): 563. 17. William Paley, *Moral and Political Philosophy* (Boston: Etheridge, 1795), xii, iv. 18. North, *Economic Growth of the United States,* 53. See also J. E. Crowley, *This Sheba, Self: The Conceptualization of Economic Life in Eighteenth-Century America* (Baltimore: John Hopkins University Press, 1974). 19. *Notable American Women* 3:111. 20. Ruth E. Finley, *The Lady of Godey's: Sarah Josepha Hale* (Philadelphia: J. B. Lippincott, 1931), 35–36. 21. Sarah J. Hale, *Northwood: A Tale of New England,* 2 vols. (Boston: Bowles & Dearborn, 1827), 1:3–4. 22. Hale, *Northwood* 2:241. 23. Martin Smart, *The Female Class Book; or Three Hundred and Sixty-Five Reading Lessons, adapted to the use of schools for every day of the year: consisting of moral, instructive, and entertaining extracts selected principally from Female writers, or on subjects of Female education and manners* (London: Lackington, Allen, 1813), 19. 24. Sarah Josepha Hale, *Flora's Interpreter; or, The American Book of Flowers and Sentiments* (Boston: Thomas H. Webb, 1832), iv. 25. *Notable American Women* 2:111. 26. Sarah Joseph Hale, "Introduction," *American Ladies' Magazine* 1, no. 1 (1828): 3. Hale inaugurated the magazine under the title *Ladies' Magazine,* changing the title to *American Ladies' Magazine* in 1934. This title will be used in all citations for the purpose of clarity. 27. Alexis de Tocqueville, *Democracy in America,* vol. 2, ed. J. P. Mayer and trans. George Lawrence (1835; reprint, New York: Harper & Row, 1969), 527. 28. Sarah Josepha Hale, "To Our Friends," *American Ladies' Magazine* 2, no. 12 (December 1829): 584. 29. Sarah Josepha Hale, *American Ladies' Magazine* 4, no. 1 (1831): 3–4, also quoted in Douglas, *Feminization of American Culture,* 93. 30. Hannah More, *Coelebs in Search of a Wife* (London: Printed for T. Cadell and W. Davies, 1808). 31. Sarah Josepha Hale, *American Ladies' Magazine* 2, no. 11 (November 1829): 489. 32. Ibid., 490. 33. "Lucilla," "To Coelebs," *American Ladies' Magazine* 2, no. 11 (1829): 492. This article was a response to "Coelebs in Search of a Wife," in ibid. 2, no. 10 (1829): 442–45. 34. Sarah Josepha Hale in *American Ladies' Magazine* 8, no. 1 (1835): 10. 35. Sarah Josepha Hale in *American Ladies' Magazine* 9, no. 12 (1836): 670. 36. Sarah Josepha Hale in *American Ladies' Magazine* 7, no. 5 (1834): 215. 37. Ibid. 38. Sarah Josepha Hale, "Literary Notices," *American Ladies' Magazine* 1, no. 8 (1828): 430. 39. Ibid., 431. This was not the first book on political economy by a woman; see Mrs. [Jane Haldimand] Marcet's *Conversations on Political Economy* (Philadelphia: M. Thomas, 1817), in which the elements of that science are familiarly explained 40. Sarah Josepha Hale, "Literary Notices," *American Ladies' Magazine* 3, no. 1 (1830): 43. 41. Sarah Josepha Hale, "The Worth of Money," *American Ladies' Magazine* 3, no. 2 (1830): 50. 42. See Karcher, *First Woman in the Republic,* 132–33, for a related discussion of Hale's review of *The Frugal Housewife.* 43. Sarah Josepha Hale, "The Worth of Money," *American Ladies' Magazine* 3, no. 2 (1830): 52 44. Mills,

Cultural Reformations, 7. Child was also strongly influenced by Franklin. 45. Sarah Josepha Hale, "The Worth of Money," *American Ladies' Magazine* 3, no. 2 (1830): 53, 54. See also Linda K. Korber, *Women of the Republic: Intellect and Ideology in Revolutionary America* (Chapel Hill: University of North Carolina Press, 1931) for a related discussion about republican motherhood. 46. Finley, *Lady of Godey's,* 64; "The Editor's Table," *Godey's Lady's Book* 54, no. 2 (1858): 180. Tudor and Everett were editors and contributors to the *North American Review.* 47. Hale, "Worth of Money," 54. 48. Sarah Josepha Hale, "Literary Notices," *American Ladies' Magazine* 5, no. 7 (1832): 381. 49. Sarah Josepha Hale in *American Ladies' Magazine* 8, no. 1 (1835): 54. 50. Sarah Josepha Hale, "To Our Subscribers,"*American Ladies' Magazine* 9, no. 7 (1836): 424. 51. Sarah Josepha Hale, "The '*Conversazione,*'" *Godey's Lady's Book* 14, no. 1 (1837): 1. 52. Nicole Tonkovich, *Domesticity with a Difference: The Nonfiction of Catharine Beecher, Sarah J. Hale, Fanny Fern, and Margaret Fuller* (Jackson: University of Mississippi Press, 1997), 30–31. One of the most famous of these clubs was the Transcendentalist Club, which held its first meeting in September 1836. Elizabeth Peabody also held a series of conversations in 1832, and Margaret Fuller, who came to Boston in the fall of 1836 to teach school and assist Bronson Alcott in the publication of the third volume of his *Conversations with Children on the Gospels* (the first two volumes had been published in 1836–37), participated in these conversations and continued the tradition in the late 1830s. Hale and Fuller, both friends of Eliza Farrar, shared an interest in the education of women. See Charles Capper, *Margaret Fuller, an American Romantic Life: The Private Years* (New York: Oxford University Press, 1992), 1:96, 189–200; Bruce A. Ronda, "Print and Pedagogy: The Career of Elizabeth Peabody," in *A Living of Words: American Women in Print Culture,* ed. Susan Albertine (Knoxville, University of Tennessee Press, 1995), 37–38; Sandra M. Gustafson, "Choosing a Medium: Margaret Fuller and the Forms of Sentiment," *American Quarterly* 47 (1): 45; Donald M. Scott, "The Popular Lecture and the Creation of the Public in Mid-Nineteenth-Century America," *Journal of American History* 66 (4): 792; Lawrence Buell, *Literary Transcendentalism: Style and Vision in the American Renaissance* (Ithaca, NY: Cornell University Press, 1973), 77–101. 53. See Anderson, *Imagined Communities.* 54. Hale, "*Conversazione,*" 4–5. 55. Foletta, *Coming to Terms with Democracy,* 222–26. 56. See Ruth H. Bloch, "Religion, Literary Sentimentalism, and Popular Revolutionary Ideology," in *Religion in a Revolutionary Age,* ed. Ronald Hoffman and Peter J. Albert (Charlottesville: University Press of Virginia, 1994), 308–30, for a related discussion.

2. Telling Tales

1. Samuel Miller, *A Brief Retrospective of the Eighteenth Century* (New York: T. and J. Swords, 1803). Samuel Miller became a professor at Princeton Theological Seminary in 1813. 2. Agnew, *Worlds Apart,* 172. 3. Miller, *Brief Retrospective,* 427–28. 4. Ibid., 167. 5. Ibid., 173. 6. Ibid., 174. 7. Ibid., 175. 8. Ibid., 429, quoted from *Monthly Review* 29, p. 302. 9. Miller, *Brief Retrospective,* 171. 10. See Brown, *Knowledge Is Power;* William Gilmore, *Reading Becomes a Necessity: Material and Cultural Life in Rural New England, 1780–1835* (Knoxville: University of Tennessee Press, 1989). 11. Lehuu, *Carnival on the Page,* 18; see also Ronald J. Zboray, *A Fictive People: Antebellum Economic Development and the American Reading Public* (New York: Oxford University Press, 1993). 12. In "Lydia Maria Child and the *Juvenile Miscellany:* The Creation of an American Children's Literature," in *Periodical Literature in Nineteenth-Century America,* ed. Kenneth M. Price and Susan Belasco Smith (Charlottesville: University Press of Virginia, 1995). Carolyn L. Karcher argues that children's literature helped disseminate the bourgeois work ethic, and in the case of Lydia Maria Child, children's authors also tried to teach moral lessons within that

scope. In Child's case, it was the lesson of racial tolerance and equality. 13. Cott, *Bonds of Womanhood*, 113. 14. Gilmore, *Reading*, 262. 15. Most discussions of market fiction focus on the 1850s without considering its relation to earlier texts: Brown, *Domestic Individualism*; Samuels, *Culture of Sentiment*; and Merish, *Sentimental Materialism*. 16. Johnson, *Shopkeeper's Millennium*; Ryan, *Cradle of the Middle Class*; Blumin, *Emergence of the Middle Class*; Ginzberg, *Women and the Work of Benevolence*. 17. Nathan O. Hatch, *The Democratization of Christianity* (New Haven, CT: Yale University Press, 1989), 126. 18. David Paul Nord, "Benevolent Capital: Evangelical Book Publishing in Early Nineteeth-Century America," in *God and Mammon: Protestants, Money, and the Market, 1790–1860*, ed. Mark A. Noll (New York: Oxford University Press, 2001), 155–56. 19. *American Tract Magazine* 1, no. 1 (June 1824): 17 (New York: American Tract Society). 20. Ibid., 21. 21. Jon Butler, *Awash in a Sea of Faith: Christianizing the American People* (Cambridge: Harvard University Press, 1990), 285–86; Charles Sellers, *The Market Revolution: Jacksonian America, 1815–1846* (New York: Oxford University Press, 1991), 202–36. 22. Mark S. Schantz, "Religious Tracts, Evangelical Reform, and the Market Revolution in Antebellum America," *Journal of the Early Republic* 17 (fall 1997): 426, 429; see also Paul E. Johnson and Sean Wilentz, *The Kingdom of Matthias* (New York: Oxford University Press, 1994); Nord, "Benevolent Capital," 147–70. 23. *American Tract Magazine* 1 (June 1825): 160–61 (New York: Daniel Fanshaw, 1826); Hatch, *Democratization of Christianity*, 141. 24. *American Tract Magazine*, August 1826, 44. 25. Butler, *Awash*, 256, 273–75, 277. 26. *American Tract Magazine*, August 1826, 108. 27. Carol Sheriff, *The Artificial River: The Erie Canal and the Paradox of Progress, 1817–1862* (New York: Hill and Wang, 1996), 156. 28. Mark Y. Hanley, *Beyond a Christian Commonwealth: The Protestant Quarrel with the American Republic, 1830–1860* (Chapel Hill: University of North Carolina Press, 1994), 150. 29. Hatch, *Democratization of Christianity*, 138–39. 30. See Sellers, *Market Revolution*, 212–13, for a discussion of the influence organizations of Christian British businessmen on American voluntary associations. 31. *The Address of the Executive Committee of the American Tract Society to the Christian Public* (New York: American Tract Society, 1825), 7, 10, 14. 32. Sellers, *Market Revolution*, 202–36. 33. *Address of the Executive Committee*, 1825, 4. 34. Arjun Appadurai, "Introduction: Commodities and the Politics of Value," in *The Social Life of Things: Commodities in Cultural Perspective*, ed. Arjun Appadurai (New York: Cambridge University Press, 1986), 4. 35. *A Brief History of the American Tract Society*, 20. 36. Nord, "Benevolent Capital," 162. 37. *General View of Colportage as Conducted by the American Tract Society in the United States* published by the American Tract Society (New York: Daniel Fanshaw, 1845), 1. The books referred to are Richard Baxter's *Call to the Unconverted* and *The Saints Everlasting Rest*. 38. Nord, "Benevolent Capital." 39. David Paul Nord, "Religious Reading and Readers in Antebellum America," *Journal of the Early Republic* 15 (summer 1995): 245. 40. Hanley, *Beyond a Christian Commonwealth*, 28. 41. *American Tract Magazine* 1, no. 1 (June 1824): 15. 42. Sellers, *Market Revolution*, 213. 43. Nord, "Benevolent Capital," 251. 44. Reverend L. C. Wilcoxon to American Tract Society, February 24, 1840 [?], quoted in Zboray, *Fictive People*, 92. 45. Nord, "Religious Reading," 251. This is not unlike the logic that drives Christian network television and Christian music today. 46. Schantz, "Religious Tracts," 430. 47. See Wilentz, *Chants Democratic*; Stanley, "Home Life," 74–98. 48. The tension between middle-class reformers and the women and men whom they attempted to reform is well documented, see Stansell, *City of Women*, and Ginzberg, *Women and the Work of Benevolence*. 49. Some scholars have read the nostalgic pastoralism of this tale as the rejection of, or at least an ambivalence about, the market revolution. Schantz, "Religious Tracts," 431. 50. *The Closet Companion; or a Help to Self-Examination* (New York: American

Tract Society, n.d.), 7. 51. See Sellers, *Market Revolution*, 215–16. See also T. S. Arthur, "Living It Down," in *Sketches of Life and Character* (Philadelphia: J. D. Bradley, 1850), 292–300. In this story, Mr. Coleman, an honest businessman whose reputation had been ruined by the false accusations of his niece's husband, chooses not to confront his accuser, but to live down the slander. While he does manage to rehabilitate his own reputation, his actions cause the widow of one of his former business associates to lose much of her inheritance because her husband chooses another man instead of Mr. Coleman as executor of his will. This man embezzles half of the widow's inheritance before she come to Mr. Coleman for advice. Although he comes to the widow's aid, it is too late. The widow's lawyer tells Mr. Coleman that he is in part to blame for the widow's plight. If he had not succumbed to the false pride of "living it down" he would have remained her executor and the tragedy would have been avoided. Thus Christian businessmen have the obligation to maintain the integrity of that community beyond their personal interest: "If we do not, we are responsible for any injury that society may sustain in consequence of our influence for good being lost" (300). 52. Rev. Austin Dickinson, *Appeal to American Youth on Temperance, A Premium Tract*, Tract no. 233 (New York: American Tract Society, n.d.). 53. Ibid., 1–2. 54. *Advice to the Keeper of a Turnpike Gate together with Useful Hints to Travellers* (New York: American Tract Society, [1825]), 3. 55. Ibid. 56. *American Tract Magazine*, August 1826, 215. 57. Anne M. Boylan, *Sunday School: The Formation of an American Institution, 1790–1880* (New Haven, CT: Yale University Press, 1988), 15,16. 58. Ruth K. MacDonald, *Literature for Children in England and America from 1646 to 1774* (Troy, NY: Whitston, 1982), 11. 59. Boylan, *Sunday School*, 73, 77, 169; Rosalie V. Halsey, *Forgotten Books of the American Nursery: A History of the Development of the American Story-Book* (1911; reprint, Detroit: Singing Tree Press, 1969) 204. 60. Boylan, *Sunday School*, 48–50. 61. Ibid., 17. 62. Halsey, *Forgotten Books*, 164. 63. *Pretty Stories for Good Children*, Tract no. 18 (New York: American Tract Society, n.d.), 31, 22, 29. 64. [Sarah J. Hale], "Cause and Cure; or, Conversations by the Fireside," *Godey's Lady's Book* (February 1842): 114. 65. Ibid. 66. See Woloson, *Refined Tastes*, 32–65, for a related discussion on the temptations of candy. 67. *Pretty Stories for Good Children: The Hymn Book*, 82–94; "Morning and Evening," 97–111; "Dialogue Between a Brother and a Sister Concerning Salvation by Christ," 129–43; "Reading the Bible," 207. 68. Some tracts explicitly engaged questions of commerce. *The Little Merchants*, by Maria Edgeworth, tells the story of two little boys, cunning Piedro and honest Francisco, who work as vendors in Naples, and presents the ethics of business through their exploits. Maria Edgeworth, *The Little Merchants* (Baltimore: F. Lucas Jr., J. Vance & Company, and Anthony Mittenberger, 1811). 69. Anne Scott MacLeod, *American Childhood: Essays on Children's Literature of the Nineteenth and Twentieth Centuries* (Athens: University of Georgia Press, 1994), 97. 70. Not all gift books had new stories. The same book was often republished several times under a new name. See Frederick W. Faxon, *Literary Annuals and Gift Books* (Boston: Boston Book, 1912); Ralph Thompson, *American Literary Annuals and Giftbooks, 1825–1865* (New York: H. W. Wilson, 1936); and Lehuu, *Carnival on the Page*, 76–101. 71. Karcher, *First Woman in the Republic*, 60. 72. Ibid., 58. 73. Carolyn L. Karcher, ed., *A Lydia Maria Child Reader* (Durham, NC: Duke University Press, 1997), 97–100. 74. Sally Michalski, Samuel Goodrich Collection, University of Pittsburgh Special Collections, Elizabeth Nesbitt Room, www.library.pitt.edu/libraries/is/enroom/goodrich. 75. Max J. Herzberg, *The Reader's Encyclopedia of American Literature* (New York: Thomas Y. Crowell, 1962), 396. 76. Samuel Goodrich, *Recollections of a Lifetime* 1:165–166, 174, as quoted in David D. Hall, *Cultures of Print: Essays in the History of the Book* (Amherst: University of Massachusetts Press, 1996), 71. 77. Jacob Abbott, *The Young*

Christian: Or a Familiar Illustration of the Principles of Christian Duty (New York: American Tract Society, 1832). 78. Halsey, *Forgotten Books*, 215. 79. See *Abbott's Young Christian: A Memorial Edition with a Sketch of the Author by One of His Sons* (New York: Harper & Brothers, 1882). 80.*Child's Paper* 1, no. 9 (September 1852): 34 (New York: American Tract Society). 81.*Child's Paper* 1, no. 1 (January 1852): 6 (New York: American Tract Society). 82. Ibid. 83. Ibid., 7. 84. *Child's Paper* 1, no. 6 (June 1852): 23 (New York: American Tract Society).

3. Cents and Sensibility

1. Bertha Monica Stearns, "Louis Antoine Godey," *Dictionary of American Biography* (New York: Charles Scribner's Sons, 1960), 4:343–44; Ellis Paxson Oberholtzer, *The Literary History of Philadelphia* (Philadelphia: George W. Jacobs, 1906), 229–32. 2. Frank Luther Mott, *History of American Magazines* (Cambridge: Belknap Press, 1957), 2:582. Mott comments on Godey's ability to balance the imperatives of business with his "native sentimentality." 3. Ibid., 2:514–15. In many ways, the discussion of delinquent subscriptions in the editorial pages of *Godey's Lady's Book* was typical of the magazine business in its early years, although perhaps more constant than in many magazines. *Graham's Lady's and Gentleman's Magazine*, 1841–58, on of Godey's most serious competitors, rarely included discussions of delinquent subscriptions. Many issues did not have an Editor's Table. 4. See Benedict Anderson, *Imagined Communities: Reflections on the Origin and Spread of Nationalism* (New York: Verso, 1991). 5. See Fred Lewis Pattee, *The First Century of American Literature, 1770–1870* (New York: Cooper Square, 1966). 6. *Godey's Lady's Book* has been an important source for the study of middle-class domesticity, but primarily as evidence for the doctrine of separate spheres and the "Cult of True Womanhood." Mott saw *Godey's Lady's Book* as an important part of the early history of popular magazines. Pattee saw it as a quaint expression of the ideas and mores of yesteryear. Biographies of Sarah Josepha Hale present the magazine as a vehicle for Hale's championship of women's education and authorship: Finley, *Lady of Godey's*; Isabelle Webb Entrikin, *Sarah Josepha Hale and "Godey's Lady's Book"* (Philadelphia: Lancaster Press, 1946); Olive Burt, *First Woman Editor: Sarah J. Hale* (New York: Julian Messner, 1960); and Sherbrooke Rogers, *Sarah Josepha Hale: A New England Pioneer, 1788–1879* (Grantham, NH: Tompson and Rutter, 1985). In her seminal essay, "The Cult of True Womanhood" (1966), Barbara Welter inaugurated a new examination of nineteenth-century womanhood. In subsequent studies of nineteenth-century women *Godey's Lady's Book* has often stood for the "cult," although Welter rarely refers to it in her article, and to only a few of its earliest volumes. As the study of sentimentalism matured, significant challenges to Welter's formulation were made: Tompkins, *Sensational Designs*; Harris, *Nineteenth-Century American Women's Novels*; Frances B. Cogan, *All-American Girl: The Ideal of Real Womanhood in Mid-Nineteenth-Century America* (Athens: University of Georgia Press, 1989); and Isabelle Lehuu, "Sentimental Figures: Reading *Godey's Lady's Book* in Antebellum America," in Samuels, *Culture of Sentiment*, 73–91. Laura McCall's work on the fiction in *Godey's* has helped to complicate our understanding of its relationship to the tropes of middle-class ideology: Laura McCall, "'The Reign of Brute Force Is NOW OVER': Content Analysis of *Godey's Lady's Book*, 1830–1860," *Journal of the Early Republic* (summer 1989): 217–36. Nicole Tonkovich's serious examination of Hale's nonfiction has also broadened our understanding of her understanding of sentimentalism in important ways: Tonkovich, *Domesticity with a Difference*. As the ideology of women's history shifted, and sentimentalism became a form of empowerment rather than oppression, *Godey's Lady's Book* became shorthand for the cultural context in which the cultural work of sentimental-

ism was done. Although it was no longer disparaged quite so virulently, it was still primarily a foil for the important works of sentimentalism. It was used to demonstrate the ways in which these works had risen above the mainstream commercialism of "ordinary sentimentalism." The contents of *Godey's*, both fictional and nonfictional, performed important cultural work in their own right. Laura McCall's survey of the fiction in *Godey's* demonstrates that visions of womanhood presented in the fiction were far from static and did not strictly conform to a limited ideological vision. Nicole Tonkovich's study of Sarah Josepha Hale' s editorial writing demonstrates the complexity of her opinions, rescuing her from the separate spheres caricature that she had become. 7. "The Book of the Nation. Godey's Lady's Book for 1851. Literary and Pictorial, Devoted to American Enterprise, American Writers, and American Artists," *Godey's Lady's Book* 42, no. 1 (1851): 72. 8. "The Editor's Table," *Godey's Lady's Book* 11, no. 12 (1835): 285. 9. Ibid. 10. Ibid. 11. Clark, *Roots*, 125, 218–27. 12. "The Editor's Table," *Godey's Lady's Book* 12, no. 6 (1836): 283. The enterprise was the *Saturday News and Gazette*, a joint venture with Morton McMichael and Joseph C. Neal. 13. Glenn Porter and Harold C. Livesay, *Merchants and Manufacturers: Studies in the Changing Structure of Nineteenth-Century Marketing* (Chicago: Ivan R. Dee, 1989), 13–36; Pierre Bourdieu, *Distinction: A Social Critique of the Judgement of Taste*, trans. Richard Nice (Cambridge: Harvard University Press, 1984), 1–7. 14. Mott, *History of American Magazines* 2:351. See Richard Brodhead, *Cultures of Letters: Scenes of Reading and Writing in Nineteenth-Century America* (Chicago: University of Chicago Press, 1993) for a related discussion. 15. "The Editor's Table," *Godey's Lady's Book* 12, no. 6 (1836): 283. 16. Ibid. 17. L. A. Godey and Co., Miscellaneous Collection, Rare Books and Manuscripts, New York Public Library. 18. Mott, *History of American Magazines* 2:506. 19. "The Editor's Table," *Godey's Lady's Book* 15, no. 12 (1837): 284. In 1845, Congress passed a law that provided fixed postage rates based on weight rather than distance. This contributed to increased magazine subscriptions. Mott, *History of American Magazines* 2:518. 20. "The Editor's Table," *Godey's Lady's Book* 12, no. 2 (1836): 96. 21. "The Editor's Table," *Godey's Lady's Book* 14, no. 1 (1837): 48. Godey had also warned his readers not to give the money to persons whose names did not appear on the cover of the magazine. *Godey's Lady's Book* 12, no. 6 (1836): 283. 22. Ibid. 23. Ibid. 24. To make his point on this clear, Godey "answered" a letter from Trenton, Tennessee, in the editorial pages as a way to make it clear that he would not honor subscriptions paid to fraudulent agents. "The Editor's Table, *Godey's Lady's Book* 12, no. 6 (1836): 283. 25. "The Editor's Table," *Godey's Lady's Book* 14, no. 2 (1837): 95. 26. Kelly, *In the New England Fashion*; Sheriff, *Artificial River*. 27. Clark, *Roots*, 195, 220 28. "The Editor's Table," *Godey's Lady's Book* 14, no. 2 (1837): 95. 29. See Karen Halttunen, *Confidence Men and Painted Women: A Study of Middle-Class Culture in America, 1830–1870* (New Haven, CT.: Yale University Press, 1982), for a discussion of the literary incarnations of the confidence man. Halttunen has described the relationship between confidence men and their unwitting victims in terms of romantic chicanery and moral ruin. She also identified it as an urban phenomenon that targeted unsuspecting rural men newly arrived in the city, or unsuspecting women too trusting of strangers. The confidence men described in *Godey's* invert this model. They were "urban" figures in rural places, and they perpetrated economic swindles but without the moral overtones. These confidence games were a form of financial inconvenience but not moral ruin. 30. "The Editor's Table," *Godey's Lady's Book* 14, no. 6 (1837): 285. 31. "The Editor's Table," *Godey's Lady's Book* 18, no. 8 (1839): 113. 32. In 1835, Barnum launched his career with his first exhibit, Joice Heth, whom he advertised as George Washington's nurse. When interest in the exhibit began to wane, Barnum wrote an anonymous letter to Boston newspaper denouncing Heth as a fraud, encouraging many who had come to see Heth to return for another visit to see how they had been fooled. This marketing strategy served Barnum well throughout his career. Neil Harris, *Humbug: The Art of P. T. Barnum* (Chicago: University of Chicago Press, 1973), 20–24. 33. "The Editor's Table," *Godey's Lady's Book* 17, no. 10 (1838): 190. Some of Godey's financial resilience may have come from his marriage in 1833 to Maria Duke, who came from a wealthy family. *Dictionary of American Biography* 4:344. 34. Sellers, *Market Revolution*, 204. 35. "The Editor's Table," *Godey's Lady's Book* 17, no. 10 (1838): 190. Some of Godey's financial resilience may have come from his marriage in 1833 to Maria Duke, who came from a wealthy family. *Dictionary of American Biography* 4:344. 36. "The Editor's Table," *Godey's Lady's Book* 17, no. 10 (1838): 190. 37. Ibid. Godey and Hale made it clear that they understood the pressures of the market: "The hard times will scarcely afford a sufficient excuse for all those who delay the remittance of their subscriptions. While some of the delinquents are forgetful and careless, there are others who are waiting for expected payments to themselves, or expected earnings in order to meet their long arrears. For such we are willing to wait a while longer." "The Editor's Table," *Godey's Lady's Book* 25, no. 4 (1842): 204 38. "The Editor's Table," *Godey's Lady's Book* 17, no. 12 (1838): 283. 39. Her allusion to Portia's "The quality of mercy is not strained" speech from *The Merchant of Venice* underlined her point and tacitly congratulated her readers on their education. 40. "The Editor's Table," *Godey's Lady's Book* 17, no. 12 (1838): 283. 41. "The Editor's Table," *Godey's Lady's Book* 18, no. 12 (1839): 287. 42. Ibid. 43. In January 1838, Hale threatened to append an alphabetical list of delinquent subscribers with accompanied by the amount due. Some of Godey's contemporaries also threatened to publish the names of their delinquents, and one, the *Ladies Companion*, actually carried out this threat in 1842, publishing both the names and the amounts due. Mott, *History of American Magazines* 2:515. 44. "The Editor's Table," *Godey's Lady's Book* 18, no. 12 (1839): 287. 45. "The Editor's Table," *Godey's Lady's Book* 20, no. 7 (1840): 46. 46. See issues from 1853, 1854, and 1855. It is possible that some of these letters were fictitious, but there are so many that it seems unlikely that they all were. 47. T. S. Arthur, "Can't Afford It," *Godey's Lady's Book* 38, no. 10 (1848): 207. 48. "The Editor's Table." *Godey's Lady's Book* 20, no. 7 (1840): 46. 49. Many volumes had advertisements for subscription clubs or discussion of their terms on the editorial page. For an example, see *Godey's Lady's Book* 45, no. 11 (1852): 494. 50. "The Editor's Table," *Godey's Lady's Book* 40, no. 5 (1850): 355. 51. Ibid. 52. "The Editor's Table," *Godey's Lady's Book* 21, no. 6 (1840): 282. 53. "The Editor's Table," *Godey's Lady's Book* 41, no. 12 (1850): 380. Despite his protestations, it appears Godey continued the practice of sending subscriptions in advance of payment. 54. *Godey's Lady's Book* 30, no. 4 (1845): 192. 55. "The Editor's Table," *Godey's Lady's Book* 43, no. 1 (1851): 60–61. 56. "The Editor's Table," *Godey's Lady's Book* 41, no. 10 (1850): 254. 57. "Godey's Arm Chair," *Godey's Lady's Book* 45, no. 9 (1852): 299. 58. "Godey's Arm Chair," *Godey's Lady's Book* 48, no. 11 (1853): 469. 59. For an example, see *Godey's Lady's Book* 71, no. 12 (1865): 545. 60. See Bourdieu, *Distinction*, 1–7, for a discussion of the importance of distinctions of taste in defining the aspirations of class. 61. See Sellers, *Market Revolution*, and Robert Abzug, *Cosmos Crumbling: American Reform and the Religious Imagination* (New York: Oxford University Press, 1994). Abzug argues that evangelicals infused worldly matters with spiritual understanding, viii.

4. The Economy of Domestic Happiness
1. See Cott, *Bonds of Womanhood*. 2. Lydia Maria Child, *The American Frugal Housewife* (1833; reprint, Bedford, MA: Applewood Books, n.d.), 7. Originally published as *The Frugal Housewife* in 1832, its name was changed to distinguish it from a British book with the same title. 3. Lydia Maria Child, *The*

Mother's Book (1831; reprint, Bedford, MA: Applewood Books, 1992), v. 4. Child, *American Frugal Housewife*, 91. 5. Ibid., 111. 6. Ibid., 95–96. 7. See Hemphill, *Bowing to Necessities*, for a related discussion of class identity. 8. Child, *American Frugal Housewife*, 90. 9. Nathaniel P. Willis, "On Furnishing a Home," in *The Rag Bag: A Collection of Ephemera* (New York: Charles Scribner, 1855), 35. 10. See Katharine C. Grier, *Culture and Comfort: Parlor Making and Middle-Class Identity, 1850–1930* (Washington, DC: Smithsonian Institution Press, 1997). 11. Catharine Sedgwick, *Live and Let Live, or Domestic Service Illustrated* (New York: Harper and Brothers, 1837); *Means and Ends, or Self Training* (Boston: Marsh, Capen, Lyon and Webb, 1840). 12. See Horowitz, *Morality of Spending*. 13. Catharine Maria Sedgwick, *Home* (Boston: James Munroe, 1841), 9. 14. Ibid., 13–14. 15. Ibid. 16. See Carolyn J. Lawes, "Capitalizing on Mother: John S. C. Abbott and the Self-Interested Mother," *Proceedings of the American Antiquarian Society* 108 (2): 372–73, for an interesting discussion of the economic value of motherhood; see Richard H. Brodhead, "Sparing the Rod: Discipline and Fiction in Antebellum America," in *Cultures of Letters: Scenes of Reading and Writing in Nineteenth-Century America* (Chicago: University of Chicago Press, 1993), 13–47, for an related discussion of the importance of the moral economy of the home for antebellum middle-class families; Mensh, *Sentimental Materialism*, 116–34, for a related discussion of *Home*. 17. Sarah J. Hale, "Editor's Table," *Godey's Lady's Book* 14, no. 3 (1837): 143. 18. Sarah J. Hale, "Editor's Table," *Godey's Lady's Book* 33, no. 1 (1846): 47. 19. Hannah F. Lee, *Three Experiments of Living: Living within the Means; Living Up to the Means; Living Beyond the Means* (Boston: W. S. Damrell and S. Colman, 1837), i. 20. Ibid., 36–37. 21. Sarah J. Hale, *The Good Housekeeper; or, The Way to Live Well and Be Well While We Live* (Boston: Weeks, Jordan, 1839), 1. 22. Ibid., 105. 23. Indian pudding is made from cornmeal, molasses, and milk and baked in a slow oven. 24. Sarah J. Hale, "The Editor's Table," *Godey's Lady's Book* 21, no. 1 (1840): 45. 25. Ibid. 26. Ibid. 27. Catharine E. Beecher, *A Treatise on Domestic Economy for the Use of Young Ladies at Home and at School*, rev. ed. (New York: Harper & Brothers, 1850), 9. 28. Ibid., 65. 29. Kathryn Kish Sklar, *Catharine Beecher: A Study in American Domesticity* (New York: W. W. Norton), 125–26. 30. Ibid., 143. 31. "Timothy Shay Arthur," *Dictionary of American Biography* 4:377–79. See my dissertation, "Sentimental Enterprise," for more discussion of Arthur's fiction, and Tim Ruppel, "Gender Training: Male Ambitions, Domestic Duties, and Failure in the Magazine Fiction of T. S. Arthur," *Prospects* 24:311–38. 32. Blumin, *Emergence of the Middle Class*, 1. He quotes Walt Whitman, who used this figure to distinguish a middle class. 33. T. S. Arthur, "The Clerk's Marriage," in *Hidden Wings and Other Stories*, by T. S. Arthur (1866; New York: Sheldon, 1970), 40. This is a collection of previously published stories. 34. T. S. Arthur, "History of a Day and a Life," in *Sketches of Life and Character* (Philadelphia: J. W. Bradley, 1850), 153. This is a collection of previously published stories. 35. T. S. Arthur, *Sunshine at Home and Other Stories* (1866; reprint, Freeport, NY: Books for Libraries, 1970), 39–60. This is a collection of previously published stories. 36. Arthur, *Hidden Wings*, 50. 37. T. S. Arthur, "Is It Economy: An Experience of Mr. John Jones," in *Sketches of Life and Character* (Philadelphia: J. D. Bradley, 1850), 383, 387. See Mrs. A. M. F. Annan, "The Cheap Dress. A Passage in Mrs. Allanby's Experience," *Godey's Lady's Book* 31, no. 3 (1845): 86–91, for a similar story from a woman's perspective. 38. T. S. Arthur, *Sketches of Life and Character* (Philadelphia: J. D. Bradley, 1850), 317–24. 39. See also T. S. Arthur, "Marrying a Merchant" *Godey's Lady's Book* 25, no. 4 (1842): 160–66, in which Josephine Allison prides herself on not being an economical wife, choosing instead to marry for financial security rather than love, only to find that her husband's own lack of economy ends in his own bankruptcy and the financial ruin of her own father. Her friend Mary, on the other hand, married a young clerk who worked his way up through the business, and together they established a happy and prosperous home together while Josephine was left without money and without love. 40. Arthur, *Hidden Wings*, 212. 41. I am indebted to Jean-Christophe Agnew for his insight on Charlotte Perkins Gilman. See Boydston, *Home and Work*, for an discussion of the strategies of making housework invisible. Gilman was Catharine Beecher and Harriet Beecher Stowe's grandniece. 42. T. S. Arthur, "Taking Boarders," *Godey's Lady's Book* 42 (1) (1851): 13–20; 42 (2) (1851): 81–87; and 42 (3) (1851): 160–67. 43. Taking boarders was a fairly common practice among middle-class families in small cities. By 1828, 28 percent of the employed males in Utica were boarders. Middle-class households frequently took in boarders to supplement the family income. Ryan, *Cradle of the Middle Class*, 62. Ryan suggests that this kind of domestic enterprise by the women of the family augmented the family income in place of the wages of a son who was preparing for a career. But while keeping boarders was common among middle-class families before the Civil War, after the war the number of families who kept boarders began to decline. Magazine fiction often discussed the pros and cons of taking boarders: "The Boarding House," *Godey's Lady's Book* 9, no. 4 (1834): 157–60; Mrs. H. Seely Totten, "Keeping a Few Genteel Boarders," *Godey's Lady's Book* 31, no. 1 (1845): 25–26; and another series by T. S. Arthur, "Country Boarding" *Godey's Lady's Book* 41 (1): 46ff.; 41 (2): 106ff.; and 41 (3): 141ff., which goes as far as to equate ill health and eventual death with boarding. 44. Arthur, "Taking Boarders," 15. 45. Ibid., 16. 46. Louis Godey sent his daughters to the school run by Sarah Hale's daughter. The school was often advertised in the "Editor's Table" of the magazine. 47. See Halttunen, *Confidence Men and Painted Women*, for a discussion of middle-class anxieties. 48. See C. A. Gregory, *Gifts and Commodities*, 41, for a related discussion of class- and clan-based economies and the distinctions made between gifts and commodities. 49. See Catharine Beecher and Harriet Beecher Stowe, *The American Woman's Home* (1869; reprint, Hartford, CT: Stowe-Day Foundation, 1987). Harriet Beecher Stowe also fictionalized the crusade for a domestic system in *Uncle Tom's Cabin* by juxtaposing Miss Ophelia's Northern ideas about domestic management with the chaos of Dinah's kitchen; see Brown, *Domestic Individualism*, 13–40. 50. Sklar, *Catharine Beecher*, 263 51. Beecher and Stowe, *American Woman's Home*, 241. 52. Ibid., 247. 53. Sklar, *Catharine Beecher*, 264. 54. Marion Harland, "Stumbling Blocks," *Godey's Lady's Book* 84, no. 3 (1872): 229–36; and 84, no. 4 (1872): 325–33. Although I refer to Terhune by her real name in the text, all citations will be under her pseudonym. Kelley, *Private Woman*, 175; *Notable American Women* 3:441. 55. The rhetorical bait and switch that Terhune performs here is a prime example of what Mary Poovey has called "the work of making ideology." See Poovey, *Uneven Developments*, 2. 56. Harland, "Stumbling Blocks," 84, no. 3 (1872): 232. 57. Ibid., 234. 58. Ibid. 59. Ibid. 60. Ibid., 230. 61. Harland, "Stumbling Blocks," 84, no. 4 (1872): 330. 62. Ibid., 235. 63. See Leonore Davidoff and Catherine Hall, *Family Fortunes: Men and Women of the English Middle Class, 1780–1850* (Chicago: University of Chicago Press, 1987) for a discussion of the importance of women's work and capital in the development of middle-class business in England. 64. Harland, "Stumbling Blocks," 84, no. 4 (1872): 329. 65. Ibid. 66. Ibid. 67. Harland, "Stumbling Blocks," 84, no. 3 (1872): 235. 68. Edwin T. Freedley, *Home Comforts; or, Things Worth Knowing in Every Household; Being a Digest of Facts Established by Science, Observation and Practical Experience, Respecting the Important Art of Living Well and Cheaply, Preserving Health and Prolonging Life* (Philadelphia: S. A. George, [1878]), 5. 69. Stanley, *From Bondage to Contract*, 166–72.

5. This Land of Precarious Fortunes

1. S. A. Frost, *Frost's Laws and By-Laws of American Society: A Condensed but Thorough Treatise on Etiquette and Its Usages in America, Containing Plain and Reliable Directions for Deportment in Every Situation of Life* (New York: Dick and Fitzgerald, 1869), 33. 2. See Bushman, *Refinement of America,* for an extended argument about emulation and class formation. 3. See Poovey, *Uneven Developments,* 9–13. 4. See Halttunen, *Confidence Men and Painted Women.* 5. See Katherine Grier, *Culture and Comfort.* 6. [Louis A. Godey], "The Cabinet Council; or How to Make a Lady's Book," *Godey's Lady's Book* 2, no. 1 (1831): 9–11. Godey is only identified as "the author." The name of Godey's magazine changed several times during the course of its history. For the purposes of clarity, I will refer to it only as *Godey's Lady's Book.* Mott, *History of American Magazines,* notes that the *Louisville Varieties* called *Godey's Lady's Book* the "Banquet of the Boudoir," and "Mr. Godey commented: 'There is something very pretty about that.'" Mott gives no dates for this exchange (2:594). 7. The characters in this story suggest the gradations of class and status possible within a single family. Godey distinguishes between the cousins; he does not give Penelope an honorific, which suggests that although the cousins are peers, Miss Mary may have a more elevated social status. Aunt Elinor is clearly defined by her spinsterhood. Godey as the author, and family member, also calls attention to his own status as a successful man of business, suggesting that boudoirs and business were not incompatible. This family portrait conveys the spectrum of the genteel class in America in the 1830s. 8. Godey, "Cabinet Council," 9–10. Miss Mary also makes the point that taste is not always supported by the means to express it. 9. Ibid., 9. 10. Ibid. 11. See Nancy Bercaw, "Solid Objects/Mutable Meanings: Victorian Fancywork and the Construction of Bourgeois Culture," *Winterthur Portfolio* (winter 1991): 231–47, for a related discussion of the continuing importance of the relationship of production and consumption in consumer culture. 12. Ladies who already had boudoirs did not need their contents cataloged, but Godey framed it this way to give his aspiring middle-class readers confidence that their interests were compatible with the kind of women depicted in the story. 13. Susan Stewart, *On Longing: Narratives of the Miniature, the Gigantic, the Souvenir, the Collection* (Durham, NC: Duke University Press, 1993), 151. This is not dissimilar from Martha Stewart's suggestions that even if one has not inherited family linens or silver, it is possible to appropriate the cast-off treasures of other families who have lost the sensibility that one has now gained for fine things and old things. 14. See Tonkovich, *Domesticity with a Difference,* 60, for a discussion of the ways in which the term "lady" was used as an umbrella term to describe the aspirations of readers as well as their actual social status. 15. For example, "Reminiscences of a Juris-consult. No. 5: The Destroyed Will," *Godey's Lady's Book* 4, no. 5 (1832): 222; "Jean Baptiste Say," *Godey's Lady's Book* 6, no. 4 (1833): 189. 16. "Women of Business," *Godey's Lady's Book* 3, no. 6 (1831): 347. 17. Child, *Mother's Book,* 136. 18. See Lee Virginia Chambers-Schiller, *Liberty a Better Husband: Single Women in America: The Generation of 1780–1840* (New Haven, CT: Yale University Press, 1994). 19. Sarah Josepha Hale to Mr. Childs, December 1, 1859. Sarah Josepha Hale Papers, Folder 1, Schlesinger Library, Radcliffe Institute, Harvard University (hereafter cited as Hale Papers). 20. Hale, *Flora's Interpreter.* First published in 1833, an improved sixth edition appeared in 1837 with new introductory remarks; in 1848, after fourteen editions and three publishers, it was again improved, and a new section, "Flora Fortuna," was added. This edition was reprinted each year through 1854. It was revised and enlarged in 1856, and in 1860 another revised edition was issued. Hale prepared another set of revisions for a final edition that was never published. 21. Hale, *Flora's Interpreter,* 1840 ed., v. 22. Hale, *Flora's Interpreter,* 6th ed., 1837.

23. Hale, *Flora's Interpreter*, 1840 ed., v. Thomas Jefferson also used this metaphor: "Editors are but cooks who must consult the palates of their customers." Quoted in Joyce Appleby, *Inheriting the Revolution: The First Generation of Americans* (Cambridge: Harvard University Press, 2000), 96. 24. Hale, *Flora's Interpreter*, 1848 ed., v. 25. "I send you a new poem that seems to me more worthy of a place in your new work than the one you selected—'W Snows' has appeared in so many collections of poetry that readers may consider it the only poem I have written. I shall be obliged if you will make the change. I hope my Thanksgiving Hymn will prove popular." Sarah Josepha Hale to Mr. Laird [?] Simons, [1870], Hale Papers. 26. Hale, *Flora's Interpreter*, 1848 ed., v. 27. "The Ladies' Mentor," *Godey's Lady's Book* (January 1837): 47–48. 28. [Lydia Maria Child], *The Little Girl's Own Book* (Glasgow: John Reid, 1837), v–vi. 29. Sarah Josepha Hale to Mr. Childs, December 1, 1859, Hale Papers. 30. Godey and Hale received many letters from gentlewomen in reduced circumstances asking for employment or at least advice about ways to earn money. Although the magazine could not offer employment to all women who applied, Godey emphasized how many women he did employ: "The establishment of Godey's Lady's Book gives employment to one hundred and fifty females in the coloring and binding departments alone. This at least should gain us some credit among our female patrons." *Godey's Lady's Book* (February 1851): 138. 31. Alice B. Neal, "Employment of Women in Cities: No. I. The Mint Coin Adjusters," *Godey's Lady's Book* 45, no. 2 (1852): 125. 32. Ibid., 127. 33. Alice B. Neal, "Employment of Women in Cities: No. II. The Philadelphia School of Design," *Godey's Lady's Book* 45, no. 3 (1852): 277. 34. Alice B. Neal, "Employment of Women in Cities: No. III. Shopkeeping," *Godey's Lady's Book* 45, no. 4 (1852): 369–70. 35. Sarah J. Hale, "Editorial," *Godey's Lady's Book* 45, no. 4 (1852): 389. 36. Sarah J. Hale, "Colporteurs in America," *Godey's Lady's Book* 45, no. 3 (1852): 293. 37. This book was enthusiastically reviewed in *Godey's Lady's Book* 45, no. 7 (1852): 99. 38. Mrs. L. G. Abell, *Woman in Her Various Relations: Containing Practical Rules for American Females* (New York: William Holdredge, 1851), 215. 39. "Studies toward the Life of 'A Business Woman' being conversations with Mrs. R. P. Clarke in the winter of 1864–65," unpublished manuscript, Caroline H. Dall Papers, vol. 2, Schlesinger Library, Radcliffe Institute, Harvard University. 40. Ibid., 48. 41. Abell, *Woman in Her Various Relations*, 315. 42. Eliza Leslie, *Miss Leslie's Behavior Book: A Guide and Manual for Ladies* (1859; reprint, New York: Arno Press, 1972). Leslie was prolific; she edited gift books, *The Violet or Juvenile Souvenir: A Christmas and New Year's Gift or Birthday Present* (Philadelphia: E. L. Carey & A. Hart, 1837) and *The Gift: A Christmas and New Year's Present for 1837* (Philadelphia: E. L. Carey & A. Hart, 1836), among others. One of her best-known books was *The American Girl's Book; or Occupation for Play Hours* (New York: C. S. Francis, 1831). 43. Leslie, *Miss Leslie's Behavior Book*, 261. 44. Charles Leslie to Eliza Leslie, November 12, 1829, in Tom Taylor, ed., *Autobiographical Recollections by the Late Charles Robert Leslie* (Boston: Ticknor and Fields, 1860), 283. 45. Ibid., 284. 46. Charles Leslie to Eliza Leslie, May 20, 1830, in ibid., 289–90. 47. Ibid., 290. 48. Leslie, *Miss Leslie's Behavior Book*, 276. 49. Ibid., 259. 50. Ibid., 283. 51. Ibid., 282–83. 52. Harriet Martineau, *Society in America* (Gloucester, MA: Peter Smith, 1968), 306. 53. Virginia Penny, *The Employments of Women: A Cyclopedia of Woman's Work* (Boston: Walker, Wise, 1863), vi. Penny had collected her evidence in New York City from 1859 to 1862. 54. See Stansell, *City of Women*. Middle-class reformers tried to impose sentimental ideals of womanhood on the poor women to whom they offered charity, using middle-class notions of domesticity to determine who the "worthy poor" were. This was a sources of tension between the two groups, poor women did not find the tenets of middle-class womanhood very useful in any in practical way. Penny offered this book as a source of practical rather than

ideological solutions to women's poverty. 55. Penny, *Employments of Women*, xiv. 56. Mrs. Maria Gilman [Charles Barnard], *My Ten-Rod Farm; or How I Became a Florist* (Boston: Loring, 1869), 118–19. 57. Charles Barnard, *Co-operation as a Business* (New York: G. P. Putnam's Sons, 1881), iv. 58. Ibid., 174. 59. Ibid., iv. 60. Ibid., 214. 61. Ibid., 224. 62. Ibid., 226. 63. Amy Dru Stanley, *From Bondage to Contract: Wage Labor, Marriage, and the Market in the age of Slave Emancipation* (New York: Oxford University Press, 1998), 166–74. 64. M. L. Rayne, *What Can a Woman Do; or, Her position in the Business and Literary World* (Petersburg, NY: Eagle Publishing, 1893), iii–iv.

6. Fancy That

1. Material culture studies have become an increasingly important part of historical inquiry. Jules Prown introduced a method of close analysis based on sensory rather than intellectual data in "Mind in Matter: An Introduction to Material Culture Theory and Method," *Winterthur Portfolio* 17, no. 1 (spring 1982): 1–2. This approach placed objects at the center of analysis and drew its method and theory from the history of art. Anthropology, archaeology, folklore, and studies of the built environment also offered theoretical models for the study of material culture. See Thomas J. Schlereth, ed., *Material Culture: A Research Guide* (Lawrence: University of Kansas Press, 1985). In his introduction to this collection of essays, Schlereth noted that while the bulk of material culture studies remained case studies of object types, new work in the field was integrating material culture into a larger historical narrative in an attempt to balance the different kinds of evidence rather than privilege one genre over another. See Rhys Isaac, *The Transformation of Virginia, 1740–1790* (Chapel Hill: University of North Carolina Press, 1982), for a seminal example of this kind of scholarship; Thomas J. Schlereth, *Cultural History and Material Culture: Everyday Life, Landscapes, Museums* (Ann Arbor: UMI Press, 1990), for a collection of his writings on material culture; Harvey Green, *The Light of the Home: An Intimate View of the Lives of Women in Victorian America* (New York: Pantheon, 1983); Robert St. George, ed., *Material Life in America, 1600–1800* (Boston: Northeastern University Press, 1988); and John R. Stilgoe, *Common Landscapes of America, 1598–1845* (New Haven, Conn.: Yale University Press, 1982). See also Kenneth L. Ames, *Death in the Dining Room and Other Tales of Victorian Culture* (Philadelphia: Temple University Press, 1992). Ames uses objects, primarily furniture, to read the cultural activities of the home and to demonstrate the ambiguity and ambivalence about market culture in nineteenth-century middle-class culture. See Bushman, *Refinement of America*. 2. Kathleen D. McCarthy, *Women's Culture: American Philanthropy and Art, 1830–1930* (Chicago: University of Chicago Press, 1991), 47. 3. Although Beverly Gordon's more positive interpretation of fancywork suggests that "given a limited, constricted arena of acceptable activity and behavior, women's 'airy trifles' and 'fancies' were imaginative expressions of amusement and play, fantasy, escape and transformation," her argument is only the positive inverse of the previous condemnation; it does not change the assumptions of its negative counterpart. Gordon, "Victorian Fancywork in the American Home: Fantasy and Accommodation," in *Making the American Home: Middle Class Women and Material Culture, 1840–1940*, ed. Marilyn Ferris Motz and Pat Browne (Bowling Green, OH: Bowling Green State University Popular Press, 1988), 49. 4. Gordon, "Victorian Fancywork," 53–55. 5. Bercaw, "Solid Objects/Mutable Meanings," 231–32, 240. 6. In the dual household economy of the farm, butter production provided cash for agricultural women. Butter making was an essential capital-generating activity that helped to strike a balance between new and old market forms. See Joan M. Jensen, "Butter Making and Economic Development in Mid-Atlantic America from

1750–1850," *Signs* (summer 1988): 813–29; and *Loosening the Bonds: Mid-Atlantic Farm Women, 1750–1850* (New Haven, CT: Yale University Press, 1986). See also Cott, *Bonds of Womanhood;* Boydston, *Home and Work;* Strasser, *Never Done;* and Laurel Thatcher Ulrich, *Good Wives: Image and Reality in the Lives of Women in Northern New England, 1650–1750* (New York: Vintage Books, 1991) for further discussion of the changes that took place in domestic production. 7. "The Early Field of Employment," in *Women in Industry: A Study in American Economic History,* ed. Edith Abbott (New York: D. Appleton, 1909; BoondocksNet Edition, 2002), 2. 8. Clark, *Roots,* 179–91. 9. Matilda Pullan and Eliza Warren, *Treasures in Needlework* (1855; New York: Lancer Books, 1973), v; S. Annie Frost, *The Ladies' Guide to Needle Work, Embroidery, Etc.: Being a Complete Guide to All Kinds of Ladies' Fancy Work* (New York: Henry T. Williams, 1877), 3. This story of the origins of the Bayeux Tapestry is apocryphal. It was embroidered by nuns as political propaganda. Odo, William's half-brother, commissioned it to justify William's claim to the throne. James Snyder, *Medieval Art: Painting, Sculpture and Architecture* (New York: Prentice-Hall, 1989), 291–93. 10. Florence Hartley, *The Ladies' Hand Book of Fancy and Ornamental Work* (Philadelphia: G. G. Evans, 1859). 11. Ibid., 239. 12. Alice Kessler-Harris, *Out to Work: A History of Wage-Earning Women in the United States* (New York: Oxford University Press, 1982), 77. 13. Susan Warner, *The Wide, Wide World* (1851; reprint, New York: Charles L. Bowman, 1909), 41. 14. Hartley, *Ladies' Hand Book,* 5. 15. Ibid., 239. 16. Ibid., 239–40. 17. Ibid., 240. 18. Katharine Morrison McClinton, *Antique Collecting for Everyone* (New York: McGraw-Hill, 1951), 183–84. 19. Felice Hodges, *Period Pastimes: A Practical Guide to Four Centuries of Decorative Crafts* (New York: Weidenfeld and Nicolson, 1989), 67. 20. Ibid., 117. 21. Virginia Penny, *How Women Can Make Money, Married or Single, in All Branches of the Arts and Sciences, Professions, Trades, Agricultural and Mechanical Pursuits* (Philadelphia: John E. Potter, [1862]), 42. 22. Sarah E. Herman, *Instructions in Madame Herman's New Method of Making Wax Flowers* (New York, [1873]); She published *Instructions in Wax Foliage* simultaneously. See also Lizzie S. Patten, *Wax Flowers and Fruit: Modelling Without a Teacher* (New York: J. L. Patten, 1876); Marie LeFranc, *How to Make Waxflowers* (New York: Wynckoop & Hallenbeck, 1882); and George Worgan, *The Art of Modelling Flowers in Wax* (Brooklyn, NY: H. H. Dickinson, 1867). 23. Penny, *How Women Can Make Money,* 277. 24. Mrs. Bosen, a New York manufacturer, ran her own wholesale Imitation Hair Works, trafficking in waterfalls, braids, curls, Empress coils, and Japan switches. Hair: Box 1, Warshaw Collection of Business Americana, Archives Center, National Museum of American History, Smithsonian Institution. A present-day hair augmentation system called "Perfect Hair" is advertised on late-night television infomercials. 25. Penny, *How Women Can Make Money,* 278. 26. Ibid. 27. "Hair Work," *Godey's Lady's Book* 41, no. 6 (1850): 377. 28. Advertisements in *Le Bon Ton* for hair jewelers in the late 1850s included Schmitt and Stubenraugh, 1858–65; Vincent Brandly, 108 Canal Street, 1857 and 1859; J. Shaffner, Artist in Hair and Jewelry, 339 Canal Street, New York, 1859; and Robert Link and Brother, Artists in Hair and Jewelry, 753 and 537 Broadway, N.Y., 1860. I am grateful to Shelley Foote, Division of Costume, National Museum of American History for this information from the archival files. 29. Mrs. C. S. Jones and Henry T. Williams, *Ladies' Fancy Work: Hints and Helps to Home Taste and Recreation* (New York: Henry T. Williams, 1877), 49. 30. L. Shaw, 54 West 14th Street, New York, *Harper's Bazaar,* January 14, 1876, Hair: Box 1, Warshaw Collection of Business Americana, Archives Center, National Museum of American History, Smithsonian Institution. 31. Mrs. C. S. Jones and Henry T. Williams, *Ladies' Fancy Work,* 52. 32. There is a collection of hair wreaths in the Division of Domestic Life, National Museum of American History, Smithsonian Institution. I am grateful to Rodris Roth for showing these to me. m 33. The pleasure of this sensation had the opposite effect of a hair shirt. 34. *Godey's Lady's Book* 45, no. 2 (1862): 204. 35. Penny also recommended that ladies patronize stores in which saleswomen were employed and petition merchants, like Mr. Stewart of New York, to employ saleswomen. 36. Penny, *How Women Can Make Money*, 105. 37. See Julia A. Parker, "The Fancy Store; or, My Friends of the Cottage," *Ladies National Magazine* (October 1848): 115–22. British stores included, Ackermann's Repository, and S. J. Fuller's "Temple of Fancy"; Hodges, *Period Pastimes*, 26–27. 38. See also Michael Anesko, *Friction in the Marketplace: Henry James and the Profession of Authorship* (New York: Oxford University Press, 1986), 61–77; and Michael T. Gilmore, *American Romanticism and the Marketplace* (Chicago: University of Chicago Press, 1985), 96–112, for two alternate discussions of market symbolism of the Pyncheon shop front. 39. Nathaniel Hawthorne, *The House of Seven Gables* (1851; reprint, New York: Bantam Books, 1986), 58–60. 40. Ibid., 60. 41. "The Ornamental Artist," *Godey's Lady's Book* 2, no. 4 (1831): 177. 42. "The Toilet," *Godey's Lady's Book* 8, no. 1 (1834): 25; 8 (2): 88; 8 (3): 121; 8 (5): 229; 8 (6): 271; and 9, no. 5 (1834): 329. 43. *Godey's Lady's Book* 42, no. 3 (1851): 204. 44. Margaret Vincent, *The Ladies' Work Table: Domestic Needlework in Nineteenth-Century America* (Hanover, NH: University Press of New England, 1988), 45. 45. "Instructions for Making Ornaments in Rice-Shell-Work," *Godey's Lady's Book* 48, no. 1 (1854): 22–25; 48 (2): 154; and 48 (3): 240–42. 46. There is a painting in Tate Gallery in London by William Dyce, c. 1859, which depicts middle-class women gathering shells and seaweed to use for fancywork; illustrated in Hodges, *Period Pastimes*, 143. 47. *Martha Stewart Living*, February 2003, has instructions for simple shell work. 48. "Everyday Actualities—No. XVII: The Manufacture of Artificial Flowers," *Godey's Lady's Book* 48, no. 4 (1854): 295–300. 49. White velvet was the preferred medium because it showed the colors well and give the painting a soft texture. Black velvet is now the preferred medium, and Elvis Presley is the most popular subject. 50. N. B., "Carrie Lee's Talisman," *Godey's Lady's Book* 47, no. 1 (1853): 30–32; also *Carrie Lee's Talisman* (Philadelphia: T. K. Collins, 1856), quoted in Catherine E. Kelly, "Lives and Letters: Female Literary Culture in Provincial New England," in "Between Town and Country: New England Women and the Creation of a Provincial Middle Class, 1820–1860" (PhD diss., University of Rochester, 1992). 51. Jane Weaver, *Dictionary of Needlework* (Philadelphia: Peterson's Magazine, 1860). It was originally published in *Peterson's* in 1858. 52. Eliza Warren and Matilda Pullan, *Treasures in Needlework: Comprising Instructions in Knitting, Netting, Crochet, Point Lace, Tatting, Braiding and Embroidery* (1855; reprint, New York: Lancer Books, 1973), i. 53. Ibid., vi. 54. Ibid., xv. 55. Matilda Pullan, *The Lady's Manual of Fancy-Work: A Complete Instructor in Every Variety of Ornamental Needle-Work* (New York: Dick & Fitzgerald, 1859). 56. America, which she described as "the Paradise of women," provided her with the strength to undertake such an ambitious project. 57. See Charlotte Allen, "Purl Jam," *Washington Post Magazine*, January 22, 1995, for a humorous essay about recreating the domestic culture of cooking and fancywork that her mother, a skilled practitioner herself, never taught her. 58. Pullan, *Lady's Manual*, xvi. 59. Ibid., xi. 60. Ibid., xv. 1858 was the year the first Atlantic telegraph cable was laid. 61. Ibid., 208. 62. "HAIR ORNAMENTS—Ladies wishing hair made into Bracelets, Pins (which are very beautiful) Necklaces or Ear rings, can be accommodated by our Fashion Editor. A very large number of orders have recently been filled, and the articles have given great satisfaction." Prices ranged from $1.50 to $15.00, and items included "Fob chains, Hair studs, sleeve buttons etc." *Godey's Lady's Book* 65, no. 6 (1862): 613. 63. *Godey's Lady's Book* 64, no. 1 (1862): 102. 64. "Some Hints," *Godey's Lady's Book* 64, no. 1 (1862): 102. 65. *Godey's Lady's Book* 64, no. 2 (1862:, 303. 66. "Pincushion," *Godey's Lady's Book* 74, no. 4 (1867): 165.

67. See Mrs. C. S. Jones and Henry T. Williams, *Household Elegancies* (New York: Henry T. Williams, 1877). 68. Mrs. C. S. Jones and Henry T. Williams, *Ladies' Fancy Work: Hints and Helps to Home Taste and Recreation* (New York: Henry T. Williams, 1877), 60. 69. From *Cassell's Household Guide* (1875), quoted in Hodges, *Period Pastimes*, 142. 70. Jones and Williams, *Ladies' Fancywork*, 196. 71. Edmund Parrish, *The Phantom Bouquet: A Popular Treatise on the Art of Skeletonizing Leaves and Seed-vessels, and Adapting Them to Embellish the Home of Taste* (Philadelphia: J. B. Lippincott, 1863). 72. Aquariums and herbariums were another fashionable decoration for the parlor. Virginia Penny suggested making them as a possible source of income. The aquarium at Barnum's Museum had inspired a fashionable interest in marine creatures. Herbariums were collections of dried plants arranged according to botanical classification or as ornaments for the parlor. Books detailing the techniques for setting up an aquarium or creating a herbarium had just appeared on the market, Penny told her readers, and might furnish useful information in these pursuits. See H. D. Butler, *The Family Aquarium; or Aqua Vivarium* (New York: Dick & Fitzgerald, c. 1858). This volume was also recommended by the *New York Times*. 73. Shirley Hibberd wrote a whole series on gardening published by Groomsbridge and Sons: *The Amateur's Flower Garden* (1871), *The Amateur's Kitchen Garden* (1877), and *The Amateur's Greenhouse and Conservatory* (1880). Henry T. Williams published several books on gardening, including Daisy Eyebright [Mrs. S. O. Johnson], *Every Woman Her Own Flower Gardener* (New York, 1877) and Henry T. Williams, *Window Gardening* (New York, 1878). Williams also edited *The Ladies Floral Cabinet*, a magazine that included gardening prominently among its other amusements. Virginia Penny reported that being a florist was "a delightful business for a lady," as long as she had someone to do the manual labor. Bouquets offered a tasteful expression of sentiments. It was often a business conducted by husbands and wives together. 74. Advertised in the back of Frost, *Ladies' Guide to Needle Work*. The vines were patented in 1874. See also Shirley Hibberd, *Rustic Ornaments for Homes of Taste* (London: Groomsbridge and Sons, 1870). 75. Virginia McAlester and Lee McAlester, *A Field Guide to American Houses* (New York: Alfred A. Knopf, 1988), 197–209. See also Sweeting, *Reading Houses and Building Books*. 76. Advertisement for *Fret Sawing for Pleasure and Profit* (New York: Henry T. Williams, c. 1877), in Frost, *Ladies' Guide to Needle Work*. 77. Advertisement for *Women's Ornamental Designs for Fret-Work, Scroll Sawing, Fancy Carving, and Home Decorations* (New York: Henry T. Williams, c. 1877). 78. Ibid. 79. Advertisement for *Women's Ornamental Designs*.

7. Charitable Calculations

1. Arjun Appadurai, ed., *The Social Life of Things: Commodities in Cultural Perspective* (Cambridge: Cambridge University Press, 1986), 11. 2. See Marcel Mauss, *The Gift: Forms and Functions of Exchange in Archaic Societies*, trans. Ian Cunnison, introduction by E. E. Evans Prichard (Glencoe, IL: Free Press, 1954), 18, 22. 3. Sarah J. Hale, *Traits of American Life* (Philadelphia: E. L. Carey & A. Hart, 1835), 260. 4. Penny, *Employments of Women*, 105. Penny noted that flirtation was a common part of shopping, women shopping took longer because they spent time flirting with the clerks. 5. Kathleen Waters Sander, *The Business of Charity: The Women's Exchange Movement, 1832–1900* (Urbana: University of Illinois Press, 1998), 14–15. 6. Ibid., 4–6 7. Ginzberg, *Women and the Work of Benevolence*, 36, 43. 8. Ibid., 57–59. 9. See Boydston, *Home and Work*. 10. Ginzberg, *Women and the Work of Benevolence*, 46. 11. *Salem Gazette*, May 17, 1833. I am grateful to Cassandra Cleghorn for bringing this fair to my attention. 12. Ibid. 13. Ibid. 14. Hale, *Traits of American Life*, 259–67. 15. Ibid., 257. 16. Ibid., 262.

17. The opera as the site of spectacle appeared in the end of the nineteenth century in the work of Mary Cassatt and Edith Wharton, who both took a slightly different view of the seriousness of the gaze of others in this circumstance. See Mary Cassatt, *At the Opera* (1880) and Edith Wharton, *The Age of Innocence* (New York: D. Appleton, 1920). 18. Hale, *Traits of American Life*, 263. 19. Mauss, *Gift*, 18. See also Lewis Hyde, *The Gift: Imagination and the Erotic Life of Property* (New York: Vintage Books, 1983), 56. "It is the cardinal difference between gift and commodity exchange that a gift establishes a feeling-bond between two people, while the sale of a commodity leaves no necessary connection." 20. Louisa May Alcott, *Little Women* (1868; reprint, New York: Penguin Books, 1989), 306. 21. Hale, *Traits of American Life*, 261–62. 22. Ibid., 264. 23. Lee, *Three Experiments*, 34. 24. Penny, *Employments of Women*, 1863; Caroline Dall, *The College, the Market and the Court; or, Woman's Relation to Education, Labor and Law* (1859; reprint, Boston: Memorial Edition, 1914); [Dinah Maria Mulock], *A Woman's Thoughts About Women* (New York: John Bradburn, 1866). 25. Hale, *Traits of American Life*, 265. 26. Ibid., 263. 27. Hyde, *Gift*, xiv: "The spirit of the gift is kept alive by its constant donation." 28. Hale, *Traits of American Life*, 260–61. 29. Hyde, *Gift*, 138. "Charity is a way of negotiating the boundary of class. There may be gift circulation within each class, but between classes there is a barrier." 30. Ginzberg, *Women and the Work of Benevolence*, 46. Philadelphia Quakers criticized the fairs as "light-minded," so Lucretia Mott called her fairs "sales" and held them privately in her home. 31. See Campbell, *Romantic Ethic*. 32. Nancy Hewitt, *Women's Activism and Social Change: Rochester, New York, 1822–1872* (Ithaca, NY: Cornell University Press, 1984), 150–51. 33. For another discussion of charity fairs, see Elizabeth Alice White, "Charitable Calculations: Fancywork, Charity, and the Culture of the Sentimental Market," in *The Middling Sorts: Explorations in the History of the American Middle Class*, ed. Burton J. Bledstein and Robert D. Johnston (New York: Routledge, 2001) and Jeanne Attie, *Patriotic Toil: Northern Women and the American Civil War* (Ithaca, NY: Cornell University Press, 1998), 198–219. 34. *Speech of the Rev. Dr. [Henry Whitney] Bellows, President of the United States Sanitary Commission, Made at the Academy of Music, Philadelphia, Tuesday Evening, February 24, 1863* (Philadelphia: C. Sherman, Son & Company, 1863), 17. 35. [Elisha Harris], *The United States Sanitary Commission* (Boston: Crosby & Nichols, 1864), 48–49. Reprinted from an article in the *North American Review* 203 (April 1864). 36. George M. Frederickson, *The Inner Civil War: Northern Intellectuals and the Crisis of the Union* (1965; reprint, Chicago: University of Illinois Press, 1993), 103–8. 37. *Speech of the Rev. Dr. Bellows*, 32. 38. Preserves, dried apples, cookies, and other food were also included in these boxes. 39. Mary Livermore, *My Story of the War: A Woman's Narrative of Four Years Personal Experience* (Hartford, CT: A. D. Worthington, 1888), 137. 40. "Letter from a Lady of New England," in "Editor's Table," *Godey's Lady's Book* 66, no. 1 (1863): 93. 41. Ibid. 42. Livermore, *My Story*, 410. 43. Marjorie Barstow Greenbie, *Lincoln's Daughters of Mercy* (New York: G. P. Putnam's Sons, 1944), 186. 44. Livermore, *My Story*, 411. 45. Ibid., 455. 46. Ibid., 412. 47. Ibid., 456. 48. Ibid., 457. 49. Katharine Wormley, *The Cruel Side of the War* (Boston: Roberts Brothers, 1898), 11, estimates the total at $2,736,868.84, an exact number that she observed did not include the value of the labor expended in making materials to donate and running the fairs. A truer estimate, she suggested in a footnote, would approach $25 million. It is testimony to the increased respect for and awareness of women's business activities that Wormley acknowledges the value of women's "voluntary" labor. 50. Livermore, *My Story*, 153. 51. "Articles that Children Can Make for Fancy Fairs or Holiday Presents," *Godey's Lady's Book* (January 1862): 100. Nine of the twelve issues of *Godey's Lady's Book* for 1862 contained instructions for children's fancywork for this purpose. See also Lucretia P. Hale and Margaret E. White, *Decorative and Fancy Articles for Presents and Fairs* (Boston: S. W. Tilton, 1885).

52. Attie, *Patriotic Toil*, 202–8. 53. Quoted from Philadelphia Sanitary Fair Catalogue, 1864, in Vincent, *Ladies Work Table*, 24. 54. Greenbie, *Lincoln's Daughters of Mercy*, 206. 55. Ginzberg, *Women and the Work of Benevolence*, 152. 56. See Kathleen Waters Sander, *The Business of Charity: The Women's Exchange Movement, 1832–1900* (Urbana: University of Illinois Press, 1998) for further discussion of the Women's Exchange movement. 57. McCarthy, *Women's Culture*, 61. 58. Ibid., 40. 59. Ibid., 43.
60. Candace Wheeler, *Yesterdays in a Busy Life* (New York: Harper and Brothers, 1918), 211, quoted in Isabelle Anscombe, *A Woman's Touch: Women in Design from 1860 to the Present Day* (New York: Penguin Books, 1985), 36. 61. "Nonprofit entrepreneurship" is Kathleen McCarthy's term (*Women's Culture*, 62); Sander, *Business of Charity*, 2. 62. McCarthy, *Women's Culture*, 62, 63; Lucy M. Salmon, "The Women's Exchange: Charity or Business?" *Forum* 13 (May 1892): 394–406.

8. Roses Are Read

1. Schmidt, *Consumer Rites*, 40. 2. See Norma Basch, *In the Eyes of the Law: Women, Marriage, and Property in Nineteenth-Century New York* (Ithaca, NY: Cornell University Press, 1982). 3. See Karen Lystra, *Searching the Heart: Women, Men and Romantic Love in Nineteenth-Century America* (New York: Oxford University Press, 1989) for a related discussion of the intersections of individualism and romantic love. Lystra emphasizes the compatibility of romantic love and individualism. 4. Erica Harth, "The Virtue of Love: Lord Hardwicke's Marriage Act," *Cultural Critique* 9 (spring 1998): 136. 5. Ibid., 134.
6. Frank Staff, *The Valentine and Its Origins* (London: Lutterworth Press, 1969), 24. 7. The origins of Valentine's Day have been (naturally) romanticized. The feast day of St. Valentine, bishop of Terni, martyred about AD 270, falls on February 14. Another St. Valentine of Rome also claims the fourteenth as a feast day, but he is thought to have been invented in the fifth century, whereas the bishop of Terni is considered the authentic saint. Neither saint had any official tie to lovers; there is, however, an apocryphal story that draws the connection. St. Valentine, as the story goes, befriended the daughter of his jailer during his imprisonment and she, in turn, fell in love with him. She was absent at the time of his execution, and he left her a farewell note signed "Your Valentine." While this is a charming, if macabre, origin for the tradition of expressing one's love on February 14, it is more likely that the connection to lovers came from the Roman festival of Lupercalia, a fertility rite held on February 15. It was common practice in the Middle Ages to merge pagan festivals with saints' feast days to encourage participation, and the rituals of Lupercalia were adapted over time to the service of Valentine's Day.

One Chaucer scholar, Henry Ansgar Kelly, in *Chaucer and the Cult of Saint Valentine*, Davis Medieval Texts and Studies, University of California, Davis (Lugduni Batavorum: E. J. Brill, 1986), attributes the origin of the lover's association to Chaucer himself, suggesting that Chaucer invented and popularized the association through his poetry, which contains a number of references to Valentine's Day as a lover's holiday. Whether or not Chaucer can be seen as the originator of the association, Kelly makes a convincing case that the St. Valentine of Chaucer's *Parlement of Bryddes, or the Assembly of Foules* and other contemporary poetry is St. Valentine of Genoa, whose feast day falls on May 2. This later date would explain the images of spring that accompany Chaucer's discussion of Valentine's Day and his equation of the holiday with the day on which birds chose their mates, all of which correspond to similar customs associated with the first of May. The February 14 feast day was, however, more commonly included on calendars, and this may have contributed to the acceptance of the February date over the May date. The custom of choosing a valentine was akin to the choice made by birds, who were thought to choose one mate for life; to choose a valentine was a year-long commitment, and the one who was chosen often became the betrothed. By the sixteenth century, the association between courtship and the feast of St. Valentine was firmly entrenched; Ben Jonson condemned the association, which he declared besmirched the name of St. Valentine, who was the good and gentle patron saint of epileptics. For a more complete history of Valentine's Day, see Lee, *History of Valentines*, and Staff, *Valentine and Its Origins*. 8. Attempts to reform folk holidays were common practice in the nineteenth century. Schmidt, *Consumer Rites*, 889. 9. See Hickory Broom, "The Dream of St. Valentine's Eve," *Godey's Lady's Book* (February 1853): 149–50, for a fictional exploration of this valentine custom. 10. Mrs. J. Y. Foster, "The Valentine Party," *Peterson's*, February 1850, 78–85; "Valentine Games; or, Amusements for the Fireside," *Godey's Lady's Book* 46, no. 2 (1853): 147–48; "Parlor Games," *Peterson's*, February 1856, 178–79. 11. Samuel Pepys kept his diary between 1660 and 1669 while he was secretary to his cousin, Edward Montagu, earl of Sandwich, who was a personal friend of Oliver Cromwell. O. F. Morshead, ed., *The Diary of Samuel Pepys* (New York: Harper & Brothers, 1926), x–xi. 12. Schmidt, *Consumer Rites*, 70–71. 13. "Editor's Table," *Peterson's*, February 1851. 14. Mary Moore, "Saint Valentine's Day," *Godey's Lady's Book* 62, no. 2 (1861): 119–22. 15. Ibid. 16. See Schmidt, *Consumer Rites*, 30, for a related argument. 17. Campbell, *Romantic Ethic*, 10. 18. "Hints for and Essay on Presents," *Godey's Lady's Book* 30, no. 1 (1845): 27. 19. Marcel Mauss, *The Gift: Forms and Functions of Exchange in Archaic Societies*, trans. Ian Cunnison, introduction by E. E. Evans-Pritchard (Glencoe, IL: Free Press, 1954), 3. 20. "Hints for and Essay on Presents," 27. 21. See also a discussion of related essays by Caroline Kirkland and Ralph Waldo Emerson in Schmidt, *Consumer Rites*, 85–87. 22. See Merish, *Sentimental Materialism*, for a related discussion of these ideas in sentimental fiction. 23. Schmidt, *Consumer Rites*, 49. For this reason, I use British and American valentines as evidence interchangeably. 24. See C. T. Hinckley, "Everyday Actualities.—No. XVII—The Manufacture of Paper," *Godey's Lady's Book* 48, no. 3 (1854): 199–207, for a contemporary discussion of innovations in paper-making technology. The article primarily discusses foreign manufacturers. 25. Lee, *History of Valentines*, 42. 26. Ibid., 34–35. 27. *Hymen's Revenge against Old Maids, Old Bachelors and Impertinent Coxcombs or a* NEW *Valentine Writer for the Present Year, Being a Choice Collection of Valentines, Humorous and Satirical Chiefly Organized and Written Expressly for this Work* (London: A. Kidwell, c. 1805); *The New Cupid's Bower Being a Poetical Garden of Love Abounding with Original Valentines Calculated to Convey the Sentiments of the Heart in Language Neat, Chaste and Expressive* (London: Dean, n.d.). 28. Mr. Turner of Norfolk, *The New English Valentine Writer or the High Road to Love for Both Sexes* (London, 1784). 29. Ibid., 56. 30. *A Collection of New and Original Valentines— Serious & Satirical, Sublime & Ridiculous* (London: Ward & Lock, [1857]). This book was part of Ward and Lock's Railway series; other titles in the series included *Money: How to Get It, How to Keep It and How to Use It, a Guide to Fortune; The Best Method of Doing Common Things; The Railway and Parlour Song Book; Etiquette for Ladies and Gentlemen;* and *The School of Life*. 31. *A Collection of New and Original Valentines—Serious & Satirical, Sublime & and Ridiculous*, 9–10. 32. Ibid., 15. 33. Series II, Box 28, Norcross Historical Greeting Card Collection, Archives Center, National Museum of American History, Smithsonian Institution (hereafter cited as Norcross Historical Greeting Card Collection). 34. Another hapless lover, who felt the printed sentiment of his valentine did not truly convey his feelings, inscribed in his own handwriting along the side of the poem "I really do love you." This anonymous lover found the mass-produced valentine he had chosen to lack the emphasis with which he wished to express himself. But by asserting his sincerity too vehemently, he called its very existence into question. Without intimate knowledge of the exchange, it is not possible to know whether this protestation of love was a corrective to some previous action or a profession of love so ardent that no printed poetry could articulate its passion. Series II, Box 28, Norcross Collection. 35. The flyleaf is inscribed "Library of Carlos Smith, Whitehall, NY." The volume, which is in the Norcross Historical Greeting Card Collection, contains two writers bound together. The first is *Strong's Universal Valentine Writer*, the second is *Saint Valentine's Budget Being a Choice Miscellany of Elegant Poetical Pieces Gay and Sentimental Suitable for Valentines of Compliment, Friendship and Love for Gentlemen and Ladies, single and married, maids and bachelors, young and elderly by a Literary Lady* (New York: T. W. Strong, n.d.). The home of T. W. Strong's Valentine Depot was 98 Nassau Street, New York. This was, of course, a private book that Smith did not intend for the kind of public scrutiny an archive offers. 36. Abraham Fisher and Frederick Turner, of Fisher and Turner, and the Robert H. Elton and Company produced lithographed valentines in the early 1830s, Elton in New York, Fisher and Turner in Philadelphia and then Fisher alone in New York. The valentines produced by these companies were primarily hand-colored lithographs with a printed poem beneath. Both firms claimed to be the oldest valentine manufacturer in America. Thomas W. Strong, also of New York, was another early and successful wholesaler and retailer of valentines. Strong went into business in 1842 and advertised his store at 98 Nassau Street as "Strong's Grand Valentine Depot." It was a valentine address of long standing; Robert H. Elton and Company started at 98 Nassau Street in 1834, moving ten years later as T. W. Strong moved in. Strong stayed until 1869, and in 1874, Abraham Fisher advertised at 98 Nassau Street. Staff, *Valentine and Its Origins*, 136–37. Other New York valentine sellers included the American Valentine Company, active in the 1860s; Berlin and Jones, 1859–69; Philip J. Cozans, 1850–62; Pasqual Donaldson, 1839–55; T. Frere, 1852–55; G. S. Haskins and Company, 1861–63; Charles P. Huestis, 1841–53; McLoughlin Brothers, 1849–50; Charles Magnus, 1854–70; Richard Marsh, 1850–54; Edward Whaites, 1836–68; James Wrigley, 1846–70; John A. Lowell and Company, Boston, Mass., 1882; George Dunn and Company, Richmond, Va., 1860s publisher of Civil War valentines; John Windsor and Sons, 1840s–1850s; and J. Childs, 46 1/2 Walnut St., Philadelphia, c. 1850. List complied from appendices in Staff, Lee, and the Norcross Historical Greeting Card Collection. 37. Lee, *History of Valentines*, 54. The advertisement ran for two weeks. 38. *Boston Globe*, February 14, 1901, p. 6. Ruth Webb Lee estimated Howland's gross as high as $100,000; Lee, *History of Valentines*, 57. 39. On one of these trips in the early 1860s, she fell and injured her knee and was forced to run her business from a wheel chair for several years. Lee, *History of Valentines*, 60. 40. The New England Valentine Company was still listed at 68 Summer, but Southworth's advertisement for his insurance company indicated that 325 Main Street was also the office of the New England Valentine Company. The year 1876 was the first that Esther Howland had a separate credit history; R. G. Dun and Company reported that she had taken over the business. The same year, Howland mortgaged her stock and fixtures for $2,500. The credit reporter from R. G. Dun indicated that this was not a business-related loan but a personal one. In 1877, she mortgaged the business again. There is no indication in the credit record that the mortgages were due to mismanagement; it is possible that the money was for Southworth Howland's medical expenses. Esther gave up the valentine business and nursed her father until his death in 1882. Massachusetts, vol. 2, 683, R. G. Dun & Co. Collection, Baker Library, Harvard University Business School. 41. *Boston Globe*, February 14, 1901, p. 6. 42. Ibid. 43. Schmidt, *Consumer Rites*, 18. 44. After 1865, she no longer appeared in the city directory. Lee, *History of Valentines*, 67. 45. Despite the popularity of her valentines, Howland was not able to pay off the mortgages and G. Henry Whitcomb, holder of the second mortgage threatened to foreclose in June 1879. Charles Howland sold Esther's stock at auction to

George Whitney claiming that Whitcomb's mortgage was worthless. Although Whitney bought Howland's business in a state of disarray, the credit reporter was confident of Whitney's judgment: "Doing his usual business which at this season of the year is necessarily moderate as it consists a great measure of Valentine Manufacturing. We understand that he has bought out the effects of the New England Valentine Company.... Appearances indicate that there will be some trouble before the matter is finally adjusted. 'Whitney' is pretty shrewd however and parties here think he knows what he is about. He says he looked the matter over thoroughly before taking hold of it and feels confident that it will not affect him in any way, merely bought it for the sake of getting rid of the competition and says he paid all it was worth." Massachusetts, vol. 3, 868, R. G. Dun & Co. Collection, Baker Library, Harvard University Business School.

The patterns of family business that characterized the Howland and Whitney families in the valentine business also characterized the business of Jonathan King, a prominent London valentine merchant. In 1845, King was a stationer who sold valentines on the side. The valentines he sold were made at home by his wife, Clarissa, whose skill and artistry in the art of valentine manufacture is trumpeted by valentine antiquarians. By 1848, King's twelve-year-old son, Jonathan Jr., had joined the enterprise. When Jonathan Jr. married, some years later, his wife, Emily Elizabeth, ran the business while he worked as a traveling salesman for his father. When Jonathan Jr. inherited the business in 1869, he and Emily Elizabeth consolidated the business in two neighboring villas in suburban London and opened the Fancy Valentine Shop. Emily Elizabeth was listed as the proprietor, Mrs. E. E. King, and her daughter Ellen Rose King supervised the manufacture of the valentines by the women and girls who worked twelve hours a day in a valentine factory that abutted the shop. Staff, *Valentine and Its Origins*, 85. 46. "Cupid's Manufactory," *All the Year Round*, February 20, 1864, 36–40. The article was based on the valentine business of Joseph Mansell. Staff, *Valentine and Its Origins*, 126. 47. "Cupid's Manufactory," 36. 48. Ibid., 36–37. 49. Ibid., 38. 50. This was an another account of Eugene Rimmel's business on the Strand. Staff, *Valentine and Its Origins*, 134. 51. "Cupid's Manufactory," 40. 52. Ibid. In 1863, 430,000 valentines passed through the London Post Office, and the following year, 20,000 more were added to that number. 53. Ibid. 54. *Niles National Register*, February 22, 1845, p. 400. I am indebted to Carol Sheriff for this information. 55. Mary Moore, "Saint Valentine's Day," *Godey's Lady's Book* 63, no. 2 (1861): 119. 56. "A New Fashion for Valentines," *Godey's Lady's Book* 40, no. 2 (1849): 73–74. A year later, *Peterson's* proposed its own valentine fashion, while *Godey's* congratulated itself on the success of its new fashion. 57. Ibid., 73. 58. Ibid. 59. Ibid. 60. Ibid. 61. Series II, Box 21B, c. 1863, Norcross Historical Greeting Card Collection. 62. See Viviana Zelizer, *Morals and Markets: The Development of Life Insurance in the United States* (New Brunswick, NJ: Transaction Books, 1983) for another discussion of the importance of the idea of "pricelessness." 63. An item from the February issue of *Peterson's* in 1860 confirmed the success of such a gift: "HOW TO GET A WIFE—a gentleman, remitting two dollars to us for his wife's subscription says, "Last year I noticed an editorial in 'Peterson' stating that any lover, who would present his Dulcinea with a copy of the Magazine for one year, might be sure of success, and I wondered if such would be my happy lot. Accordingly, I sent a copy to Miss——, and she now bears the later clause of my name. So, I advise all young men, if they would succeed, to present a copy of Peterson to the object of their affections." He adds: "By way of caution, I will inform my young friends, that I had been betrothed for four months, and had begun to repudiate the old adage, 'the course of true love never does run smooth,' when I thought I would subscribe to a different magazine for my Dulcinea, when lo! the very first visit I made to her after the reception of the other monthly, I had to bear the ordeal of passing from a happy betrothed to a discarded lover. So, as for me and my household we will go for Peterson" (169). 64. "New Fashion for Valentines," 73–74. 65. "Godey's Arm Chair" *Godey's Lady's Book* 46, no. 2 (1853): 182. 66. "Godey's Arm Chair" *Godey's Lady's Book* 48, no. 2 (1854): 181. 67. "Godey's Arm Chair" *Godey's Lady's Book* 46, no. 4 (1853): 375. 68. R. Shelton MacKenzie, "Wives by Advertisement" *Godey's Lady's Book* 15, no. 4 (1837): 181. 69. Ibid., 182. One of these *mesalliances* led to murder, an outcome MacKenzie implies was the natural result of such an unnatural union. 70. Ibid. 71. Ibid. 72. See Agnew, *Worlds Apart*, 12, for a discussion of the role of individual as commodity in the cultural reproduction of market relations. 73. See Brown, *Domestic Individualism*, 15, for a related discussion of the sentimental economics of slavery. 74. Hannah More, *Coelebs in Search of a Wife* (London: T. Cadell and W. Davies, 1809). 75. This system resembled the valentine custom of drawing lots, which was frequently recounted in the histories of Valentine's Day. 76. "Letter to the Editor," *Godey's Lady's Book* 16, no. 5 (1838): 194. 77. See Georg Simmel, *The Philosophy of Money*, trans. Tom Bottomore and David Frisby (London: Routledge & Kegan Paul, 1978), 380–84 for a similar view of marriage advertisements. Simmel suggests that marriage advertisements are peculiar to the middle class. Because such a high premium is placed on the emotional compatibility of marriage and the predestination of the right partner, the advertisement becomes an important factor in maximizing the search. And yet advertisements are scorned because the one piece of information that is most easily represented in an advertisement is the financial situation of the advertiser, and middle-class ideals of romantic love rejected money as the primary impetus for marriage. 78. "Editor's Table," *Godey's Lady's Book* 17, no. 2 (1838): 95. 79. Ibid. 80. "To Coelebs," *Godey's Lady's Book* 17, no. 4 (1838): 167. 81. "Cahokia," *Godey's Lady's Book* 17, no. 4 (1838): 168. 82. "To Coelebs," *Godey's Lady's Book* 17, no. 4 (1838): 168. 83. "Editor's Book Table," *Godey's Lady's Book* 41, no. 4 (1850): 253. 84. *Godey's Lady's Book* commented on the marriage business: "GOOD EYE TO BUSINESS a Meadville (PA) paper keeps this advertisement standing 'Cupid and Hymen—The little brown cottage at Cambridge Pa, is the place to call to have the marriage knot promptly and strongly tied. Inquire of Rev. S. S. Whitcomb. We would ask whether his knots are so strongly tied that an Indiana divorce court can't untie them.'" "Godey's Arm Chair," *Godey's Lady's Book* 82, no. 1 (1871): 101. 85. Series 2, Box 16, Norcross Historical Greeting Card Collection. 86. Emma Bradford, *Roses Are Red: Love and Scorn in Victorian Valentines* (London: Michael Joseph, 1986), plate 10. 87. Quoted from a valentine in the Collection of English Valentines at the British Art Center, Yale University. 88. Quoted from a valentine, ibid. 89. Cathy N. Davidson, *Revolution and the Word: The Rise of the Novel in America* (New York: Oxford University Press, 1986), 219. 90. Harry Sunderland, "Kate's Valentine," *Godey's Lady's Book* 40, no. 2 (1850): 119–21. The same story appeared in the *Orleans American* published in Orleans County, NY, February 28, 1850. I am indebted to Carol Sheriff for this information. 91. Ibid., 119. 92. Ibid. 93. Moore, "Saint Valentine's Day," 120. 94. Sunderland, "Kate's Valentine," 121. 95. Ibid. 96. See Michel Foucault, *The History of Sexuality*, trans. Robert Hurley (New York: Vintage Books, 1980), 58–73. 97. Sunderland, "Kate's Valentine," 121. 98. S. Annie Frost, "St. Valentine's Day," *Godey's Lady's Book* 68, no. 2 (1864): 143–47. 99. Ibid., 144. 100. Ibid., 147. 101. See Campbell, *Romantic Ethic*, 77–97.

9. A Tempest in a Teacup

1. Davidson, *Revolution and the Word*, 73. 2. Pattee, *First Century*, 87. 3. See Robert Darnton, "Readers Respond to Rousseau: The Fabrication of Romantic Sensitivity," in *The Great Cat Massacre and Other*

Episodes in French Cultural History, by Robert Darnton (New York: Vintage Books, 1985), 215–56.
4. Cathy N. Davidson, "The Life and Times of *Charlotte Temple,*" in *Reading in America: Literature and Social History,* ed. Cathy N. Davidson (Baltimore: Johns Hopkins University Press, 1989), 168, 178.
5. George M. Beard, *American Nervousness, Its Causes and Consequences; a Supplement to Nervous Exhaustion* (New York: G. P. Putnam's Sons, 1881). 6. Stewart, *On Longing,* 23. 7. See Robert Solomon, "On Kitsch and Sentimentality," *Journal of Aesthetics and Art Criticism* 49, no. 1 (1991): 1–14. 8. Earnest Elmo Caulkins, "St. Elmo or, Named for a Bestseller," *Saturday Review of Literature,* December 16, 1939, 11, 16. 9. Barker-Benfield, *Culture of Sensibility,* 168; Bernard Kreissman, *Pamela-Shamela: A Study of Criticisms, Burlesques, Parodies, and Adaptations of Richardson's Pamela* (Lincoln: University of Nebraska Press, 1960), 4–5; Margaret A. Doody, introduction to *Pamela; Or, Virtue Rewarded,* by Richardson (New York: Penguin Books, 1980), 7. 10. See Darnton, "Readers Respond to Rousseau," and Mullan, *Sentiment and Sociability.* See also my dissertation, "Sentimental Enterprise," for more discussion of eighteenth-century sentimental reading and spinoff products. 11. Davidson, *Revolution and the Word,* 40–41. 12. Ibid., 43. 13. A spinoff product is related thematically to the original text but does not necessarily benefit the producer of the text. A tie-in is part of a planned marketing scheme that benefits the producer directly. Today, in the consumer culture of the late twentieth century, it is often hard to distinguish where the original ends and the spinoffs and tie-ins begin. The impulse to recycle goes well beyond environmental concerns, spinning itself out in popular culture through the unending representations of narratives in material form. It is almost as if the originating text depends upon its tie-ins for its own legitimacy. It is now common practice, especially with children's movies, for tie-ins to appear in stores and at fast food restaurants before the movie opens in theaters, thus encouraging children to prompt their parents to purchase something as part of the anticipation of the movie's release, then to attend the movie, and finally to buy more products to reenact and remember the movie. This sequence is possible in part because the movie itself is marketing for the brand name of the motion picture studio—Disney, for example—and the actual narrative of the movie is secondary to its identity as the "new movie." The licensing deals made for these tie-ins are an important part of the projected profit. Occasionally a studio will misjudge the demand for spinoffs, as was the case with *Forrest Gump,* and have to scramble to produce items to satisfy consumer desire. 14. See Merish, *Sentimental Materialism.* 15. See Richard Brodhead, "Veiled Ladies: Toward a History of Antebellum Entertainment," in *Cultures of Letters: Scenes of Reading and Writing in Nineteenth-Century America* (Chicago: University of Chicago Press, 1993). 16. Ivor Guest, *Fanny Elssler* (Middletown, CT: Wesleyan University Press, 1970), 113. For a contemporary account of Elssler's tour, see *The Life of the Beautiful and Accomplished Danseuse, Mlle Fanny Elssler, Selected and Compiled by a Lady of This City* (Philadelphia: Printed for Purchaser and for Sale, [1840]). 17. Quoted in Guest, *Fanny Elssler,* 134. Mademoiselle Maria Malibran was a famous soprano, popular in the 1820s and daughter of tenor Manuel Garcia, who was Jenny Lind's voice teacher. 18. See Kelley, *Private Woman,* vii, for another example of the importance for women of maintaining a demure persona in public performances. 19. Quoted in Guest, *Fanny Elssler,* 133. 20. Ibid.; Harris, *Humbug,* 113; Lawrence Levine, *Highbrow/Lowbrow: The Emergence of Cultural Hierarchy in America* (Cambridge: Harvard University Press, 1988), 108. Elssler's name became an adjective: *La deesse: An Elssler-atic Romance by the Author of "Straws"* (New York: Carvill, 1841). 21. Guest, *Fanny Elssler,* 137, 145–47. 22. Allison Delarue, ed., *Fanny Elssler in America* (New York: Dance Horizons, 1976), 7. 23. Harris, *Humbug,* 114. 24. See Leo Braudy, *The Frenzy of Renown: Fame and Its History* (New York: Oxford University Press, 1986),

503–4. 25. Bluford Adams, *E Pluribus Barnum: The Great Showman and The Making of U.S. Popular Culture* (Minneapolis: University of Minnesota Press, 1997), 2–3. 26. Ibid., 6. 27. Ibid., 2. 28. Ibid., 7. 29. See William Lee Miller, *Arguing About Slavery: John Quincy Adams and the Great Battle in the United States Congress* (New York: Vintage Books, 1995). 30. See Eric Lott, *Love and Theft: Blackface Minstrelsy and the American Working Class* (New York: Oxford University Press, 1993). 31. Adams, *E Pluribus Barnum*, 25. 32. Harris, *Humbug*, 130. 33. *Godey's Lady's Book* 40, no. 2 (1850): 312, "Tribute to Jenny Lind"; 41, no. 5 (1850): 316, congratulation of Barnum for bringing Jenny Lind to America in the prime of her career; 41, no. 6 (1850): 353–55, "A Reminiscence of Jenny Lind"; 41, no. 6 (1850): 386, Editor's Book Table, "Sinclair 101 Chesnut Street, has sent us the neatest specimen of printing in colors we have ever seen. It is a portrait of Jenny Lind—the pure, the talented, and charitable Jenny Lind"; and (February 1851): 134–35, Editor's Table, Review of Jenny Lind's Performance. For other contemporary discussions of Lind's tour, see William Allen Butler, *Barnum's Parnassus; Being the Confidential Disclosures of the Prize Committee on the Jenny Lind Song* (New York: D. Appleton, 1850); George G. Foster, *Memoir of Jenny Lind, Compiled from the Most Authentic Sources* (New York: Dewitt & Davenport, 1850); C. G. Rosenberg, *Jenny Lind: Her Life, Her Struggles and Her Triumphs* (New York: Stringer & Townsend, 1850). 34. Sherry Lee Linkon, "Reading Lind Mania: Print Culture and the Construction of Nineteenth-Century Audiences," *Book History* 1, no. 1 (1998): 94–106. 35. "Chit Chat upon Philadelphia Fashions for December," *Godey's Lady's Book* (December 1850): 388. 36. Adams, *E Pluribus Barnum*, 64–67. 37. "Chit Chat upon Philadelphia Fashions for December," 388. 38. Harris, *Humbug*, 124. 39. The popularity of cigars as sentimental spinoffs complicates Lori Merish's gendered analysis of the cigar and calls into question her use of the cigar as a marker of the difference between masculine and feminine consumption. Spinoff cigars suggest the permeability of those spheres of consumption rather than their opposition. Merish, *Sentimental Materialism*, 287. 40. Bruce Levine, *Half Slave and Half Free: The Roots of the Civil War* (New York: Hill and Wang, 1992), 186–90. 41. Adams, *E Pluribus Barnum*, 43–47. 42. Ibid., 63. 43. Elizabeth B. Clarke, "'The Sacred Rights of the Weak': Pain, Sympathy, and the Culture of Individual Rights in Antebellum America," *Journal of American History* 82, no. 2, 486–87. 44. Harris, *Humbug*, 145. 45. Stowe included this letter in her introduction to the 1878 edition of the novel. Adams, *E Pluribus Barnum*, 63. 46. Herbert Ross Brown, *The Sentimental Novel in America, 1789–1860* (New York: Pageant Books, 1959), 259; J. T. Randolph, *Cabin and the Parlor;* Robert Criswell, *"Uncle Tom's Cabin" Contrasted with Buckingham Hall, the Planter's Home;* Mary Eastman, *Aunt Phillis's Cabin; or Southern Life as It Is;* J. W. Page, *Uncle Robin in his Cabin in Virginia and Tom Without One in Boston.* 47. "Uncle Tomitudes," *Putnam's Monthly* (January 1853): 7–102. 48. See Neil McKendrick, John Brewer, and J. H. Plumb, *The Birth of a Consumer Society: The Commercialization of Eighteenth-Century England* (Bloomington: University of Indiana Press, 1982). 49. Clarke, "Sacred Rights," 476. 50. Ibid., 481. 51. See Harriet Beecher Stowe, *Uncle Tom's Cabin*, ed. Jean Fagin Yellin (New York: Oxford University Press, 1998). 52. Agnew, *World's Apart*, 177–87. 53. See Walter Johnson, *Soul by Soul: Life Inside the Antebellum Slave Market* (Cambridge: Harvard University Press, 1999). 54. I am grateful to Margherita M. Desy of the National Museum of American History for bringing this term and the wide range of the spinoff products themselves to my attention. 55. John D. Hart, *The Popular Book: A History of America's Literary Taste* (Berkeley and Los Angeles: University of California Press, 1961), 118. 56. Ann Douglas, introduction to *Uncle Tom's Cabin* (1852; reprint, New York: Penguin Books, 1981), 9. 57. Brown, *Domestic Individualism*, 39–60, and Merish, *Sentimental Materialism*, 135–64, for a similar discussions of the market relations of Stowe's novel. Brown emphasizes the role of possessive individualism in Stowe's formulation of the economics of sentimentalism. See also Thomas Haskell, "Capitalism and the Origins of the Humanitarian Sensibility, Parts I and II," *American Historical Review* 90:339–61, 547–66, on the links of capitalism and humanitarianism. Haskell argues that the nature of capitalism itself shapes humanitarian interest, which becomes the a way to define the market interactions of a · group of people who come to be identified as a middle class. The inconsistencies of humanitarianism are not, he argues, the result of self-deception but inherent in the structural changes in market culture. 58. Adams, *E Pluribus Barnum*, 130–39. 59. See Beverly Peterson, "Mrs. Hale on Mrs. Stowe and Slavery," *American Periodicals: A Journal of History, Criticism and Bibliography* 8 (1998): 30–44 for more discussion of Hale's treatment of *Uncle Tom's Cabin*. 60. Sarah J. Hale, "Literary Notices," *Godey's Lady's Book* 6, no. 53 (1856): 561. 61. Sarah J. Hale, *Northwood; or Life in North and South, Showing the Character of Both* (New York: H. Long and Brother, 1852), iv. 62. Sarah J. Hale, *Liberia; or Mr. Peyton's Experiments* (New York: Harper and Brothers, 1853), iv. 63. "A New Story by Mrs. Stowe," *National Era* 5, no. 228 (May 15, 1851): 78. 64. Emma D. E. N. Southworth, "A Warning to the Public," *National Era* 8, no. 378 (March 30, 1854): 51. 65. Paul Christian Jones, "'This Dainty Woman's Hand . . . Red with Blood': E. D. E. N. Southworth's *The Hidden Hand* as Abolitionist Narrative," *American Transcendental Quarterly* 15 (2001): 61. 66. Jones, "Dainty Woman's Hands," 71. 67. *The Hidden Hand* appeared in the pages of the *New York Ledger* two more times before it was finally published as an independent volume in 1888, after a constant stream of appeals from both readers and publishers. In addition to multiple serializations, most of Southworth's novels remained in print, in inexpensive collections, well into the twentieth century. See Joanne Dobson, introduction to *The Hidden Hand; or, Capitola the Madcap*, by E. D. E. N. Southworth (1888; reprint, New Brunswick, NJ: Rutgers University Press, 1988), xiv. 68. Kelley, *Private Woman*, 27; Dobson, introduction, xl. 69. See David W. Blight, *Race and Reunion: The Civil War in American Memory* (Cambridge: Harvard University Press, 2001). 70. Caulkins, "St. Elmo," 11, 16; William Perry Fidler, *Augusta Evans Wilson, 1835–1909* (University: University of Alabama Press, 1951), 128–29. These towns still exist, with the exception of California, Georgia, and Missouri. St. Elmo, Tennessee, is very close to Chattanooga, Tennessee, where the novel begins. 71. Caulkins, "St. Elmo," 17; Hart, *Popular Book*, 119. 72. Caulkins, "St. Elmo," 16. Her novel *Macaria* (1864) was read by Confederate troops to boost moral, or in the case of one soldier, to save his life when his copy, which he carried in his breast pocket, stopped a Yankee bullet. Fortunately for the soldier, Evans's novels were always voluminous. The Union army declared the novel contraband and forbade soldiers to read it for fear it would damage morale. 73. Mark Twain wrote a satire of this novel: "Excerpts from Captain Stormfield's Visit to Heaven." 74. Elizabeth Stuart Phelps, *The Gates Ajar* (1868; reprint, Cambridge: Harvard University Press, 1964), 99, 103. 75. Elizabeth Stuart Phelps, *Chapters from a Life* (Boston: Houghton Mifflin, 1896), 112–13. 76. See Sarah Stage, *Female Complaints: Lydia Pinkham and the History of Women's Medicine* (New York: W. W. Norton, 1979) and T. J. Jackson Lears, *No Place of Grace: Antimodernism and the Transformation of American Culture, 1880-1920* (Chicago: University of Chicago Press, 1994). 77. Agnew, *World's Apart*, 188.

Epilogue

1. "The Funeral of L. A. Godey," *New York Times*, December 4, 1878, p. 1. 2. "Obituary: Mrs. Sarah J. B. Hale," *New York Times*, May 12, 1879, p. 4. 3. "The Late Mrs. Hale: The Illustrious List of Authors Whom

She Outlived," *New York Times,* May 12, 1879, p. 5, reprinted from the *Boston Traveller.* 4. "Obituary: Mrs. Sarah J. B. Hale," 4. 5. *Godey's* was not able to compete with *Munsey's, McClure's,* and *Cosmopolitan,* which were able with the help of advertising revenue to drop their prices to ten cents an issue, considerably less than the three dollar yearly subscription to *Godey's.* Garvey, *Adman in the Parlor,* 9. 6. Livingston, *Pragmatism,* 30. 7. Charlotte Perkins Gilman, *Women and Economics: The Economic Factor Between Men and Women as a Factor in Social Evolution,* ed. Carl Degler (New York: Harper & Row, 1966), 12. 8. Ibid., 15. 9. See Stanley, *From Bondage to Contract,* 166–72; Livingston, *Pragmatism,* 52–56. 10. See Dolores Hayden, *The Grand Domestic Revolution: A History of Feminist Designs for American Homes, Neighborhoods, and Cities* (Cambridge, Mass.: MIT Press, 1981). 11. See Alison J. Clarke, *Tupperware: The Promise of Plastic in 1950s America* (Washington, DC: Smithsonian Institution Press, 1999); Christopher M. Bryson, *Martha Inc.: The Incredible Story of Martha Stewart Living Omnimedia* (New York: John Wiley, 2002). 12. Thorstein Veblen, *The Theory of the Leisure Class* (New York: Penguin Books, 1979), 356 13. Ibid., 82. 14. See Stuart Ewen, *Captains of Consciousness: Advertising and the Social Roots of the Consumer Culture* (New York: McGraw-Hill, 1976); Elizabeth Ewen, *Immigrant Women in the Land of Dollars: Life and Culture on the Lower East Side, 1890–1925* (New York: Monthly Review Press, 1985); Fox and Lears, *Culture of Consumption; Lears, Fables of Abundance.* 15. Jean Baudrillard, "The System of Objects," in *Selected Writings,* ed. Mark Poste (Stanford, Calif.: Stanford University Press, 1988), 12. 16. Campbell, *Romantic Ethic,* 77–95. 17. This remained a convention to distinguish middle-class consumption from working-class consumption. In the 1950s, Lee Rainwater argued that working-class women uncritically accepted the contents of advertising, distinguishing them from more sophisticated middle-class consumers. See Lee Rainwater, *Workingman's Wife: Her Personality, World and Life Style* (New York: Oceana Publications, [1959]). 18. See David Brooks, *Bobos in Paradise: The New Upper Class and How They Got There* (New York: Simon and Schuster, 2001) for a similar argument about contemporary culture. 19. De Tocqueville, *Democracy in America* 2:129.

Index

Printed in the United States
by Baker & Taylor Publisher Services